A Guide to the Professional Interview

A Guide to the Professional Interview

A Research-Based Interview Methodology for People Who Ask Questions

Asbjørn Rachlew

Geir-Egil Løken

Svein Tore Bergestuen

ANTHEM PRESS

Anthem Press
An imprint of Wimbledon Publishing Company
www.anthempress.com

This edition first published in UK and USA 2022
by ANTHEM PRESS
75–76 Blackfriars Road, London SE1 8HA, UK
or PO Box 9779, London SW19 7ZG, UK
and
244 Madison Ave #116, New York, NY 10016, USA

The author asserts the moral right to be identified as the author of this work.

This translation has been published with the financial support of
NORLA, Norwegian Literature Abroad.

NORLA
Norwegian
Literature
Abroad

British Library Cataloguing-in-Publication Data
A catalogue record for this book is available from the British Library.

Library of Congress Control Number: 2021952353

ISBN-13: 978-1-78527-798-6 (Hbk)
ISBN-10: 1-78527-798-7 (Hbk)

Cover image: Stian Hole

This title is also available as an e-book.

CONTENTS

PREFACE

A reliable answer can mean the difference between life and death. In other cases, when people offer answers that skirt the issue under investigation, it can merely be a source of irritation. In either case, the quality of the question will always have a profound impact on the quality of the answer.

When a physician speaks with a patient, it is crucial for diagnosis and treatment that the patient provide reliable information that includes all relevant details. In the aftermath of a shipwreck, the accident investigation authorities must ensure the reliability of the statements of those involved to prevent further accidents. During less-dramatic, more everyday interviews and conversations, unreliable responses lead to consequential errors and inefficiency. Even when lives are not at stake, unreliable or incomplete information can lead to faulty conclusions and bad decisions, and have negative implications for individuals, organizations, the environment, the economy, and society.

Interviews are carried out in many professions as a means of obtaining information. The interview is led by a professional in the capacity of his or her given occupation, and the interviewee shares his or her experiences, knowledge, or story. When the purpose of the interview is to obtain relevant, accurate, and reliable information, which will in turn form the basis for decisions, we call this a *professional interview*. The quality and reliability of the information acquired depends on the existence of trust between the participants and, not least, on how the questions are asked.

The courts, the public health service, and the media are just a few of the many institutions for which the interview is not merely important but wholly essential. All the same, the interview is often not included in the definition of an institution's core activity, whether this be to ensure justice, save lives, or report on the authorities' execution of power. We believe *that* is why the professional interview has not been afforded sufficient priority or been understood as requiring a methodological approach in education, courses, training, and evaluation contexts. One of the ramifications of this is that professional interviews are carried out in different ways, often based on the interviewer's gut feeling, intuition, and experience, as well as the overall culture of the interviewing institution.

This was the case for the police forces in both Norway and Great Britain, and it remains the case in many countries. It has not been considered necessary to provide training in professional interview techniques. The predominant conception has been that young police detectives would learn from those with experience and, with practice, eventually master the necessary techniques. The police saw no reason to develop a research-based, quality-assured methodology for professional interviews. The result of this culture of an experience-based approach to police questioning of victims, witnesses, and crime suspects was that unreliable information was frequently mistaken for the truth. For lack of a corrective methodology, detectives followed their intuition and unconsciously searched for information that confirmed what they already believed. Innocent people were convicted, perpetrators went free. Although the aim was noble, the methodology was flimsy or completely nonexistent.

Two of the authors of this book have been a part of what can be best described as a paradigm shift within the field of investigative interviewing. We began our careers as police detectives with virtually no formal training in interpersonal communication and subsequently went on to become method developers and instructors in research-based investigative interviewing techniques, first nationally and then on an international scale. We have also adapted and taught investigative interviewing to professionals in other fields, such as financial analysts, recruitment personnel, judges, lawyers, physicians, and journalists. The book's third author has employed a corresponding interview technique in thousands of one-on-one interviews for radio and television and taught interviewing techniques at the Norwegian Institute of Journalism.

Over the years we have met many people holding different ranks and titles from various industries and different countries, all of whom employ professional interviews as an integral tool in the context of their daily work. Through these encounters, we have gradually come to understand that a surprisingly large number of people are engaged in activity similar to that of detectives and journalists: the gathering of information through professional, interpersonal encounters. Regardless of the context, the purpose of the activity remains the same: to obtain information that is as accurate, relevant, and reliable as possible.

We are therefore confident that a large number of people can benefit from leading-edge insights and research-based knowledge about interviewing methodology. We are also certain that the methodology in question has relevance far beyond the scope of law enforcement.

Doctors talk to patients, judges question witnesses in court, journalists interview sources. A manager carries out job interviews, the financial analyst acquires information before making investments or performing transactions, and those who investigate industrial, aviation, railway, or maritime accidents rely upon detailed information. Child welfare officers speak with children about the *real* challenges facing their family, and so on. The list of professions that require relevant and reliable information is a long one, whether this information is gathered through interviews, conversations, or consultations.

Our objective in writing this book is to inspire readers to improve their communication skills in professional interviews. We want to make the research-based methodology developed through the pioneering efforts of the Norwegian and British police services available to all those who use the interview as an information-gathering tool.

We understand that some readers may be skeptical about the usefulness of investigative interviewing techniques in a doctor's office, business meeting, or political interview. And we understand that the setting, requirements, and frameworks of professional interviews carried out in other occupations may diverge considerably from those of police questioning. Nonetheless, we would maintain that the purpose of the interview, the structure, the risk of influence, and cognitive bias are features common to most professional interviews. We believe this book provides a good basis for and comprehensive explanation of how the investigative interview method can also be used at your place of work.

It is our hope that the knowledge about the method and insights from the police's hard-won experiences can improve the efficiency and accuracy of your work and prevent typical errors and pitfalls in your professional daily life.

Oslo, June 1, 2021

PROLOGUE

Several weeks have passed since that rainy Friday afternoon at the end of the summer holiday in Norway. The entire world has now learned of the tragedy that struck Oslo, the international city of peace. But the worst terrorist attack in Norway's history is still impossible to comprehend.

On July 22, 2011, a terrorist detonated a car bomb in the Government Quarter in the city center of Oslo. The same terrorist then traveled to the summer camp of the Worker's Youth League (AUF) on the island of Utøya located some 24 miles northwest of Oslo. There he proceeded to shoot as many of the young people attending the camp as he could. Seventy-seven people were killed. Hundreds were injured. Thousands of mothers, fathers, siblings, and friends were scarred for life by the traumatic loss of loved ones.

The terrorist is now seated in an interview room at Oslo police headquarters. He is surprised about how he has been treated while in police custody. Initially, he thought he would be killed on the island when the responding SWAT team arrived. At the very least, he expected to be tortured during the interrogation. Instead, he is sitting in a comfortable chair explaining his ideas about a fictitious world order to an empathetic interviewer who allows him to speak without interruption. The interviewer is concerned about how he is feeling and asks whether they should take a break or if they may continue.

The interviewers and their support team are trying to ascertain whether the terrorist is just one of a number of cells in a larger operation, or if he worked alone, a lone wolf with heinous ambitions. The best way to determine this is to carry out the interviews using the exact same procedure they ordinarily use.

Although the crime in question cannot be compared to any crime ever before committed in Norway, the interview method employed is the same as used when interviewing rape victims, witnesses of traffic accidents, drug addicts, and financial directors under suspicion of embezzlement. The objective in all cases is to gather as much reliable and relevant information as possible.

The terrorist leans back in his chair and takes a sip from a bottle of Coca-Cola. The bottle is not empty until the interview is over. He smiles and cracks a self-deprecating joke. He has fallen into an easy banter with all of the three police detectives who take turns interviewing him. Although each of the detectives has different styles, they carry out the interviews using the exact same formula.

The terrorist continues to share information, politely and casually, about actions and details that most people would have difficulties stomaching. The contrast between the form and content of his explanation verges on the absurd. When the trial starts and the terrorist is asked about his alleged terrorist network, he answers matter-of-factly but dismissively: "I have already said too much during the police interviews."

The method presented in this book has been scientifically tested for decades. In the context of the long series of interviews of the July 22 terrorist in Norway, the method was also tested for several intense months while the entire world looked on. The young people who survived the Utøya attack were interviewed using the same method. Norway's worst terrorist attack in peacetime shook an entire nation. Simultaneously, the police procedure was a study in how—and why—investigative interviews addressing even the most extreme of circumstances must be conducted like all other professional interviews.

How can police interviews of terrorists—and the victims of their extreme actions—be of any relevance in your workplace? We hope the answer to that question, along with the interview method's foundation and universal features, will be clear by the time you've finished the first part of the book.

PART 1

1

INTRODUCTION

When we hear talk of police interrogations, most of us naturally picture how this situation is depicted in movies and television series. A guilty scoundrel is interrogated by a hard-nosed police officer who bends the rules for the better good. Shrewdness, strategic bluffing, and leading questions are often combined with a bit of violence and a dramatic confrontation with all the evidence. Finally, a confession is elicited.

Fortunately, thanks to science and our ability to learn from our mistakes, actual interview practice has little in common with such cinematic depictions, and with time, this holds true in increasingly more countries. But the current interview practice did not simply appear out of the blue.

The Starting Shot

Before the Norwegian police became receptive to critical research and knowledge-based interview methods, young detectives picked up techniques, tips, and tricks from their older colleagues. These were techniques that those with experience had learned in the course of an eventful career, based in turn on tips from their own older colleagues and role models. The techniques did not constitute a specific method or methodology. They were not based on recognized or relevant knowledge. To the contrary, they were based on myths and a variety of personal experiences.

The phasing out of obsolete interrogation methods through the development of research-based, investigative interviewing techniques started in Great Britain as a consequence of wrongful convictions at a number of criminal trials in the 1970s and 1980s. The 1981 report of the Royal Commission on Criminal Procedure established that the interrogation practices of the British police force were clearly in need of an overhaul. One of several important changes implemented was that all interviews of suspects were to be recorded. When researchers gained access to the recordings, they were able to document that the police were not the expert interviewers they presumed themselves to be. The nature of the interviews, at the time called interrogations, suggested that the detectives were predominantly interested in confirming their own suspicions. After having listened to 600 police interviews of suspects, Professor John Baldwin (1992) submitted a report illustrating—in correlation with other similar types of studies—that a great number of changes were necessary and that training would be required to achieve this aim. On-the-job experience was not enough. In fact, the evaluations showed that the detectives who believed they were the best interviewers were in fact the most dangerous. In a unique collaboration between researchers and the British police services, an interview methodology was developed based on eyewitness psychology and ethical, interpersonal communication principles. The method was named PEACE. The police replaced their *experience-based* interrogation technique with a *research-based* interview technique, from interrogations with a focus on the confirmation of preconceived assumptions to *investigative interviewing with a focus on gathering information.*

In the late 1990s, a similar type of recognition emerged in Norway. One of Norway's most notorious criminal cases, the Birgitte case, came to represent a turning point. In the spring of 1995, the body of 17-year-old Birgitte Tengs was found after she had been sexually abused and murdered close to her home in Karmøy on the west coast of Norway. It wasn't until almost two years after her death that Birgitte's cousin was charged and prosecuted for the murder. After several lengthy interrogations, the cousin confessed. He later recanted his confession but was still convicted by the district court, based on the confession he had given to the police. The shock was therefore substantial when he was subsequently acquitted by the Court of Appeals. Of critical importance for the acquittal was the testimony of Professor Gisli H. Gudjonsson, one of the world's foremost experts on police interviewing techniques and false confessions. Gudjonsson was crystal clear in his assessment. The cousin's confession had been coerced and was most probably false.

In the wake of the Birgitte case, we have researched the classified teaching materials of that time with an eye to determining the prevailing "methodology" (Rachlew 2003). Here we found that Gudjonsson was right. The methodology advised the use of coercion and manipulation as techniques for eliciting confessions. It was stated in black and white in the curriculum for the police academy:

> You start preparing him from the moment of initial contact with the objective of becoming the only person he can lean on in this difficult situation. You have control over with whom he has contact and thereby prevent him from receiving psychological support from others. [...] Have a box of tissues on hand and place it where he can see it but not reach it. When you see him struggling, show consideration by handing

him the box of tissues to demonstrate your compassion and your under-standing of his pain.[1]

The Birgitte case was a wake-up call. A legal scandal had to occur for the Norwegian police to recognize the fact that research had been done on police questioning techniques, the police detectives' most important tool. This was to be the starting shot for the development of an upgraded investigative interviewing methodology in Norway. Asbjørn Rachlew had the opportunity to study investigative interviewing at the University of Liverpool in Great Britain, where the research on police questioning techniques was the most advanced. It was like being a medicine man or a witch doctor and suddenly gaining access to medical science. These studies led to a master's degree and CREATIVE: the Norwegian version of the investigative interviewing methodology.

The Method

CREATIVE constitutes the foundation for this book. The method has been developed for the Norwegian Police Service and employs the methodology of the English PEACE interview model and thereby the research and ethos underpinning investigative interviewing. The essence of the method highlights the ethical questions such interviews raise, applying knowledge about psychology and communication in a systematic approach designed to obtain the most relevant and reliable information.

Whereas the letters in the acronym PEACE stand for the phases of the model, **P**lanning and preparation, **E**ngage and explain, **A**ccount clarification and challenge, **C**losing, **E**valuation, the letters of the acronym CREATIVE represent the principles behind the method.

Communication. To obtain information, we must communicate well. Good interpersonal communication is crucial.

Rule of Law. As professionals in an interview situation, we must strive for objectivity by exploring reasonable doubt and eliminating arbitrary processes.

Ethics and empathy. The method is based on ethical principles. Guiding precepts are honesty, integrity, and predictability—all of them the

---

1. See Fahsing and Rachlew (2009) for a critical review of the manipulative interrogation techniques cited here.

opposite of manipulation and trickery. The interviewees are viewed and treated as an end in themselves, never solely as means to an end.

Awareness. Change starts with a recognition that the prevailing mentality and practice must be revised and developed. Cognitive bias is human. The method acknowledges this and heightens the interviewer's awareness of such bias so as to counteract the inherent pitfalls it represents.

Trust won through openness. Trust is a prerequisite for a good professional interview. In contrast to the approach of formerly applied methods, in the investigative interview, openness and transparency are key.

Information. The purpose of the interview is to obtain relevant and reliable information. The goal is not to acquire information that confirms prior assumptions.

VErified scientific research. The most important difference between former and current practice is the methodology's basis in science and research. The experience-based approach and gut instincts are replaced by or adapted to methods that have been proven effective. The work of the police is to be based on knowledge.

Like PEACE, CREATIVE contains a model of the interview phases. See Figure 1.

As can be seen in Figure 1, the interview is divided into six phases.

The model is both straightforward and practical, while also being flexible and dynamic. It is therefore applicable to most professional interviews. In countries where the police have addressed the failings of former practices and introduced research-based methods, the same methodology is applied, regardless of whether a suspect or a witness is being interviewed. The detectives who were tasked with the difficult challenge of questioning the young people who survived the terrorist's deranged attack on the island of Utøya on July 22, 2011, have been through the exact same training as the detectives who interviewed the terrorist.

We will cover each individual phase of the model in Part 2.

Broad Scope of Application

When we claim that the method is suitable for virtually all professional interview situations, this claim is primarily based on two key factors.

The first is the method's scientifically verified effectiveness and continued evaluation. Investigative interviewing has become the subject of extensive research. What is unique about police interviewing is that unlike most other forms of professional interviews, an audio or video recording is made of the

1. PLANNING AND PREPARATION

The interviewer carries out physical, mental, and case-related/strategic preparations for all phases

2. ESTABLISHMENT OF RAPPORT (ENGAGE AND EXPLAIN)

Interviewees are greeted with empathy and receive information about the interview objectives and process—promoting a mutual understanding.

3. FIRST FREE RECALL

The interviewer facilitates and encourages the interviewee to provide a free recall.

4. EXPLORATION AND CLARIFICATION

In this phase, clarification and follow-up questions are asked. Information is presented if necessary.

5. CLOSING THE INTERVIEW

The interview is closed in an informative manner. Predictability and trust are preserved.

6. EVALUATION

The information obtained and the interview phases are evaluated. Self-reflection.

Figure 1 The interview phases. *Source:* Author.

entire interview. These recordings have provided researchers with comprehensive and true-life data. In their analyses, the researchers have culled insights from findings in the fields of psychology, sociology, criminology, human rights, and ethics. Investigative interviewing has thus been developed through an interdisciplinary approach and adapted to years of research on what works and doesn't work in an interview situation. Police interviews are also evaluated daily in a large number of investigations and in the courtroom. The basis in research, the ongoing evaluation, and application of lessons learned also ensure that the investigative interviewing methodology is constantly evolving.

The second reason why we maintain that the method is ideal for many professions is its practical structure and inherently dynamic flexibility. The tools of the method make it suitable for interviews with with individuals that are motivated to tell everything they know, parts of what they know, or nothing. We can use the same methodology in both cases. The flexibility of the method allows you to adapt it to each unique interpersonal encounter. The structure is designed to counteract unconscious, and thereby automatic, decision-making processes. An open mindset in the interviewer is stimulated through use of a method that counters the tricky aspects of cognitive bias through the testing of relevant hypotheses (i.e., alternative explanations). Objectivity and reliability are also strengthened by an informed clarity about the nature of questions and their formulation. The method is like a toolbox, in which some tools are used in virtually every interview, while others are more context specific. Tools used to foster communication, for example (such as balancing the relation of power in the interview), will be helpful in most professional interviews. Memory enhancement tools, on the other hand, serve no purpose in an interview when the recollection of prior events is not significant but can be crucial in cases where it is.

The book is written in two parts. The first part is about the foundation of the method: cognitive and social psychology research on memory, interpersonal communication, and decision-making. In the second part, the method itself is explained.

To demonstrate the method's broad-reaching relevance and illustrate the scope of its application, throughout the book we will employ both factual and invented examples from a variety of professions. The majority of the examples are naturally from police interviews, but the book also cites examples from interviews conducted by doctors, headhunters, journalists, child welfare officers, financial analysts, scholars, and teachers. This is of course not an exhaustive list of all the professions that use the interview to obtain relevant and reliable information. Nonetheless, it is our hope that the scope of the examples is broad enough to allow readers to apply them to their own context.

Since our claim is that the book's method is relevant for a number of professions, and even necessary in order to increase the professionalism of interview techniques, it is therefore also implicitly a critical assessment of the interview practices of other professions.

In the lectures we have held internationally for a wide range of professions, we have received feedback that the method is not only highly relevant but also a practical and necessary supplement to professional training and development. In some cases, professionals will acknowledge that they actually have no methodological approach to the interview whatsoever, even though it is the most important source of information in their daily work.

In the following we have addressed the doctor–patient interview, the journalistic interview, and research interview based on Norwegian reference materials. Of course, we do not have an overview of all the available literature, research, and case studies from these professions, but we have attempted to collate a selection of relevant sources that will illustrate the methodological foundation for training and instruction in a range of professions that use the interview as an important source of information.

The Doctor–Patient Interview

The ethical guidelines issued by the Norwegian Medical Association highlight trust and respect as key objectives: "The physician shall safeguard the interests and integrity of the patient. The patient is to be treated with compassion and respect. The collaboration with the patient should be based on mutual trust."

The ethical guidelines of medical practice do not specify anything about the communication between physician and patient, but substantial research has been done on the subject, and medical communication is a part of the curriculum in medical school.

According to one textbook from the reading list of this curriculum in Norway, entitled *Skreddersydde samtaler* (Tailormade Interviews) (Gulbrandsen & Finset 2019), the physician's communication with patients is a topic of interest because the experiences are quite mixed. The guidelines have also been amended to better address patients' expectations, which are wholly different from the expectations of 45 years ago. Today the patient is to be well informed and "they are to be involved in decisions about diagnosis and treatment."

A great deal of new knowledge about doctor–patient communication has been generated over the past 20 years: "This type of communication requires a number of skills that must be practiced regularly and systematically."

The textbook explains the fundamental principles for how health-care personnel should obtain information and how patients should be involved in treatment. The authors give the following advice:

Save your answers for the summary! Say something showing empathy at least once! Think before you speak and speak less. Patients are not stupid. It is easy to overestimate people's knowledge, but it is just as easy to underestimate their intelligence. Remember that you are on your home turf, and the patient is not! Good news can wait, always. Bad news cannot. (Gulbrandsen & Finset 2019)

The textbook also introduces the authors' three-phase model *BIS* (beginning, information gathering, summary and conclusion). The BIS model is based on The Four Habits Model (for effective medical communication) created by the US health-care company Kaiser Permanente. The four good habits are: (1) invest in the beginning, (2) elicit the patient's perspective, (3) demonstrate empathy, and (4) invest in the end.

The attentive reader may have noticed that the model presented in Figure 1, which forms the basis for investigative interviewing, includes the key steps promoted in research findings about the doctor–patient interview. Another key concept in the health-care sector that is also of relevance to the findings we present in this book is the *clinical interview*. This is the professional interview between a therapist and a client. Volume II of *Det kliniske intervjuet* (The Clinical Interview) (von der Lippe & Rønnestad 2011) defines the two primary objectives of the clinical interview as being to gather information and establish a relationship. Neither of these objectives can be viewed in isolation since "a good relationship usually promotes the possibility of acquiring good information."

In a professional interview as fraught with asymmetry—power imbalance— as an interview between doctor and patient, the risk of undue influence will be considerable. Despite this, there are few articles in the above-mentioned book describing the kinds of questions health-care personnel should ask, how the questions should be asked, and the order in which they should be asked. Neither is a strategy for avoiding the unfortunate consequences of cognitive traps provided.

In our opinion, the relevance of research on police interviews to this setting is considerable. Physicians also have a need for knowledge about relevant sources of error and a method to counteract these when making decisions that can mean the difference between life or death.

The Research Interview

Professional interviews are the most frequently employed research method in qualitative research. They are often described as structured interviews or qualitative research interviews. The Norwegian scientific literature about the research interview method points out that "the interview provides a particularly solid foundation for gaining insight into the experiences, thoughts, and emotions of an individual" (Thagaard 2018, p. 89). A number of researchers have written books about the research interview[2] and in more general methodology books about qualitative research methods, a chapter or two is always dedicated to the research interview.[3]

In the methodological literature used in the Norwegian social sciences, reference is often made to Kvale and Brinkmann (2015a) and their work *Det kvalitative forskningsintervju* (The Qualitative Research Interview), which illuminates the qualitative research interview from a variety of perspectives. In the chapter about interview quality, the authors explain what as researchers they hold to be "the criteria for the good and ideal interview, as well as standards for the interview as craftmanship." We recognize most of the qualities singled out here, but on one point our book distinguishes itself from theirs. At first glance, Kvale and Brinkmann appear to draw from George Ritzer's (2008) concept of the McDonaldization of society, or "rationalization" as Weber defines it in his work about the same phenomenon: everything is to be efficient, calculable, predictable, and controlled. That is a problem for qualitative research and therefore also for the research interview, Kvale and Brinkmann argue. On the basis of this, Kvale and Brinkmann place a greater emphasis on experience, craftsmanship, and the art of asking good questions than on a more methodical approach to data collection.

It is, however, our impression that the practical advice given to researchers who are supposed to learn the "craft" is, by and large, the same advice we outline in the presentation of our method in Part 2. If we are correct in this assessment, perhaps there are no contradictions, precisely because this craft—the implicit knowledge—is explained and thereby made more accessible through the findings of 30 years of critical research on police investigative interviewing. It is this production of knowledge that has led to the method we are describing. The method employs the central qualities that Kvale and Brinkmann and others describe, not least those related to their explanation of the fact-based interview, in which it can "be critical to gather valid, factual information" (Kvale & Brinkmann 2015a, p. 180).

2. Internationally, reference is often made to *Handbook of Interview Research* (Gubrium et al. 2010). Note that Kvale and Brinkmann's book is also available in English: *InterViews: Learning the Craft of Qualitative Research Interviewing* . The book was translated as a contribution to the SAGE Qualitative Research Kit (Kvale & Brinkmann 2015b), which consists of 10 volumes that provide practical and accessible advice on how to conduct qualitative research.

3. Thagaard (2018) and Tjora (2017) are two of several Norwegian sources on qualitative research method. In an international context, *The Oxford Handbook of Qualitative Research* (Leavy 2014) and *The SAGE Handbook of Qualitative Research* (Denzin & Lincoln 2011) are common references.

The Journalistic Interview

In the European tradition, the press and news media are often referred to as the fourth state power, in the United States, as the Fourth Estate or fourth power. The concept is predominantly a reflection of how the press has defined its own role as an independent and free agent, the objective of which is to evaluate and write about the other three estates in a critical fashion. With this mandate follows power. For that reason, the press—like medicine and other professions—has established ethical guidelines with which traditional media outlets worldwide endeavor to comply.

In Norway, the role of the press is defined in the Ethical Code of Practice for the Norwegian press and the joint declaration signed by both the Association of Norwegian Editors and the Norwegian Media Business Association. The purpose of the journalistic interview is not clearly laid out, but the Ethical Code of Practice operationalizes the ethics of the journalistic working method.

> Good press ethics stipulate transparency regarding the terms of interview situations as well as in relation to sources and contacts. [...] Conduct yourself considerately in the journalistic work process. In particular be considerate when dealing with people who cannot be expected to understand the impact of their statements. Do not abuse the feelings, ignorance, or faulty judgement of others. Remember that people in a state of shock or grief are more vulnerable than others.

In short, journalists are supposed to show consideration for the people they encounter when carrying out professional interviews. They are not to operate on the basis of hidden agendas and thereby mislead the people they interact with in interviews. The core values stipulate respect for the fact that we all have different points of view, roles, and experiences.

But in much the same way that the police's experience-based interrogation method pushed the ethical envelope—they were designed to elicit confessions—it is natural that in the media's search for news, the financial requirements driving speedy publication and a clickbait culture constantly challenge news media's ethical principles, especially in an interview setting.

It is not a bold claim to state that journalists often resort to closed questions and the proposing of answers to confirm their assumptions and hypotheses. There is no need to research this; it is enough to count the number of open versus closed questions. In the 1970s, 1980s, and 1990s, there was even material on the syllabus at the Norwegian Institute of Journalism advocating closed interviewing techniques. In the Norwegian textbook *Innføring i journalistikk* (Introduction to Journalism) (Wale 1996), journalists were actually encouraged to use closed questions, as a means of creating headlines, as in the following:

> Open questions elicit general statements, while closed questions lead to more specific answers. It can make sense to start an interview by asking a few open questions. But as soon as possible you should switch to closed questions that can generate answers from which headlines can be created!

Similar literature was used in Denmark, bearing similarity to the confession-focused interrogation techniques used by the police. The purpose of the interview was to induce the interviewee to make specific statements, "so that by the end of the interview, the interviewee will speak the already formulated phrases" as recommended in the Danish author Kurt Strand's book *Spørg bedre: Interview og intervjuteknik i radio og TV* (Ask Better Questions: Interviewing and Interview Techniques for Radio and TV) (1998). The method raises ethical questions and recommends a questionable mentality, insofar as it gives cognitive traps free rein. That is not recommended for anyone, journalists included.

The book *Som journalister spør: Om intervju som arbeidsmetode i nyhetsjournalistikken* (As Asked by Journalists: About the Interview as a Work Method in News Journalism) (Lamark 2001) is based on qualitative studies done at Bodø University College in Norway (Lamark 1997), in which the author has analyzed recordings of 20 interviews done by five news journalists.

Lamark's analysis shows that open questions made up only 10 percent of the questions asked, while all of 36 percent were leading questions or statements. The author's hypothesis was that the journalists had an interview method, but she concluded that it was in fact more a matter of an interview strategy, which was primarily based on experience, and trial and error.

In more recent textbooks the different types of interview methods that are covered have more in common with this book's approach. In *Intervjuteknikk for journalister* (Interviewing Techniques for Journalists) (2008) by Brynjulf Handgaard, the author is clear about how interviews aiming to "take down the interviewee" are seldom successful. Handgaard cites sociology professors Steven Clayman and John Heritage, who concluded that this type of confrontational interview strategy seldom generated admissions. Handgaard concludes:

> Good questions are defined by an attitude of a wish to ascertain something. The result of the interview can still be that a person is outed or unmasked, but that is then a consequence of the questioning technique, not a goal for the interview.

2

THE FOUNDATION OF THE METHOD

The technique for police questioning of victims, witnesses, and crime suspects has undergone fundamental revision in a number of countries. Both the recognition that errors have been made and the understanding of where those errors lie have been crucial for the positive development. Thousands of police interviews have been researched and evaluated. This has led to a better understanding of what was defective and who was responsible.

When something goes wrong in a professional interview, it is easy to blame the person in charge of the interview. But errors never arise in a vacuum. The professional interview takes place within a context, in an environment. It takes place within an organization or institution with its own routines, methods, and culture.

Errors of Justice—Procedural Aberrations

An error of justice is defined as any aberration from the optimal outcome of a criminal procedure (Forst 2004). This implies that innocent parties are not to be charged or convicted and guilty parties are to be appropriately sanctioned. In the judicial system, an error of justice committed during police questioning can lead to a case never being solved or, in the worst-case scenario, a wrongful conviction. The latter is often referred to as a miscarriage or failure of justice. Here we will use the term *error of justice*, because this book is about the prevention of both large and small procedural errors. The consequences of an error of justice can be enormous, the most apparent being personal tragedies. Rectifying the often-extreme ramifications of errors of justice that propagate and are disseminated throughout a system can also be costly and resource intensive. Large and small errors of justice will also undermine the overall trust in the judicial system and even trust in democracy.

Errors of justice are usually caused by human error. But the reason why the error was committed in the first place is often related to the larger system within which it occurs and the underlying culture. Although the manipulative interrogations and confession in the Norwegian "Birgitte case," discussed in the introduction chapter, at first glance appear to be errors committed by individuals, the errors of justice in this case ran much deeper. It was the system as a whole—the Norwegian police and the prosecution—that failed, not the detective from the National Crime Investigation Service . He was given the task of interrogating the cousin because he was reputed to be the best. He had developed and refined the experience-based approach to interrogation, the guidelines of which at the time were found in documents classified as "secret"—for internal use only. The system had failed. The education offered at the Norwegian Police Academy and later at the Norwegian Police University College was not of a professional standard that sufficiently compensated for the cultural legacy of the police as an institution, in which eliciting a confession was regarded at the primary goal of the interrogation.

If we are to translate the term *errors of justice* so as to make it relevant in other contexts, it can be described as a *procedural error:* an error arising in the course of a procedure or process that leads to a less-than-optimal outcome. In this book we will address procedural errors that occur in the professional interview.

Let's take as an illustration the case of an investor who for lack of an interview method fails to obtain sufficiently relevant or reliable information from a head of industry about his assessments of quarterly figures, information the investor needs in order to make the right investments. The outcome in this case could be that he or she invests too much or too little and therefore risks losing money. Hiring the wrong person can also be extremely expensive. This can occur when a headhunter's questions fail to elicit enough relevant information about a candidate. Incorrect diagnoses in the health-care system do not just cost money but also have huge human costs. Such errors can also be due to a flawed methodological approach in consultations with the patient.

Cases of erroneous whistleblowing and the need to reinforce and protect whistleblowing as an institution led to a new amendment in the Norwegian Working Environment Act relating to the duty of notification in Norway in 2019. The law states that employers are bound to have written procedures for obtaining, processing, and following up on notifications of blameworthy conditions. One of the most important "tools" throughout the entire process in this context is without doubt the interviews held with the whistleblower and the person who is the focus of the notification. Without training or methodology for professional interviews, the protection the Act is intended to provide will never reach its full potential.

If procedural errors are made during the fact-finding phase, these errors can have unfortunate consequences for the outcome and damage the trust in and reputation of an organization or institution. When a procedural error is detected, it should be carefully examined so as to clarify the cause and determine whether the system can be improved. If an employer has not taken appropriate measures to ensure that the investor, human resources (HR) department, or physician has the knowledge and skills required to carry out professional interviews or consultations, then the procedural error is a systemic error and must be handled as such. If, on the other hand, the interviewer in question fails to follow procedures taught in formal training or ignores established workplace routines, the procedural error lies in the practice of the individual.

In order to be able to analyze a nonconformity in an interview context, an organization must have an established method for the professional interview: we must know *what* we are evaluating. Physicians, HR employees, journalists, and detectives must have a recognized methodology, a minimum standard for their own profession. Without such a methodology, it is in practical terms impossible to ensure the professionalism of interviews. The absence of a methodology exposes organizations, agencies, and entire professions to the risk of recurring procedural errors that can damage an enterprise's achievement of goals, reputation, and perceived trustworthiness.

Research on errors of justice as the source of incorrect inferences resulting in wrongful convictions shows that the criminal justice chain tends to ratify errors committed at an early stage in a case—typically during the information-gathering phase. Or to put this differently, in cases referred to as errors of justice, the error may have occurred during police questioning and been propagated. The greater the scope of dissemination of error into the (criminal justice) system, the lesser the chances of the error being discovered and corrected (Huff et al. 1996). An exception here are cases where the error consists of obvious violations of basic rights. It goes without saying, but the point is of such central importance that it merits emphasis: every time an error provides a basis for action, its impact is compounded (Ramsey 2003; Rachlew 2009, p. 19).

Although we have greater knowledge about errors of justice thanks to research on the judicial system, it is not difficult to imagine correspondingly destructive processes in other sectors, such as when a news desk chooses to publish a quote that has been garbled through the leading questions of the journalist. Norway's largest newspaper was convicted on five counts in a historic ruling by the Norwegian Press Complaints Commission for having asked extremely leading questions.[1] Or think about the chief physician who adheres to an incorrect diagnosis arrived at through defective questioning and listening techniques on the part of the examining physician. The Norwegian Patient

---

1. https://presse.no/pfu-sak/099-19/.

Association has highlighted this as an important source of error and huge challenge:

> There are a number of reasons why patients are not heard when they share their problems and ailments with the health care system. Some of the most common causes include personnel who don't have time and haven't received proper training in how to ask questions, listen, and understand what the patient is telling them.[2]

The Benefits of a Methodology

The above quote describes the former situation of the Norwegian police. The Norwegian Police Academy had never established or taught a quality-assured method for the gathering of information when questioning victims, witnesses, or crime suspects. Police detectives did not receive adequate training and had received virtually no guidance on *how* a professional interview should actually be carried out. A long series of errors of justice occurred due to a lack of professionalism. The police were just as interested in doing a good job then as they are today—in apprehending culprits and avoiding the arrest of innocent parties—but without theoretical knowledge and a quality-assured method, the police remained at risk of committing the typical errors stemming from a reliance on human intuition.

The faulty questioning techniques did not only elicit unreliable information. The errors had large consequences for those the police were meant to serve—the victims, witnesses, and suspects. When the sources of the error were brought to light in Norway through the Birgitte case, several members of the police force understood that something had to be done. The errors of justice undermined the trust not just in individual detectives but also in the police and the prosecution—in the entire justice system.

It is not only governmental agencies that depend on a high level of trust. Regardless of the industry or profession you represent, trust is crucial for ensuring good outcomes. The legitimacy of a company, an institution, or an organization depends upon people trusting that the enterprise follows and makes decisions based on a sound code of practice. As long as decisions depend upon relevant and reliable information obtained through professional interviews, as a professional you must ensure the application of methods designed to counteract the most common procedural errors. The design of investigative interviewing is suited for strengthening relations and thereby the

---

2. https://www.pasient.no/pasienters-problemer/jeg-blir-ikke-hort.

trust between yourself and the person with whom you are speaking, whether this be a customer, patient, job applicant, or others.

The Power Structure of the Interview

In most cultures, children learn that they are to respect their elders—their parents, persons of authority, those who have experience, and those who have knowledge. Communication is also characterized by this. Politeness, respect, humility. But do we learn just as much about how we should communicate with those who are younger or who are vulnerable, those who don't have knowledge or power?

Because the power structure in an interview situation is inherently imbalanced, it is critical for the professional interviewer to understand how such asymmetry influences communication and the information acquired. A physician must understand the inherent imbalance of a doctor–patient consultation, journalists must understand that they usually hold the power when interviewing sources, and the police must understand the same thing in their interviews. Asymmetric communication can also affect the flow of information in an enterprise. Just think of how a middle management employee relates to an authoritarian boss who has power over advancement in the company. In a given situation we can even end up saying the opposite of what we actually think. By gaining an understanding of asymmetric communication, professionals can learn how to minimize the adverse effects of unequal power structures. In most professional interviews, a power differential will play an important role in the workings of communication. Without reflection and a method, the risk of unconscious influence increases.

In her dissertation "Berätta din sanning" (Speak your truth) (2005), the Swedish educator Harriet Öhrn addressed power structure imbalances found in interviews between professionals and laymen, in other words, interview asymmetry. Öhrn began her research by investigating *institutional interviews*: interviews in which a professional is expected to lead the conversation, ask questions, and give a report of the meeting. The asymmetric power structure is an inherent component of the interview situation, regardless of whether it is the police, the health-care sector, job recruiting, schools, or courts who are doing the interviewing.

Öhrn's analysis is based on Drew and Heritage's (1992) three features of an institutional interview. First, interview participants have a mutual understanding that the interaction will have an *outcome*. Nonetheless, the participants may have different objectives, and these objectives can be either clearly or poorly defined. The accused in a criminal case may have an objective of hiding the truth during questioning, while a detective will want to uncover the truth. A victim may feel compelled to speak about his or her feelings, while the detective will be primarily interested in establishing the facts of the case.

Second, the *context* will influence the interaction. Many institutional interactions have rules or expectations that control the actions of participants. There are, for example, clear legal rules regulating a police interview and court testimony. One such rule stipulates that a suspect is to be informed that he is not obliged to offer an explanation. The context can naturally influence a lot of what takes place in an interview or in a courtroom. In a doctor's office, there is an expectation that the patient will speak about his or her ailments. The doctor should keep in mind that the patient may consciously or unconsciously withhold relevant information, but the expectation of a collaboration is there. The patient expects the doctor to investigate the symptoms and help the patient find a cure.

Third, each individual institution will have frameworks defining what is considered to be *acceptable communication*. Some figures of speech, humorous turns of phrases and words, would be inappropriate in a conversation between a bereaved individual and a priest. We find similar frameworks in an interaction between a teacher and a pupil. And it is expected that the person leading an institutional interview will behave professionally and not share emotional reactions. This requires mental preparation. Such preparations are also included as a key component of the model we present in the second part of this book.

The asymmetry of an institutional interview is obvious. The professional from the institution carries out such interviews as a part of his or her job. The interviewer has the entire institution behind him, while the interviewee is often alone and must rely on himself and his own assessments. The professional usually comes prepared, has experience, and knows the rules, parameters, and structure of the interaction. The professional is also in possession of knowledge about the subject matter the interview will address. Furthermore, the professional has the power to decide or influence the outcome of the interview: benefits, sanctions, or in-between. Some decisions may even be life changing. Will you get the job? Did the physician prescribe the right medicine? Will the police press charges?

The interviewee may take part in this type of interaction only once in their lifetime, without any particular prior knowledge of the frameworks for the interview or how it will unfold. Many people therefore feel insecure in the context of a professional interview. For example, an inexperienced source may experience a meeting with the media as frightening. The source is not in a position to understand how the interview will be used. If the interviewer also lacks awareness and a method developed to curb undue influence, the risk of the production of unreliable information increases.

The professional also has power over where, when, and how the interview will be conducted, the contents, and allocation of roles. Further, the professional decides on the conceptual framework and the definitions forming the basis for the interaction.

> The asymmetry between parties in an interaction is an expression of the professional's social position of power. The interaction is controlled by the professional and the layman is guided through the phases. The layman has limited opportunities to take any initiative in the interaction and therefore limited opportunities to express himself. What is to be said, when it shall be said and how it shall be said is defined and limited by the institutional structure and the professional party in the interaction. (Harriet Öhrn 2005, p. 5)

For a suspect in a criminal procedure, a source for a newspaper article, a job applicant, or a patient who is dependent upon the help and advice of her doctor, the unbalanced power structure of the interaction gives the interviewer an advantage. To foster optimal communication, in other words, to increase the interviewee's ability and willingness to provide relevant, accurate, and reliable information, the professional must mitigate the power asymmetry in the interaction. Because it is the professional who has the power, it is the professional who holds the responsibility for doing something about the imbalance.

The elimination of all asymmetry is neither possible nor desirable. The interview is a part of a professional process through which decisions are to be made. If nobody is given professional responsibility, we risk having the entire interaction unravel into an informal and seemingly casual chat. It will not improve accuracy and will open the door to sources of error. Nonetheless, the professional can do many things to limit the experience of asymmetry without abandoning the expertise that should define the professional interview. The communication of empathy and treating others with respect and courtesy, as equals, are fundamental conditions for all professional interviews.

When the interviewer shows respect and empathy through transparency and sincerity, professional trust is formed. That trust is something professional interviewers rely on to achieve respect and ensure that interviewees will be inclined to share information. Those who are going to share information must experience that they are taken seriously and that they can exercise personal discretion regarding what information they will or will not share. They must also be able to trust that the information they provide will be handled in a professional manner. Transparency alleviates some of the power imbalance (asymmetry), making it easier for the interviewee to respond openly. At the very least, professional trust strengthens communication and reduces distractions.

And if the interviewee is not ready to communicate there and then, the invest-ment is not wasted. Building trust can take time. Through professional con-duct, we can open the door for good communication down the line.

Different types of courses are held in Norway on "interviewing the patient." Pediatrician Bård Fossli Jensen has done extensive research on the subject of doctor–patient communication.[3] In the article "Lær kommunikasjon—bli bedre lege" (Learn communication—become a better doctor), Fossli Jensen stresses the critical significance of trust when the patient is being asked to divulge information:

> Communication in the health care sector is based on one main compo-nent: trust. Everything we do should foster trust, at the very least preserve it, and above all, not undermine it. Unfortunately, this does not always come to pass. It is therefore important that trust constitute the basis for everything we do. We see that a good interview structure fosters more trust than improvised strategies, strategies such as being cheerful, helpful or funny.[4]

Establishing rapport—whereby the communication of empathy is initi-ated—is such a central component that it is highlighted as a separate phase in research-based interview techniques. In Part 2, we will explain in further detail how this fundamental phase is best carried out and the components it should include. At this point, we can already establish that the greater the amount of straightforward information the interviewer provides about (a) *con-text*, why the interview is being held, (b) *the framework* for the interview, and (c) *how* the interview will proceed, the less the interview will generate undesir-able consequences stemming from asymmetry.

In short, it is a matter of the professional surrendering some of his or her power by sharing information about what will take place. Clarifying frameworks, roles, and expectations creates predictability. It reduces stress and

---

3. Bård Fossli Jensen, "Hospital Doctors' Communication Skills. A Randomized Controlled Trial Investigating the Effect of a Short Course and the Usefulness of a Patient Questionnaire," Defense of doctoral thesis at the University of Oslo, Institute of Clinical Medicine, 2011.

4. "Lær kommunikasjon—bli en bedre lege?" (Learn communication—become a better doctor?), *Tidsskrift for Den norske legeforening* (Journal of the Norwegian Medical Association), vol. 21, November 11, 2014, 134.

nervousness and stimulates communication. This can be demanding, but the best interviewers are able to reduce the feeling of asymmetry without stepping out of their professional role.

Öhrn's research was based on interviews between professionals and laymen. However, asymmetry can also arise in interviews between two professionals. What creates asymmetry is the power inherent to the different roles. Imagine that somebody is being investigated by their colleagues for alleged errors. Even though both parties carry out professional interviews in conjunction with their jobs and know the language and rules of both the professional context and the interaction, the one party's power over the outcome of the interview will potentially produce asymmetry. The greater the consequences, the greater the asymmetry. In a meeting between two professionals from different fields, the asymmetry will be even more pronounced.

A number of studies have identified systematic social differences in the way doctors communicate with patients.[5] We know that cultural background, skin color, language, clothing, age, and gender have an impact on all relationships, also in the doctor's office. A systematic review of relevant literature documents that doctors provide better information, explain more, engage more, and are more emotionally supportive in meeting with patients with a high socioeconomic status. The opposite is the case for patients with a lower socioeconomic status. In the latter case, the communication is characterized more by "direct questions, biomedical information, physiological measurements and examinations—and less socio-emotional conversation or involvement of the patient."[6]

An Open Mind

Most civilizations endeavor to formulate some general moral principles. Such principles will often explain basic, universal rules for how people should treat one another. In Christianity, this is translated as *the golden rule, the ethic of reciprocity*, and *brotherly love*. These values find expression in Article 1 of the UN Universal Declaration of Human rights (1948): "All human beings are born

5. E. Verlinde, N. De Laender, S. De Maesschalck, M. Deveugele, & S. Willems, "The Social Gradient in Doctor-Patient Communication," *International Journal for Equity in Health* 11, no. 12 (2012).
6. "Den sosiale gradienten på legekontoret" (The social gradient in the doctor's office), https://tidsskriftet.no/2019/09/legelivet/den-sosiale-gradienten-pa-legekontoret.

free and equal in dignity and rights. They are endowed with reason and conscience and should act towards one another in a spirit of brotherhood."

The connection between fundamental human rights and research-based interview methods has over the years become increasingly evident. Two of the leading pioneers behind the introduction of the methods presented in this book, the forensic psychologists Tom Williamson and Eric Shepherd, raised ethical questions in their groundbreaking research. Their article "Ethical Interviewing" (Shepherd 1991) was made part of the compulsory syllabus for police detectives in the Oslo police district when investigative interviewing was introduced in Norway 10 years later. Today the connection to human rights is obvious. The ongoing development of investigative interviewing has a primary focus on the safe and effective integration of human rights as an inherently operational component of the interview practice (Griffiths & Rachlew 2018).

The ethos underpinning investigative interviewing implies that professional interviewers shall always carry out their interviews, conversations, or consultations in the same way that they would want to be treated had the tables been turned, as if they themselves, or a family member, were seated in the other chair.

The close connection between investigative interviewing and human rights was in many ways recognized and made manifest when Juan Méndez, the UN special rapporteur on torture, made a recommendation before the General Assembly in New York to develop UN standards of conduct for police interviewing worldwide, standards designed according to the research-based methods (Méndez 2016). Méndez substantiated his recommendation to the UN by emphasizing how investigative interviewing contributes to safeguarding the presumption of innocence, while strengthening the case against the suspect in the event the latter is found guilty. According to the presumption of innocence, everyone has the right to be treated as if they were innocent until such time when they have been proven guilty under the law.

Méndez understood that the method is effective, while it simultaneously protects fundamental human rights. The presumption of innocence is a so-called normative ideal that in many ways constitutes a guiding star for how actors in the legal system should treat the people they meet in their daily work.

The presumption of innocence is not about what the police should think or believe regarding material innocence or guilt. The principle gives actors a guideline for how to carry out their job (Packer 1969). In other words, the principle is not a guess about the outcome of the case, but more a mindset intended to prevent judgment, moralizing, precipitated conclusions, and tunnel vision. From a perspective of decision-making psychology, the principle reminds us of the importance of keeping an open mind—a mindset that interviewers should endeavor to uphold throughout the entire interview process.

Sometimes it appears obvious that one is face-to-face with a guilty suspect. In the case of the terrorist attacks in Norway of July 22, 2011, there was little doubt about the identity of the culprit. He was arrested still holding the murder weapon on the island of Utøya. In the interviews he was nonetheless treated with respect and given the opportunity to explain his actions and motives, like everyone else under suspicion of having committed a crime. The suspected terrorist did have to accept being handcuffed on his way to and from the police station, but he was interviewed using the same interview techniques as those employed with witnesses and victims in the same case (Rachlew 2017).

When the police proceed according to a presumption of innocence and allow the inherent values of the principle to define their conduct, this creates some clear guidelines. Interviewees leave the session with a feeling of having been respected without judgment and of having been allowed to tell their story.

The ethical principles constituting the foundation of investigative interviewing are clearly applicable to a series of other professional interviews and interactions. Nobody is to be prejudged—not by the media, the child welfare authorities, the asylum services, employers, or any other investigating, examining, or evaluating parties. The former director of Økokrim, the national authority for investigation and prosecution of economic and environmental crime in Norway, lawyer, and forensic detective Erling Grimstad (2015) highlights the same fundamental principles in his book on the investigation of fraud and compliance and writes: "It is also good practice to treat anyone accused of something as if they are innocent and give the person in question a fair opportunity to rebut any allegations and present their story."

There are many stories from the health-care sector of patients who claim that their condition was aggravated because their doctor had not listened well enough or been sufficiently interested in what they had to say. As an anonymous doctor (Anonymous 2017) wrote in the *Journal of the Norwegian Medical Association* under the headline "Nå skjønner jeg" (Now I understand) after contracting a serious illness:

> I believe what was lacking was one experienced doctor who was willing to take responsibility, listen to what I had to say, ask me questions, follow up, examine information with others from an interdisciplinary perspective, give the matter thought, and provide me with a proper explanation.

When we open up to listening without judgment in our interactions with others, communication is stimulated. This holds true regardless of whether or not the other person has anything to hide. In the daily life of the police, innocent parties receive a genuine opportunity to strengthen their case. A guilty party wishing to provide a truthful account will have the opportunity to tell their story in a nonjudgmental interview. Nonjudgmental listening also increases the chances that a person who initially wants to withhold information will reconsider and decide to share (Bull & Rachlew 2020). Research into the psychology of lying has revealed something that most of us understand intuitively; that the more information we acquire, the better equipped we will be for assessing the credibility of that information.

Later in the book we will explain in detail how professional interviewers should prepare and carry out strategic interviews. Strategic interviewing is essentially about how we handle critical information during an interaction. In police investigations, critical information is referred to as *evidence* or *potential evidence*. In other professional interviews, this can be information that is sensitive in nature, which others may find difficult to address. How we handle such critical information can determine the outcome of the fact-finding process. It is important to keep in mind that some people consciously withhold information while others may forget details or simply misunderstand.

The strategic aspect of investigative interviewing is also clearly applicable to a number of professions, such as doctors, job recruiters, financial analysts, journalists, and child welfare employees—all of whom must be aware that not everyone they speak with wants to share critical and relevant information. Handling such situations in an ethical and effective manner requires strategic thinking and a method for applying that strategy in practice. In the second part of the book, we explain how critical information should be handled and "strategically" disclosed.

A financial analyst may work in an investment firm that places funds in different companies—they buy shares. In the process of reaching a decision regarding an investment, a financial analyst will gather and analyze a large amount of information about the company in question. Some of that information is in the form of figures, but in order to understand what lies behind the figures, the analyst must search for information from other sources. This part of the financial analyst's work is therefore not unlike the work of a police detective.

Whether you are a financial analyst or a police detective, interviews will often be an important component of the information-gathering process. If you are going to invest in a company, you will be interested in acquiring more information than that made available in annual reports and quarterly results. It is important to obtain relevant and reliable information about operations and future prospects. For that reason, you will have many questions for the management of the company. Simultaneously, you will want to treat the management in a way that fosters a good climate of collaboration for the future. A financial analyst will often have interviews with customers, competitors, and suppliers to gain a complete picture of how the company's operations and strategy are perceived by other key stakeholders. Again, this is comparable to the police questioning of witnesses in a criminal case. When we consider the job of a financial analyst from such a perspective, it is perhaps not surprising that an investment fund was one of the first enterprises, after police services, to offer a training course on the methodology, theory, and exercises found in this book.

The principles informing the presumption of innocence help us to meet people with an open mind, prompting a fundamental attitude of curiosity and respect. What at the outset could have been merely a meeting with a customer/client/patient/student—and someone about whom you have already begun drawing conclusions—becomes an interaction between two people in which the outcome is not given. The interpersonal encounter will then be experienced as professional, and the chance of obtaining more reliable information and drawing correct conclusions is heightened.

It becomes a win–win situation. The presumption of innocence encourages productive interpersonal communication while safeguarding any ethical concerns that may arise. The professional becomes more objective and the chances of procuring relevant, accurate, and reliable information are hereby increased, which in turn provides a better foundation for decision-making. In short, professional interviews foster trust in you, your organization, and your profession.

The Aim of Professional Interviews

A key feature of the interview techniques presented in this book is that they preserve the integrity of the interviewee. When it became evident that changes in police questioning procedures were required, the police had to take a step back and ask themselves some basic questions: "Why are we doing an interview? What is the aim of what we are doing?"

The questions may seem banal, but the answers did in fact reveal that several of the experience-based techniques the police were using were not in compliance with the law's ideal of objectivity and safe, fair processes. Of course, questioning, interviews, and professional interactions are means we employ to achieve an end. But when researchers began their studies of police interrogations, they discovered a fundamental ethical problem: the objective of solving the crime dominated to such an extent that it supplanted considerations for the integrity of those being questioned. The police detectives violated the ethical principle defined by Immanuel Kant (1895) in his work *Fundamental Principles of the Metaphysics of Ethics*: "the categorical imperative," which holds that we must never treat another human being solely as a means, but always also as an end in themselves.

When professional interviewers are planning and carrying out interviews, a clear awareness of *the purpose*—or the intention—of an interview is an important guiding standard. In 2002, the Council of Europe's anti-torture committee established a standard procedure for the questioning of suspects (CPT 2002). The aim is clearly defined in Article 34:

> First and foremost, the precise aim of such questioning must be crystal clear: that aim should be to obtain accurate and reliable information in order to discover the truth about matters under investigation, not to obtain a confession from someone already presumed, in the eyes of the interviewing officers, to be guilty.

By specifying the purpose of the interview, we are building a broad foundation for an outcome that encompasses mutual interests, as opposed to having the professional interviewer design the interaction on the basis of their desired or anticipated outcome.

Every professional interview must be adapted to the predominant objectives of the investigation. How a concrete interview or a consultation can best help to achieve that objective is something we will address in further detail under the phase *planning and preparation*. Here, by way of introduction, we will concentrate on the general purpose—or intention—of most professional interviews, namely, to obtain sufficiently detailed, relevant, and reliable information. The purpose expresses the fundamental principle behind the design of the entire method.

In most contexts, information is obtained to substantiate a conclusion or to be shared with others. A doctor speaks with his or her patient to determine the type of treatment the patient needs. A journalist interviews a source to shed light on a news story. Any decision or presentation is only as solid as the information on which it is based. To avoid procedural errors, the underlying information must be as relevant, accurate, and reliable as possible.

The method presented in the following chapters is based on the premise that the purpose of virtually all professional interviews and interactions is to obtain sufficiently detailed, relevant, accurate, and reliable information.

The first and most obvious purpose of the interview is to seek information that is *relevant* to the matter under investigation. But this alone is not adequate if we also want to ensure that procedural errors are not made. Second, the information we acquire must also be *reliable*. When making a choice or decision, it is important to be aware of the degree to which the information on which we are basing that choice or decision is trustworthy. In an interview situation, this requires knowledge about how you and others taking part in the interview are influencing one another and the answers that emerge. It also requires an awareness of the best way to corroborate the information gathered. Third, the information must be sufficiently *detailed*. Even if the information is relevant and reliable, it is not sufficient if it doesn't contain the details you need. It would be like asking for an address and receiving only the name of a country and city. Both pieces of information are presumably relevant and reliable, but you still won't find your way without the details, such as the street name and preferably also the number of the building.

Even if the information we gather is relevant, reliable, and detailed, we are still at risk of making bad decisions. This is the case if we haven't succeeded in gathering information covering all aspects of the matter under investigation or if we have failed to meet objectivity requirements. It is human nature to seek information that confirms our preconceived notions about how the world is put together.

We must establish the case's relevant, alternative hypotheses and subsequently test them with systematic precision in the interview, in order to compel ourselves to see all relevant sides of the case. Without such a professional approach, we are more susceptible to being misled by unconscious cognitive traps that influence us more than we suspect. They are called traps because we walk into them, all the time, in a wholly natural and human attempt to *confirm* what we already believe.

Knowledge about cognitive traps (biases) and research-based counter-strategies have been central components in the development of the interview methods addressed in this book. In decision-making psychology, the various types of cognitive traps are referred to as cognitive simplification processes (Kahneman 2011). In simple terms, the unconscious strategies help us notice and search for information in support of our assumptions, or in the opposite case, to explain away or ignore whatever doesn't fit those assumptions. Overcoming the effects of cognitive simplification processes is tricky because we don't notice their influence. We will soon return to *how* we are influenced—and what we must do to reduce the inexpedient effects of cognitive simplification processes.

In the following quote, forensic psychologists David Canter and Laurence Alison (1999, p. 30) outline a normative ideal for how we should think in an interview context. It is an ideal, and full compliance is probably impossible. But in the same way that the presumption of innocence serves as a guideline for how we should approach the interviewee, the quote expresses an ideal for how we should think: "good thinking is represented by a thorough search for an alternative without favouring the one already on mind."

One unavoidable quality requirement is that our interview methods must be effective. Effective processes are also a part of the purpose. Time is a limited resource in almost all interview situations. The methods must both balance and include all objectives. Quick clarifications are of little help if they are based on unreliable information. Erroneous inferences can be extremely costly. Balancing all these elements with professional precision is such a demanding exercise that we need the support of a method. The method stimulates an open mindset and upholds requirements for relevance, precision, and reliability. One of the keys to success lies in the first phase of the method: the planning and preparation phase. But before moving on to this, we must first explore in greater depth the underlying psychology of the methods.

3

PSYCHOLOGY

Knowledge from psychology research has been integral to the development of the police investigation methods in general and investigative interviewing techniques in particular. The findings of cognitive and social psychology experiments have proven especially important. Modern cognitive psychology emerged in the 1960s at a time when computer technology was on the rise and psychological processes in humans were compared with electronic data processing done by computers. From the late 1960s, the research findings were actively applied in other fields, including eyewitness and decision-making psychology.

In its online dictionary, the American Psychological Association (APA) defines cognitive psychology as follows: "The branch of psychology that explores the operation of mental processes related to perceiving, attending, thinking, language, and memory, mainly through inferences from behavior."

Insights from social psychology, decision-making psychology, eyewitness psychology, and research on how the memory works have been of critical importance to the development of professional interview techniques. In many professional interviews, we search for the details or experience of an event. We then search through the memory of the interviewee. To extract the most reliable information possible from the memory, we must have knowledge about eyewitness psychology and how the memory works. In professional interviews in which we primarily look for factual information, attitudes, beliefs, and values, memory enhancement is of less importance. But regardless of the type of information we are looking for, the gathering and assessment of information and evidence will be strengthened when we employ available research findings from cognitive and social psychology. Knowledge about how decisions are made and how people influence one another in social settings is of key importance in interview situations. To understand and prevent all the sources of error the research has disclosed, we must first know a little bit about how the memory is structured.

Short-Term and Long-Term Memory

Most of us are familiar with the concepts of short- and long-term memory. The two types of memory carry out two different tasks, but they are simultaneously interdependent. Short-term memory is the part of memory that receives sense impressions and stores a limited amount of information for a short period of time, such as a telephone number, an address, or a name. It is our *attention* that determines what is registered here. Sense impressions (information) that are not transferred from the short-term memory to the long-term memory are lost forever. Short-term memory is a bit like a lost-and-found box at school. The contents remain there for a little while, but anything that is not retrieved is soon discarded. There is not much room in the box. Short-term memory is also called the *working memory* because it functions at a high gear and has limited capacity. Every single second of the day we are exposed to an inconceivable number of sense impressions. Everything we see, hear, smell, taste, and feel constitutes an enormous volume of "data" that we do not in any sense have the capacity to absorb. Most of this is lost, but we do retain some of it.

Long-term memory has far greater capacity than short-term memory when it comes to storing information. When information is transferred from the *short-term* to the *long-term memory*, we will remember that information for a long time. This transfer process is known as information *encoding* in the long-term memory.

The transfer of information from the short- to long-term memory is a complex process that we don't actually know all that much about, but numerous studies have confirmed some findings.

The information is transferred in three different ways:

1. Through *repetition* or memorization.
2. Through *association*. You won't necessarily remember four random numbers for a long time. But if you can connect and associate them (e.g., 1945), they can be stored.
3. *Emotions* assist long-term memory storage. If information in the short-term memory has an emotional connection, it is more easily transferred, sometimes automatically, to the long-term memory.

Figure 2 illustrates how our attention serves up information to the short-term memory, how most of the information is discarded, and how some of the information is transferred to the long-term memory, as the process is described by the *dual memory theory* (Chaplin 1985). There are a number of models that illustrate the functioning of short- and long-term memory. What these models

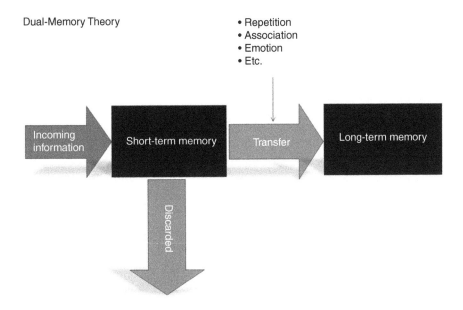

Figure 2 Dual memory theory, from CREATIV, based on Atkinson and Shiffrin (1968), also known as the Dual Store Model.

have in common is that some form of repetition seems to play a key role in the transfer and, thereby, in what is stored and can consequently be retrieved at a later date.

It is the long-term memory that is of most interest in our case, because it is from here that we retrieve the knowledge and memories we need to reconstruct events. The long-term memory is in turn divided into three different types of memory systems: (1) the procedural memory, (2) the semantic memory, and (3) the episodic memory.

The neurologist Paul McLean (1973) introduced the model of what he called the triune brain, which illustrates how the parts of the brain are connected to each of the three types of memory.

The *procedural memory* includes everything that is automated, such as work tasks that are performed as a matter of course. Once we have learned to walk, run, and ride a bike, we don't forget how to do these things. We do them without thinking. This type of memory is connected to the oldest and most basic parts of the brain: the brain stem and the cerebellum, also called the reptilian brain. The procedural memory requires a minimum amount of maintenance.

The *semantic memory* focuses on factual and conceptual knowledge, such as state capitals, multiplication tables, historical dates, language, etc. This knowledge is stored in the frontal cortex. This is the rational part of the brain that distinguishes us from other animals and is the youngest part of the human brain. This part of the brain also controls the processing of information and decisions. The semantic memory requires upkeep. Unlike riding a bicycle (procedural memory), it makes little difference that you learned in elementary school that George Washington was the first US president. Likewise, if we don't maintain our semantic memory of Norse mythology, we will lose the knowledge.

The *episodic memory* focuses on episodes we have experienced as children, adolescents, and adults. If we start to think about these episodes, more details related to the events will often begin to emerge. It is often this memory we mean when we refer to the memory in ordinary conversation. The responsibility for episodic memories is found in the limbic system of the brain. The limbic system is made up of several different parts that work together to steer autonomous reactions, feelings, and long-term memory. Sense impressions of odors are also stored in the limbic system. *For human beings, the connection of emotions, odors and memory in the limbic system is useful.* Because of this connection, memories associated with strong emotions are easier to remember and odor is the strongest memory trigger of all the senses.

An important factor that professional interviewers should keep in mind in this context is that the long-term memory is a complex network structure containing innumerable connections. The fact that you may have forgotten Stephen's name does not necessarily mean that the information is not stored somewhere in the network constituting your semantic memory. Instead, it means that the path to where the information is stored has been forgotten. We will return to how we as professional interviewers can take advantage of existing knowledge about the network structure of memory, but at this point what is important to understand is that the interview methods described step-by-step in Part 2 have been developed with this knowledge in mind, with an eye to how we as interviewers can best help the interviewee to retrieve memories—how we can help an interviewee find the right connections.

The potential of the human memory is fantastic. It is incredible what we are able to remember. The challenge for the police—and all other professionals seeking accurate and reliable information from their sources—is that the memory is fragile and easily influenced. It doesn't take much to produce erroneous connections—such as by overwriting a genuine memory with a false one. Preventing this kind of influence constitutes in many ways the core competency of the methods that were presented to the British police when they initiated their collaboration with researchers in the early 1990s. In the following, we will focus on episodic memory.

It is important to understand that an episodic memory does not function in isolation. It has no meaningful function without help from the semantic memory. Picture an eyewitness telling the police that the robbers drove away in a red car. A witness with a well-developed semantic memory for cars will easily be able to provide relevant and reliable details: "It was a Volvo xc90, 2002 First Edition. I have the same car." If on the other hand, the witness has lived his entire life deep in the Amazon rain forest, he would perhaps only be able to report that "the people got into a big box on wheels that made a fearful noise and disappeared with the swiftness of a jaguar." The point is that episodic memory is always connected to our semantic memory. Episodic memory in isolation has little import—on the whole, children and adults with a limited cognitive capacity have a more limited semantic memory than other adults.

This knowledge about the different types of memory can be of equal importance for doctors, journalists, recruiters, therapists, and detectives. A job applicant can describe herself as an extremely skilled leader and mean it but can still completely miss the mark due to a lack of knowledge about what good leadership actually entails. A child with a limited vocabulary about body parts may speak of having a pain in their "leg" and point at their foot when the problem is actually in the Achilles tendon.

The Phases of Memory

Even adults with basic cognitive skills can have difficulties remembering things, but as stated earlier, the fact that we can't remember does not necessarily mean that the information has not been stored. The connections to the memory may simply be temporarily missing. To understand the mechanisms at work when we as professional interviewers are going to retrieve memories from the long-term memory—find the paths—we must know that the memory is a process that is also divided into three parts: (1) the encoding phase, (2) the storage phase, and (3) the retrieval phase. And remember, our memory is influenced at all times, in all the phases.

Encoding Phase

In the *encoding phase* we absorb the information we have received through our senses and connected to feelings from the same experience. Research from eyewitness psychology explains what influences us and what can promote or inhibit storage of our experiences. Eyewitness psychologists have demonstrated in numerous studies that our ability to understand, interpret, prioritize, and organize our sense impressions (perception) is prone to several potential sources of error. These sources can be external (lighting conditions, the view, exposure time, barriers, disturbances), internal factors (age, perspective, experience, knowledge, interest, motivation, attention), and a combination of external parameters causing stress and/or confusion.

Knowledge about perception and the different sources of memory error improves our ability to pose good, relevant questions that are suitable for testing the reliability of the information we gather. Many police detectives make their own checklists of relevant questions—what was the lighting like, for how long did you observe the man, how far away were you, and so on.

Research has identified a number of variables that complicate the mapping of potential sources of error. Professional interviewers must acquire awareness of how different forms of experience can constitute significant sources of error. Human beings draw from previous experience to establish some basic rules, known as cognitive schemata *(heuristic techniques)*, which help us to organize sense impressions, find connections, and create understanding in our daily lives. Without such cognitive structures, we would become incapable of action, confused, and depressed. At the same time, these structures can be misleading when we unconsciously retrieve information from them to fill in the gaps in images from recent experiences, such as when we are attempting to make sense of processes we haven't properly understood.

For example, witnesses might state that a thief was wearing a balaclava without having actually seen the thief's head clearly. Our unconscious need to fill in the gaps and create a connection causes us to add information from our cognitive schemata, information that we think fits in the situation. The more demanding and complicated the external and individual conditions, the greater the chance of our unconsciously filling in the gaps. When we have done this by way of unconscious processes and experience, it can lead to unconscious errors. Such sources of error can be more difficult to disclose than conscious lies, since the person giving a statement actually believes she is reporting everything that happened, when in reality she is telling her own version, her interpretation of what actually took place. It is important for the professional interviewer to develop an awareness of the deceptive nature of the many different and unconscious simplification processes.

Storage Phase

In the *storage phase* the memory is wholly reliant on the information we have received from our senses. The memory's network structure is designed in such a way that the experiences from our senses, combined with emotions, determine how intense the memories are. The sense impressions are stored in different places in the brain, and it is the composite experience of these impressions, the emotions, that connects them into an episode. To put this differently: a particularly good memory is often characterized by a strong connection between the stored sense impressions and emotions. It is particularly important to employ this shared connection of different sense impressions when we are trying to help witnesses remember.

If a sense impression (such as an odor) triggers feelings (joy and well-being) connected to a memory, the feelings will often simultaneously trigger other sense impressions (sight and hearing). These sense impressions can in turn trigger further sense impressions (taste), which provide access to a completely new memory, a memory we might not have retrieved had we not activated the senses through free association. This means in practical terms that if we encourage a witness to focus on all kinds of details, even those considered irrelevant, such as what they ate or what they could smell in the situation, this can activate memories of what they saw and heard. For example, the memories and observations of a culprit in a rape case are enhanced or retrieved by giving the victim the chance to think about what she smelled, tasted, heard, felt—not solely by what she saw. Or a witness who doesn't remember the color of a car can be triggered in a manner that activates other information connected to the same incident, such as the smell of a leather interior, which in turn can activate a memory of the color.

It is critical that we—as professional information gatherers—understand that the memory's function and structure impose some requirements on how we should gather information. These requirements have been taken into consideration in the model presented in Part 2.

No interview situation has been subjected to more critical research than police questioning of victims, witnesses, and suspects. The research has highlighted the complexity of interpersonal encounters and identified sources of error associated with asymmetry in communication, decision-making psychology, and eyewitness psychology, as explained earlier. Here it can be expedient to pause for a moment and remember that the methods we will describe were developed in close collaboration with practitioners and researchers. In the ongoing developmental work that started more than thirty years ago, the focus has at all times been on making the recommended techniques and methodology as simple and user-friendly as possible. Anyone who learns and follows the method hereby preserves the researchers' proposed solutions. To put this another way: the cognitive and social-psychological processes informing methodology are far more complex than the method itself and its application in practice.

Storage and forgetting

The biggest threat in the storage phase is quite simply forgetting. Research shows that we start forgetting quickly and that we forget a lot of things almost

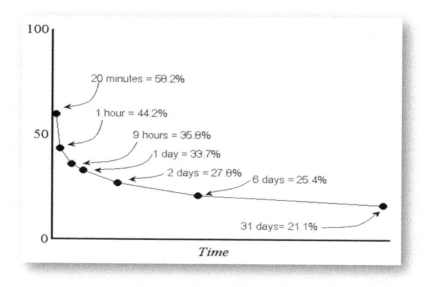

Figure 3 Ebbinghaus's (1885) forgetting curve.

immediately. Hermann Ebbinghaus's classic forgetting curve from 1885 (Figure 3) illustrates this point. As illustrated by the figure, after 20 minutes the test subjects remembered just under 60 percent of all the details they were exposed to (forgot over 40 percent). After an hour, they could remember only 44 percent (had forgotten 56 percent). Then the results *gradually* plateau.

If we don't *repeat* the information or no particular *emotions* are connected to it, the details disappear. It is therefore important to start right away and speak to sources who have experienced anything of relevance, if possible, immediately after the incident in question. There is still a great deal we don't know about memory, and nuances can be added to Ebbinghaus's forgetting curve in many ways, but all scientists agree on one point: time is not memory's best friend. To the contrary (Schacter 2001).

The storage phase and social influence

Another reason it is important to talk to sources as soon as possible after an incident is the risk of the memory being influenced in the storage phase—in other words, the time period between the event and memory retrieval.

This type of influence is often referred to as contamination and can in fact occur merely by *thinking* about what happened. A new version of the incident is stored and overwrites the old. The phenomenon known as social influence is even stronger and occurs when sources talk to one another, watch television, or read about the incident in question in the media.

A typical and disturbing example is that of children who are "interviewed" by parents, teachers, or social workers in an unprofessional manner and where there is an obvious risk of leading questions. By the time the child is finally called in for questioning by the police, his or her memory may have already been contaminated. There are many good reasons for interviewing witnesses in criminal cases individually. The risk of memory contamination is one of them.

An example taken from the murder of the Swedish foreign minister Anna Lindh in 2003 clearly illustrates what can happen when memories are subjected to social influence. The Stockholm police wanted to protect the most important eyewitnesses from the media and therefore isolated them as a group in a separate, closed room at the shopping center where the murder was committed, *before* they were questioned by the homicide detectives. That was a big mistake. One of the witnesses spoke confidently about how the culprit was wearing a military jacket and the other witnesses listened to her.

The problem was that there never was any military jacket. The culprit was wearing a light-gray, Nike sweatshirt with a hood (Figure 4). But this one witness contaminated the memories of the other witnesses by communicating her "observation" to the others. The error was propagated and when several, apparently independent, witnesses mentioned a military jacket, a national alert was sent out to all police units, border crossings, and airports to be on the

Figure 4 VG, September 15, 2003. Photo: TT Nyhetsbyraen.

lookout for a man wearing a military jacket. Of course, this doesn't mean that the eye witnesses lied. Either their original memories were overwritten, or their unconscious, cognitive schemata tricked them because the incorrect information about a military jacket fit in with their scripts or personal schemata for brutal assaults (large knife = military knife = military jacket) and filled in the gaps between fragmented sense impressions. The problem with this and other forms of contaminated memory is that false memories can be experienced as being just as real as genuine memories. After the witnesses had been questioned, they met with the press and communicated the same erroneous observation.

> Anna Lindh lay on the floor and it looked like a tall man wearing a military jacket and a baseball cap was stabbing her. When he ran away, he threw down a knife. Lindh said: "God, he stabbed me in the stomach!" Sundberg told the Associated Press. (Nettavisen, 2003)

Fortunately, the error was disclosed when the police acquired and analyzed the surveillance tapes from the crime scene. There was no military jacket to be seen there. Without the surveillance tapes, the error could have had disastrous ramifications for the subsequent investigation of the case.

Professor of psychology at the University of Goteborg Pär-Anders Granhag and colleagues decided to explore what happened in the Anna Lindh cases and concluded: "The memory is not just important; it is also extremely susceptible to (social) influence. [...] Research shows that witnesses who speak to one another perhaps constitute the greatest factor of influence during the storage phase" (Granhag et al. 2013, p. 150).

Retrieval Phase

It is not just during the encoding and storage phases that memories can be influenced. The risk of contamination is just as great in the retrieval phase and then especially if the person sharing his or her experiences is being interviewed by personnel who have no knowledge about different sources of error or the method to counteract these.

The purpose of a professional interview is to help an interviewee recount an incident as accurately and reliably as possible. The memory of the witness, the source, the applicant, the patient, or the client is then guided from the storage to the retrieval process. Here it is first and foremost the interviewer who is at risk of contaminating the witness's memory. As interviewers we can reduce the risk of influence by asking open questions and avoiding leading ones. To retrieve memories, we can use memory enhancement techniques. In short, we utilize the way the sense impressions and feelings are connected in

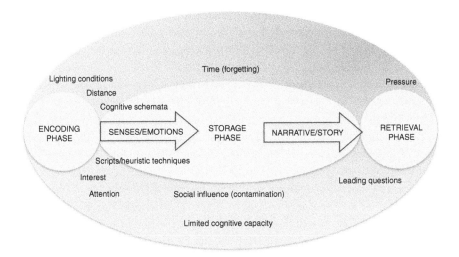

Figure 5 The phases of memory, influences, and sources of error. *Source:* Author.

memory formation. We will explain more about asking questions and memory enhancement later in this book.

Concurrent research findings from a number of studies have documented that stored information (the memory) is influenced in all three phases (Figure 5). As professionals we must be attentive to this in the memory retrieval process of an interview.

We will now move on to address a subject that can be a great challenge for professional interviewers.

False Memories

If you are at a party and begin speaking about memory with people, many will mention how they have begun forgetting names or perhaps that they have an aunt who has Alzheimer's. However, the biggest problem for the professional interviewer is not that our sources have forgotten, but that they remember things that never happened. Systematic reviews of real-life interviews also reveal that when it comes to the creation of false memories, it is the interviewer who is the largest sinner. Thousands of eyewitness psychology studies have documented that it takes relatively little to change, overwrite, create, or in another manner contaminate people's memories during the retrieval phase.

The memory does not work like a video camera. We can't just rewind it and present what really happened. Memory works more like a Wikipedia page. You can access it and make changes. As we have shown with the example from the murder of Anna Lindh, *other people* can also change our memories. When we try to remember, we supplement, remove, and are vulnerable to outside influence. The memory tries its best to reconstruct the events we have experienced. In the reconstruction, also *the conversations* about the very events we are trying to remember influence our memory of them. The original memory can be slowly erased, revised, and replaced by how you have described and thought about it after the fact. It is like your own mental whispering game. The contents change little by little every time you think about them. "I remember it like it was yesterday" is an expression we often hear. Generally speaking, that is not the case. We remember it *like it was the last time we thought about it* would be more apt, because the memory is an active, ongoing process that evolves and is influenced all the time. As professional interviewers we must therefore be aware of how we can influence the memories of those with whom we interact.

One of the most well-known experiments in the field of eyewitness psychology was carried out by the psychologists Elisabeth Loftus and John Palmer in 1974 (Figure 6). The experiment was supposed to shed light on our ability to provide reliable information in response to different questions. The experiment demonstrated that humans create false memories and was an eye-opener for all those working with memory and witnesses. And this can occur quite simply when an interviewer asks leading questions.

Loftus and Palmer divided 45 students into four groups and had them watch seven car collisions on a video. After having watched the videos, the groups were asked differently formulated questions about the events they had seen. Actually, the scientists changed only *one* word.

Figure 6 Illustration of Elisabeth Loftus's experiment. *Source:* Loftus and Palmer (1974).

The first group was asked the question: "How fast were the cars driving when they *smashed into* each other?" The second group was asked: "How fast were the cars driving when they *collided?*" The third group: "How fast were the cars driving when they *bumped into* each other?" And the last group: "How fast were the cars driving when they *hit/contacted with* each other?"

The tiny differences in the wording produced considerable variations in the answers. The average estimated speed reported by those who were asked the question using the words "smashed" and "collided" was significantly higher (65 km/h) than those who answered questions about cars that "bumped" and "hit/contacted" each other (54 km/h). The participants' recollection of speed was influenced by the word used to describe it in the question. This is an example of a leading word.

In their second experiment, 150 students were shown a video of a car accident. Again, the students were divided into different groups and asked to fill out a questionnaire with similar questions, but with indifferent verb (smashed/hit). A week later, they were given a new questionnaire. Those who had been asked questions including the word "smashed" were significantly more likely to remember having seen broken glass in the footage than those who had been asked a question using the word "hit." There was no broken glass in the accident. False memories were constructed in the process of retrieving the true memories. If on top of this, people are given erroneous information, their memories can be completely altered.

Loftus also did studies on patients who through psychoanalysis suddenly produced clear memories of extreme abuse and other incredible stories, which later proved to be purely fictitious. Loftus discovered that the methods some therapists used in psychoanalysis—interpretation of dreams, imagining and visualization, hypnosis, and exposure to false information—created the strangest and most improbable memories. False memories. Which they believed.

The studies done by Loftus have therefore helped to explain why and how children create false memories in meeting with well-meaning adults who ask difficult and leading questions. There are numerous examples of cases in which the suspicion of sexual abuse has given rise to leading questions, false memories, and in the end, errors of justice and wrongful convictions. In Norway, the best-known example of this would be the Bjugn cases from the 1990s—an infamous police investigation into alleged sexual abuse of children in the small community of Bjugn, ending in an acquittal of all the accused.

Loftus therefore emphasizes that even though somebody speaks with great conviction, a wealth of details, and a lot of emotion, the events being reported need not have happened or be true (Loftus 2018). The memory is like freedom: fantastic but also extremely fragile. Fortunately, memory enhancement is possible.

Memory Enhancement Techniques for Investigative Interviews

Based on their knowledge about the memory's structure and functions, memory researchers Edward Geiselman and Ronald Fisher initiated a study in collaboration with the US police force in 1984 to determine how to assist police information gathering, with an eye to gathering not only more information but also information that was more reliable. Because their interview methodology was developed in accordance with knowledge from the field of psychology about perception, memory, and retrieval, the method was named *cognitive interview techniques*.

Unfortunately, the police's witnesses did not remember more through the use of the method. Geiselman and Fisher investigated further and found that the police detectives lacked fundamental communication skills. In 1987 the methods were reintroduced, now under the name *enhanced cognitive interview*. After that, the memory-enhancing interview techniques were combined with elementary communication principles, including an interview structure more in accordance with how the brain retrieves memories. This achieved results.

Compared to traditional question-and-answer techniques, multiple studies have disclosed that on average, interviewers who employed the enhanced cognitive interviewing techniques obtained 40 percent more information from witnesses' memories—without increasing the probability of false or contaminated memories. The memory enhancement techniques are also suitable for interviewing children and have become popular as a research interview technique (Waddington & Bull 2007) as well as a suitable information-gathering interview technique for social workers (Ahmed et al. 2009), health-care workers, HR personnel, lawyers, prosecutors, and judges.

Based on the knowledge about memory structure and drawing from Bower's important observations of 1967 about how what witnesses report rarely corresponds with what they remember (Bower 1967), Geiselman and Fisher deduced that because our memory is made up of a network of connections, there are a number of clues (senses and emotions) we can use to retrieve information. Furthermore, Geiselman and Fisher demonstrated that mental reinstatement of the situation during which the information was encoded in the memory increases access to that stored information. Finally, as pointed out by Tulving and Thomson (1973), information we fail to retrieve through the use of one "clue" (a sense impression or emotion) will potentially become available through the use of another.

In short, and in a practical sense, it is a matter of helping an interviewee to find the path to the information stored in the semantic memory or the episodic memory. Instead of asking the interviewee to tell us "what happened," the interviewer provides some preliminary instructions designed to help witnesses mentally return to the time and place of encoding. This is done first in terms of environment (contextual reinstatement). What were the surroundings like? Then, in terms of how they felt (internal reinstatement). At the right moment, in other words, when the witness is "back" and can visualize the entire situation, he or she is encouraged to employ all the senses: Think about what you heard. Think about what you saw. What you smelled. And finally: one last request to describe everything in detail.

The memory enhancement and communicative elements are today a given component of professional interview techniques and an integrated aspect of the methods in this book. In Part 2 we will describe, step-by-step, the practical application of the methods.

Like all other skills, mastering cognitive interviewing techniques requires training and practice in order to be able to take full advantage of the inherent potential of the method. The memory enhancement techniques require good communication skills. We must help the interviewee relax and achieve an interaction in which they will feel secure and taken care of. We will address the fundamental communication principles later. Without such skills, we will not achieve the optimal collaborative climate we need. But perhaps you are thinking, what if the interviewee doesn't collaborate. What do we do then?

Lie Detection

Earlier we have essentially described the memory with a focus on variables that challenge and stimulate *the reliability* of the information we collect. Now we will address the concept and phenomenon of *credibility*. This immediately raises questions about truth and lies. Traditionally, the police have naturally had a great interest in this subject.

"How does one become a good interviewer?" the eldest of the authors of this book asked when he started his career as a detective at the Oslo Sentrum Police Station in 1993.

The question was directed to the unit's most experienced detectives. This was before the police had any formal training in questioning techniques. Without formal training or methodology, the most experienced detectives were usually considered to be the best. Techniques and tricks were passed down from one generation to the next (Fahsing & Rachlew 2009).

"You must learn to tell whether or not a suspect is lying," the older detective answered confidently. The answer sounded right. Exciting, too. But—

"How do you do that?" the young detective wondered. Lie detection had not been on the syllabus at the police academy, so it was important to pay attention now. The novice detective was about to be made privy to occupational secrets—the core of the profession. Although the senior detective's answer—"You must gain experience"—was disheartening for the young detective, as it meant there was no book to read or course to take, it was effective in terms of upholding the existing myth that experience was all that was required.

"You must gain experience." No more, no less. The secret behind the professional secret he had heard about, but had not yet quite grasped, lay of course in experience. So that was why the techniques were not discussed in the textbooks at the police academy. Experience cannot be acquired through reading.

Lie detection is surrounded by such a plethora of mystique, pseudo-science, and myths that the phenomenon enjoys widespread credence in popular culture. Just as television series depict torture as an effective means of extracting secrets from uncooperative terrorists, the reading of body language and lie detector tests are employed as fascinating tools in fiction, television, and film—and in real life as we shall see. The Internet offers an abundance of books, lectures, and YouTube videos about how to learn the art. The problem, however, is that the research says something else altogether.

In conjunction with the introduction of the new, research-based interviewing methodology that is the subject of this book, scientific findings about lie detection also emerged. The belief that police detectives developed a kind of sixth sense was one of the first myths to be dispelled through the transition from experience-based to research-based interview techniques.

A substantial number of laboratory trials have demonstrated that police detectives, psychologists, and judges are no better equipped to disclose lies by reading body language than anybody else. They are just as inept as laypeople. In the final, large-scale meta-analysis, where findings from all accredited studies were combined, we all score just above 50 percent. You may as well flip a coin (Vrij 2008).

So, how did things turn out for the young, promising detective who in 1993 was told that the secret was experience? Well, he acquired experience by taking part in hundreds of police interviews but felt he still wasn't able to tell when a suspect was lying. One day he plucked up courage and went humbly back to the eldest member of the unit.

The answer this time was: "Well, either you're a good judge of character or you're not." This was just as devastating as the previous answer had been—the fault clearly lay within himself—but was still well-suited for upholding the myth and the status of those who were viewed (and viewed themselves) as the best at detecting liars.

The story has been simplified for dramatic effect, but it is nonetheless a real-life story. In the police force, the expertise was passed down, and two of the authors of this book were apprentices. We were not the only ones looking for a shortcut to the truth. In the early 1990s, researchers carried out a number of studies on the police of Great Britain. In response to the question of what the police were interested in learning more about, police detectives replied that first and foremost they wanted to learn more about how to detect lies by reading body language (Baldwin 1992).

Body Language and Lie Detection

There are no definitive or consistent bodily responses that are produced when we lie (Vrij 2008). If the research on body language and lies shows anything consistent, it is that liars will hold your gaze—maintain eye contact—longer than those who are telling the truth. Many people think that it is the opposite, that liars will avoid eye contact. The explanation is presumably that "liars" also believe the stereotypical perception, and in an attempt to appear credible, they make sure to hold your gaze just a bit longer. But this phenomenon neither occurs in a systematic fashion that can be measured nor otherwise employed in a practical sense.

As one of Norway's foremost researchers on memory, Professor Svein Magnussen, writes: "None of us [are] any good at disclosing liars. Neither 'mentalists', police detectives, judges, psychologists nor laypeople are […] able to spot a liar based on how people talk and behave."

But even though the research shows that we can't see or measure when people are telling the truth or lying, the myth lives on in a number of countries, including the United States. Here the confession is still the goal; unlike in other democratic societies, in the United States, the police are allowed to lie during an interrogation, such as by presenting false evidence (Kassin et al. 2009). They are also avid proponents of different kinds of lie detection gadgets, not primarily to disclose whether or not a suspect is lying, but to induce suspects to confess. An example of a vintage lie detector is shown in Figure 7. Many crime suspects believe the lie detector works. The myth of the machine's excellence is perpetuated by those who use it and those who make a living selling it. Lie detection is big business. Knowledge based on research findings is suppressed, explained away, and "disproven" by new studies in which the (always) recently developed machines and methods are held to be "far more accurate than last year's model." In this way the industry survives (Rachlew 2009; Schneider 2019). There are documented cases of traveling salesmen, who often have former police experience, peddling such wares in developing countries experiencing burgeoning economic growth. These "lie detector" salesmen steal the march on critical research and offer the newest version of the most effective machine on the market: claiming it is 99.8 percent reliable—at least.

Brain scan (MRI) is one of the more recent additions to the industry. Luckily, the technology does not work as a lie detector. We say "luckily," because anyone who takes a moment to consider the type of society we would end up with if

Figure 7 An example of a vintage lie detector.

scientists were to succeed in developing a reliable lie detector will realize that the world would hardly be a better place. Think about the impact of such a machine on interpersonal relationships at different levels: the relationship between husband and wife, job applicant and employer, voter and political party, despots and the population. The implications are disturbing. Fortunately, it is only a remote possibility. Human beings are far too complex (Rusconi & Mitchener-Niessen 2013), and in the meantime, what use do we have for machines that don't work?

An approach based on the belief that it is possible to distinguish the truth from lies by reading the body language of another is not only dubious but also downright dangerous, as we will soon see. Our examples are taken from the police's painful learning process, but such an approach is just as perilous for all professions that make decisions of import, where the basis for those decisions is obtained in part through conversations, consultations, or interviews.

In 2009, the British social welfare authorities were duped into buying lie detectors that were supposed to work over the telephone. The business concept claimed that the machine distinguished the truth from lies by measuring the stress level in the voice of the interviewee. The product had already sold well in the United States. Through "effective telephone interviews," the British authorities planned to identify people who applied for social welfare benefits under false pretenses. After having invested more than USD 2 million (!) in "voice stress analysis," the pilot project was terminated. The spokesperson for the Ministry of Labour had to offer an explanation to the media, and the statement was brief: "This is the first time it has been used by the social welfare system and the conclusion is that it is not very good value for money."

Professor of phonetics Francisco Lacerda, who several years before had disclosed how the same lie detector had never been anything but a hoax (Eriksson & Lacerda 2007), praised the Ministry's decision to terminate the pilot project and added that the only thing that was surprising about the decision was that it had not been made earlier.[1]

No Shortcut to the Truth

The idea of being able to detect lies using machines or body language is an attractive one. The idea is just as appealing to overworked social workers and police detectives as it is to ambitious headhunters, financial analysts under pressure, journalists, judges, asylum and tax authorities, or federal trade commissions. But there is no shortcut to the truth. Anyone who believes in such a shortcut is ignoring the warnings of scientists and running the risk of drawing erroneous conclusions. They are also wasting time and squandering an opportunity to work effectively.

Professional interviewers work not only more effectively but also on more stable ground when they steer away from all forms of credibility analyses during their conversations and interviews. Their attention will thereby be focused on the purpose of the interview: to obtain information that is as relevant, detailed, accurate, and reliable as possible. In most cases, the interview is a part of something larger—an investigation, an inquiry, a hiring process, a review, or a study.

It is not only the police and sociologists who must keep in mind that in some interview situations they will be speaking with a person who does not want to tell the truth. The need for a strategic approach to the interview can arise in different contexts, such as when preliminary inquiries disclose information that—in the event it is correct—will incriminate, debunk, or undermine the interviewee's position in a case. In the everyday dealings of the police, such critical information is referred to as decisive or circumstantial evidence. In this book we have chosen to use the term *critical information*. The defining feature

---

1. For more on how the British authorities were fooled, see a series of articles published in *The Guardian*: https://www.theguardian.com/news/datablog/2009/mar/19/dwp-voice-risk-analysis-statistics, https://www.theguardian.com/society/2014/mar/10/councils-use-lie-detector-tests-benefits-fraudsters, https://www.theguardian.com/science/2010/nov/09/lie-detector-tests-benefit-cheats.

of critical information is that it typically stems from a suspicion, theory, or question. Journalists will find that they have potentially found a story. Members of other professions will detect indications of fraud, embezzlement, exclusion of liability, a cover-up, or (self)deception.

Our intuitive suspicion can be mistaken, and to reduce the negative influence of cognitive traps and simultaneously increase our chances of making the right choices, police and scientists have developed a methodology through which critical information is applied in a tactical manner. We maintain that financial analysts who adhere to the method will minimize the risk of costly surprises, and in the same manner, doctors, HR personnel, examiners, consultants, journalists, educators, psychologists, detectives, teachers, judges, and others can minimize the risk of erroneous inferences.

It is not the case that detectives who have understood and changed their thinking and methodology to comply with research-based investigative interview techniques have become less proficient in distinguishing the truth from lies. To the contrary. A growing body of scientific studies document that through adherence to the *investigative interviewing methodology*, accuracy is actually increased when conclusions need to be drawn (Granhag et al. 2018).

In particular, research indicates the importance of taking a strategic approach to applying critical information. The Norwegian police were possibly the first in the world to acknowledge the benefit of this concept as a crucial part of investigative interviewing (Rachlew 2002). Today the strategic application of critical information has been embraced by a growing number of law enforcement services and human rights advocates (Griffiths & Rachlew 2018).

To explain the strategy concisely and in a somewhat simplified form, the interviewer postpones the presentation of critical information until such time when all alternative explanations have been identified and tested. In contrast to the former, traditional practice where the focus was on eliciting confirmation in the form of a confession, detectives are trained to seek reliable information to prove the suspect's innocence. If they don't find information in support of a "defense hypothesis," this can help to substantiate suspicions of the suspect's likely guilt. From the perspective of scientific theory, this approach rests on the philosophical concepts developed by philosophers Charles Peirce (1839–1914) and Karl Popper (1902–1994). Detectives who apply the method need not devote a lot of time to thinking about the underlying conceptual framework. They simply follow the strategy and find it to be practical and effective (Fahsing & Rachlew 2009).

In the chapter about the planning and preparation phase in Part 2, we will explain the method in as much detail as that provided by the syllabus of the National Police University College of Norway.

Credibility versus Reliability

It is of course not only conscious lies that undermine the reliability of the information we gather in interviews. As explained in previous chapters, the reliability of the information we collect can in different ways be undermined by dubious input, such as inaccurate details and unconscious misinterpretations, perhaps triggered by leading questions. Forgetfulness and misunderstandings also threaten the reliability of the evidence we collect. As explained in the section about memory, such unconscious errors can arise during encoding, storage, and retrieval. Conscious lies and omissions are another issue altogether. Then it is no longer a question of just the *reliability* of the information we acquire but also the *credibility* of the person with whom we are speaking.

In everyday speech (and in the courts), the terms *credibility* and *reliability* are often used interchangeably. This can be dangerous, as pointed out by professors Magnussen and Stridbeck (2001):

> In the public debate about credibility in the courtroom, the terms reliability and credibility are often used interchangeably. […] It is important to distinguish between the two terms because research has shown that the memories of absolutely honest, cooperative, and credible individuals are not necessarily accurate.

Before we give an account of some central sources of error related to the evaluation of people's credibility and why such misinterpretations are especially insidious in an interview context, we will explain briefly how we define and employ the terms in this book.

How can a credible person or a credible story be unreliable, while the information from a person who is less than credible can still be reliable? The questions illustrate exactly the difference.

Credibility is about how we perceive people and what they tell us. In other words, how it all *appears*. *Reliability* is about whether the information corresponds with reality.

The answer to the question is therefore that a credible individual can give us unreliable information because credibility is based on how we perceive the person and the story, while reliability depends on whether what is said is actually correct. And vice versa.

Credibility

When we suspect that details in a story are incorrect or meet a person whose manner arouses uncertainty, it affects us. Unconsciously, it can influence how we categorize both the person and the story. Our intuition quickly tries to assist us: can we trust the person seated before us? Like all simplification processes, unconscious mechanisms help us in daily life. We see a suspicious person at a farmers' market and reach for our wallet. If we should be wrong about this person, it is of no consequence. But as professional interviewers, these unconscious simplification processes can have serious consequences. Without knowledge and a method, we become susceptible to sources of error. The risk of confusing credibility and reliability is compounded, due to an unconscious mental process that leads us to seek information to confirm our initial assumption, such as that the person we are talking with is—or isn't—"trustworthy." We will now address in detail four classic sources of error that unconsciously (mis)lead our attention away from assessing the reliability of the information we obtain and toward more uncertain, in the worst case misguided, assessments of credibility.

Body Language and Emotional Expression

We have already discussed how it is not possible to disclose lies by interpreting body language. Even with an awareness of this, body language can still deceive us when it comes to our unconscious and instinctive tendency to evaluate credibility. A big, warm smile and good eye contact will quickly give us the impression that we are talking to somebody we can trust.

There are many sources of error that complicate the task of distinguishing between our impression of a person and the statements made by that person. In their doctoral dissertation, the forensic psychologists Ellen Wessel and Guri Bollingmo (2007) investigated how emotional expression influenced test subjects' evaluation of a woman's account of a rape. In the experiment, the woman was played by a professional actress who described a fictional rape. The entire session was videotaped. The sequence of events was described using the exact same words but in three different ways. In one video, she giggled and laughed. In video number two, she remained neutral. In the third version, the actress cried and came across as clearly upset by the "incident."

The study showed that most of us will judge the crying woman as more credible than the other two. If the three statements had been written down and read, word for word, the test subject would most probably assess all three as equally reliable. The texts would have been identical. The study shows how our assessment of people's credibility contaminates our assessment of the reliability of the information they share.

The impact of the expression of emotion does not just arise in laboratory studies. A tearful witness proved to have ill-fated consequences for Stein Inge Johannessen, who was held behind bars for six months in Oslo, on charges for a murder he had not committed. The case against Stein Inge is the main topic of the doctoral thesis "Justisfeil ved politiets etterforskning" (Errors of justice in police investigations) (Rachlew 2009). The thesis asks the question: Why did the Norwegian police make such a mistake, and how may science help to prevent similar errors? In the analysis of the police detectives' in-house email correspondence, a key explanation appeared: the detectives believed the witness when she presented the false story about Stein Inge because she cried. During the interview of the witness, the detective wrote a message to his superior:

> She cried. Talked for thirty minutes about her childhood and painful things. THIS IS THE TRUTH. THE GIRL HAS A CONSCIENCE. [*sic*]

The overriding belief in "the girl's credibility" led the detectives into cognitive traps, due to which the actual information she gave—which did not correspond with other facts—was ignored and explained away. Fortunately for Stein Inge—and everyone else—the case against him was dismissed four days before the trial was scheduled to begin, when the real culprit turned himself in to the police.

Social Status

We all have an unconscious tendency to "pigeonhole" others. In decision-making psychology, this unconscious simplification strategy is called a "personal schema" (Baldwin 1992). The probability of erroneous assessments is particularly large if one has only a few, overly simplistic personal schemata. Some people come across as more credible than others simply by being themselves. Many people will consider company directors to be more credible than people who are homeless.

It may well be that a director's intention is to tell the truth. And it may well be that a welfare recipient with a criminal record will lie in order to receive welfare payments he doesn't deserve. But should we allow our unconscious perception of a group decide the fate of the individual before us?

In a professional interview we must be aware that so-called non-credible witnesses can provide perfectly reliable information. The outliers of society, drug addicts, ex-convicts, and the homeless, are often viewed as less than credible simply because they are drug addicts, ex-convicts, and homeless. A number of groups exist outside the bounds of the "establishment." But if they see or experience something, they may have information to share that is just as reliable as the information of any other witness or involved party. Still, the testimonies of stigmatized groups can quickly lose their value when the information is to be presented in the courtroom or for a committee, if the individuals receiving that information have little knowledge or awareness of their unconscious personal schemata.

Fritz Moen was in the eyes of many not a credible person. He had exposed himself to women in an area where two girls had been murdered in the space of a two-year period in Trondheim, Norway (1976 and 1977). He was what during the postwar period in Norway was called a "German child": the child of a Norwegian mother and a German World War II soldier. Fritz was also deaf–mute and had difficulties communicating. When he began by explaining that he was innocent, nobody paid attention. It was only when he broke down under the pressure of the interrogation and made a false confession that his statement was considered credible. It matched the police's theory. The detectives later claimed in a report that they could tell that Fritz was telling the truth when he confessed. Fritz Moen was in prison for eighteen and a half years for crimes he didn't commit. This tragedy would in all likelihood have been averted had the police interviewed Fritz Moen using the investigative interviewing techniques presented in this book.

Abundance of Detail

There is neither any connection between the abundance of detail included in a statement and its truthfulness. Witness psychologist Ellen Wessel emphasizes this in her doctoral thesis. In one of many newspaper interviews about her thesis, she says: "There are many factors that lead to a false story being consistent and full of detail, while a true story can appear inconsistent and lacking in detail" (Wessel 2013).

The wrongful conviction of the alleged Swedish serial killer Sture Bergwall (formerly known as Thomas Quick) is a good example of this misconception. In 1994–2001, Bergwall was convicted of eight murders, predominantly based on his own confessions. The extensive and grotesque details he shared about how he allegedly murdered his victims were of decisive significance for all involved parties—psychologists, doctors, journalists, the police, the prosecution, and the courts—all of whom perceived him as credible and, in this sense, contributed to the wrongful conviction of the mentally unstable man (Stridbeck 2020). When Bergwall withdrew his confessions in 2008, it led to a process in which he was completely exonerated in all the cases. In contrast to other potential sources of error stemming from an unconscious assessment of a person giving a statement, this error pertains to the story that is told.

Absolutely Sure!

In addition to body language, social status, and abundance of detail, our experience of credibility is affected by people's apparent certainty about their claims.

In the case of a rape committed in the neighborhood of Grefsen in Oslo, the woman who had been sexually assaulted picked out an innocent person when confronted with photographs of potential police suspects. The mistake was on the part of the police. The use of old-fashioned and outdated methods, such as an eyewitness identification parade, led to the detectives unconsciously planting a false memory in the woman's mind. The innocent suspect was put on trial and found guilty by the Oslo district court. The case is almost identical to the infamous case in the United States against the innocent Ronald Cotton, who was picked out of a lineup by Jennifer Thompson (Toreno et al. 2009). Among the causes forming the basis for the wrongful conviction in Norway, the judges wrote that "the victim's statement is highly credible."

Yes, there was never any doubt about it. The victim in the Norwegian case was, just like Jennifer Thompson, a terrific woman in every way. But the information she provided was not reliable; she was wrong. By confusing the concepts/phenomena credibility and reliability, the courts became entangled in a snarl of irrelevant details obscuring truth and lies. The evaluation of evidence should never have been about the credibility of the victim's statement. The question should have been whether the identification of the suspect was reliable. This confusion distracted the judges and led them to dismiss evidence in favor of the accused, including DNA evidence from the actual rapist (Rachlew & Rachlew 2009).

When a person appears (and is) credible, without intentions of consciously lying, those who confuse the concepts risk misjudging the reliability of the information. The confusion works in both directions. It makes no difference whether unconscious simplification processes lead us to believe (the Grefsen rape) or not believe (Fritz Moen) the person giving us information. In either case, the consequences of the mix-up can be just as disastrous.

To summarize, we can think of credibility as being like the peel on a piece of fruit. Some peels are both shiny and unblemished, while the appearance of other peels can be less attractive. Of course, the state of the peel gives us an indication, but it is only when we have bitten through it that we find out whether or not the fruit is edible. The tone, self-confidence, and details of any statement are merely the peel. When we are conscious of the difference between credibility and reliability, the significance of the peel is diminished. Instead, we focus on the information we find beneath the peel, in the fruit itself, information we must test to determine its reliability.

In an interview, in court, in consultations, in conversations, and in investigations, it is therefore crucial to distinguish between credibility and reliability. Precisely because we view some people as more credible than others, we forget that the information they give us can be unreliable. And vice versa.

Our assessment of credibility is influenced by how we experience body language, expectations about specific groups in society, the confidence people exhibit, and the amount of detail included in their explanations. To avoid having these factors undermine the collection of evidence, we must be conscious of the difference between credibility and reliability. But as stated earlier, knowledge and awareness are not enough. The world's leading researcher in the field of decision-making psychology, Daniel Kahneman, states that he also falls into cognitive traps all the time. The processes are unconscious, and we allow ourselves to be influenced, regardless of how extensive our knowledge about innate cognitive simplification processes may be. We need the support of a method, not least during information-gathering interviews and interactions that typically take place at an early stage in an investigation, consultation, or hiring process, when the danger of drawing premature conclusions is the greatest.

We will now move on from classic sources of error as disclosed by eyewitness psychology to look more closely at the underlying sources of error evidenced by decision-making psychology. Hopefully, it goes without saying at this point that a number of these errors stem from the same source: human beings' limited cognitive capacity and unconscious need for simplification processes. What is most challenging about such mechanisms is that we don't notice how they influence us.

The Psychology of Decision-Making

Our ability to think and make decisions has developed through evolution. Daniel Kahneman and other scholars explain that some components of our decision-making system—the intuitive and the unconscious—have not evolved to solve complex tasks. Kahneman (2011) calls these decision-making components System 1 and states that the evolution of System 1 has been designed to keep us safe and happy. When we must make a decision—something we do all the time—System 1 is activated immediately. This happens intuitively and unconsciously. The system makes associations with and draws rapidly from previous experiences to propose the quickest and simplest solution. System 1 tries to spare us from complicated, conscious thought processes. System 2, on the other hand, is developed to handle the types of processes that require awareness and intellect, and is a more controlled, painstaking system than System 1. That is why the title of Kahneman's best seller is *Thinking Fast and Slow* (2011). System 1 is not eradicated when we decide to mobilize System 2; System 1 continues to request priority.

As professionals we must recognize that we bring our intuitive, unconscious way of thinking into our work. At all times System 1 is trying to save us from hard work and, without our noticing it, will propose intuitive, simpler solutions to the problems we are facing. If the person before us seems dubious, System 1 will suggest that we conclude that the person is not credible. If we don't consciously engage System 2, then we proceed according to our initial intuition. End of story. Cognitive capacity has been liberated and we can relax. Our unconscious thought processes want to protect us. Without our noticing, different simplification processes are triggered and start unconsciously searching for information that will confirm that we have made the right choice. "What did I say? He's not credible." It is the simplest and the most comfortable conclusion.

Most of the decisions we make are trivial in nature. It is of little importance if we should fail to identify the optimal solution. We will live reasonably well with the choice System 1 was allowed to make. Maybe we mobilize System 2 to a certain extent when buying a new car, but we seldom invest our energy in the demanding tasks of gathering relevant data, systematization, and analyses. And usually, this works out fine. We manage perfectly well with most of the choices we make. Should some form of interference arise—a door that won't open, a flashing light—we fix it. Maybe cognitive traps help us a little bit along the way, so we don't have to suffer from irritation to any noteworthy extent: "Had I chosen another type of car, it might have caused even greater problems." Yes. Absolutely the right choice.

When we step into a professional role, however, the decisions we make can have serious consequences, not only for ourselves and our organization but also for other people's lives and interests. We have a wholly different type of responsibility. Though choosing a car is a relatively large decision for most of us, the distinctions between the choice of one or the other are negligible compared to the consequences of many of our professional decisions. There are a lot of good reasons why police detectives are bound by law to practice objectivity. The challenge is of course that System 1 and our cognitive simplification processes were never developed to comply with the normative ideal of objectivity required by law. We need assistance. Education, methods, and systems are mobilized. The challenge of the professional interview is that historically speaking it has been considered a craft that must be learned in the field. There was little research to be found—until the bubble burst in Great Britain 35 years ago and an inquiry disclosed that the seeds of wrongful convictions were sown during what back in the early 1990s was still referred to as the interrogation.

We have already covered the consequences of the unproductive confession culture championed by the police. Today we know a lot more, such as how the underlying causes of the immediate errors that arise—and are not corrected—stem from human beings' hereditary, cognitive simplification processes, otherwise known as simply cognitive traps (MacFarlane 2006; Rachlew 2009).

Another term for cognitive simplification processes is *cognitive bias*. In psychology a bias implies a predisposition for understanding and responding in a particular manner.

Over the past 40 years, a considerable amount of research has been done on human beings' decision-making abilities and what influences these. The research has predominantly been carried out by scientists working in the fields of cognitive and social psychology. But with time, a large interest has also emerged in other disciplines. Everything we do, everywhere, is affected by our decisions.

Researchers have identified more than one hundred different types of *cognitive biases*. These are unconscious processes that help us to be effective in the way we understand and process information, when making decisions in daily life.

The earliest *Homo sapiens*, who evolved in East Africa, didn't have time to consider alternative hypotheses when they spotted what they suspected was a lion hiding in the grass. Those who did didn't survive. Our forefathers instinctively concluded that a large, threatening creature could be aggressive and dangerous. In life-threatening situations, they could not absorb all the available information and process it rationally. Instead, the unconscious simplification processes kicked in. The available information was processed more or less unconsciously, leading quickly to an action. In that only those individuals who used simplification processes for processing information survived, such strategies were passed down and are a feature found in all of us. Although society has changed a great deal since anatomically modern *Homo sapiens* came into being many thousands of years ago, the biology of *Homo sapiens* has not changed as much. We still react as we did then. Because of such hereditary instincts, most people react to snakes and other dangerous animals. We also build up an experience bank throughout the course of our lives, and these experiences become a part of the unconscious processes that influence how we interpret situations and make decisions.

As we have seen, cognitive bias and simplification processes also explain how we understand and identify credibility. If we see a disheveled, unkempt person in front of us, we also intuitively believe that the person is more likely to commit a crime and is therefore less credible. Not trustworthy.

To put this simply, we unconsciously resort to simplification processes when we must remember more than we have the capacity to remember, when we have to act quickly, or when we don't have enough information to understand whatever situation it is that we find ourselves in. These processes also help us when we have too much information and must decide what is the most relevant. Different forms of pressure, such as time pressure, the pressure to find answers, or the pressure to earn money, further reduce our cognitive capacity, leading us to consider fewer alternatives. System 1 and other simplification processes are natural, unconscious cognitive systems that help us in the social interactions of our daily lives. At the same time, they put us at greater risk of drawing incorrect conclusions and undermine our ability to conduct ourselves professionally.

Consequently, these natural, unconscious processes must be counteracted if we are to minimize the negative fallout of the strategies we otherwise rely on in the comings and goings of daily life.

In cognitive and social psychology literature, a number of relevant experiments and theories are presented. Although the basic research is not focused on professional interactions or interviews, the reader is given an introduction that basically explains why decision-making psychology is relevant for all fact-seeking individuals. In recent years, forensic psychologists have applied this research and focused on members of the judicial system (Ask & Granhag 2008). The challenge remains the same: the moment a human being forms an opinion, perception, or judgment, the unconscious mechanisms start influencing us. We

1. search for information in support of what we believe;
2. interpret new information in light of what we believe;
3. use neutral information to further confirm an established opinion; and
4. ignore or dismiss information that does not fit.

The term *confirmation bias* is often used as a general, umbrella term to cover a number of cognitive simplification processes. At the core of the theories about confirmation bias lies the understanding of how psychological processes (simplification processes/cognitive traps) influence us not only as decision-makers when gathering information but also in our interpretation of the information gathered, without our necessarily realizing that we are lacking in objectivity (Nickerson 1998; Ask & Fahsing 2018).

Without corrective methods and systems, we are at greater risk of being misled by a cognitive trap. When police detectives apprehend someone whom they believe to be guilty, they will unconsciously and automatically start searching for information in support of their theory. This is natural. If a doctor suspects that a patient is a hypochondriac, the same mechanisms will kick in, and the unconscious search for information in support of that suspicion can have harmful consequences if it is not counteracted by a methodological approach. If a child welfare officer, a dentist, a kindergarten teacher, or a doctor believes that a child has been sexually abused, there will be a risk of falling into a trap during an interview with the child. It is natural to seek confirmation, but this can lead to errors in judgment of a medical, child welfare, and legal nature. Journalists are equally at risk, as are HR personnel and other recruiters.

Imagine that you have just read a wonderful resume from a job candidate from Western Norway. (Wow, we grew up in almost the same neighborhood.) He attended business school. (Yes, a sensible choice. Those were the days!) Then the day of the interview arrives. Your colleague does not share your enthusiasm about the candidate from Western Norway. "We actually need to improve the gender balance at the office." You are essentially in agreement about this, but it's not all that important. And when your colleague starts asking probing questions about why the candidate wants to change jobs and abandon his current position, you feel that the atmosphere is becoming uncomfortable. "Is it really necessary to ask such personal questions?"

Although you don't notice it, cognitive simplification processes are trying to help you. Any information that could threaten the appointment of your candidate of choice is experienced as uncomfortable. And it is not just psychology at work; it is also physiology.

Through brain scans (MRI), scientists can now observe neurophysiological activation. When test subjects receive information confirming their beliefs, the area in the brain called the ventral striatum is activated, an area that is consistently involved when the brain processes rewards. Basically, being right feels good. We are rewarded physiologically. Liberman et al. (2015) argue that this is one of the main reasons why we overlook our own biases and is the cognitive traps' contribution to erroneous inferences.

And not only does being right feel wonderful; it also feels bad to be wrong. When test subjects receive information that does not correspond with how they believe the world is put together, scientists see that the parts of the brain normally associated with the processing of pain and negative emotions are activated. The two related processes—being right activating a reward and being wrong causing pain—are key explanations for why we are so predisposed to employ unconscious simplification processes. We are motivated to seek reward and avoid pain.

Picture the exact same situation: you are going to hire a new employee, but this time the candidate is someone you intuitively disliked the moment she introduced herself. Eventually, your colleague asks why this woman wants to leave her current position. An unconscious gut feeling, or System 1 as Kahneman calls it, will immediately inform you that this is an important question. Here we can find an explanation for why she made a negative impression on you. Is she in a conflict with management? Is she a troublemaker? Perhaps someone who often calls in sick? We must ask her about that—a bit over the line, perhaps, but if you choose your words properly, it will be fine.

This is how our unconscious, cognitive simplification processes work. They steer us in the direction of information that confirms our already established convictions.

Human beings will generally gravitate toward "neutral" information that supports already established views. We are not interested, strictly speaking, in information that dispels our beliefs. If we can, we avoid or dismiss such information, and we do so unconsciously.

As professionals, we like to believe that we are more, well, professional than the employee in the earlier examples. And maybe we are, but the simplification processes illustrated here influence all of us.

An important point in this context is that people can be reasonably fair-minded at the start of a process, but their investment intensifies once they have made a decision or formed a judgment (Nickerson 1998). And remember, the more we invest, the stronger our (unconscious) need to defend our choice becomes (Baron 2008). By "investment" we mean everything that promotes a commitment. In his doctoral thesis, Police Superintendent Ivar Andre Fahsing (2016) draws from research findings on police detectives' thought processes and decisions, on the basis of which he explains that an arrest of a suspect prompts a strong experience of commitment. A "tipping point." The pain caused by being wrong will subsequently be experienced more intensely, as will the desire to be right.

Another example of investment would be if you were to step forward and make a case to the management team to persuade them to hire the candidate from Western Norway. Maybe you even play a bit on people's feelings to elicit their support. After all, you have almost twenty years of recruitment experience. The theory implies that if after such a performance (investment) any hint of negative features in the candidate from Western Norway were to arise during the interview, you would not be particularly motivated to explore it in any depth and would be more inclined to dismiss it as "insignificant" information.

Unless we have a methodology that compels us to think along alternative lines, the unconscious simplification processes become simplification traps.

Research-based interview methods were for the most part well received in Norway (Fahsing & Rachlew 2009). Some detectives were nonetheless uncertain. Their objections were especially related to the idea of discussing and describing the interview as a method. "Every interrogation is different!" After the introduction, the majority fortunately understood that this objection was unfounded; the investigative interview is both dynamic and flexible. But what the detectives feared most was that taking a methodological approach would undermine what they regarded as an important part of the task, namely, the interpersonal communication between the interviewer and the witness.

Their uncertainty was understandable. But what those who hesitated didn't initially realize was that investigative interviewing has been developed in collaboration with both researchers and practitioners. In addition to the implicit knowledge practitioners contributed to the development work, now all the social-psychology research could be brought to bear, integrated with that implicit knowledge, and where relevant correct it. It was not as if those who had studied police questioning hadn't grasped the complexity and significance of good communication. Communication principles were one of the first things they highlighted, and as pointed out by three of the pioneers in the development work on investigative interviewing, West, Bull, and Köhnken (1994), "Becoming an effective and professional investigative interviewer entails developing a better understanding of life's most complex event—a face to face encounter with another person."

4

COMMUNICATION

In the chapter "Psychology," we introduced interview techniques for memory enhancement—the enhanced cognitive interview. It is "enhanced" because the first models tested by the police did not meet their requirements or expectations. The evaluation provided a clear explanation for the poor results. It turned out that the police detectives lacked fundamental communication skills. They had problems relinquishing control to the person being interviewed, regardless of whether this person was a witness or a suspect. The detectives were used to assuming a dominant role in interrogations. In that way, people under interrogation never received a real chance to explain themselves freely. Question-and-answer techniques, accompanied by constant interruptions, impeded communication. The police also used technical jargon, and too often, the order of the questions was inappropriate.

The word "communication" comes from the Latin word *communicare*, meaning "to share." When we communicate something, we share something. Put simply, we can say that communication consists of a sender, a receiver, a message, and a communication medium. Both the sender and the receiver can be one or more person. When it comes to the communication medium, the imagination is virtually the only limit. A song, etchings, a book, an advertising pamphlet, Facebook, smoke signals, or a conversation are all communication media. Naturally, we will focus on the interview as a medium of communication in this book.

In a study commissioned by the British authorities, John Baldwin analyzed 600 police interviews (Baldwin 1992). He concluded that some detectives found it easier to communicate than others. Although members of other professions are not subjected to this type of review, we feel reasonably certain that Baldwin's findings have a general application and are valid for other professions. Some journalists are better interviewers than others. This would probably also be the case for doctors, case officers for welfare and labor administrations, researchers compiling data through structured interviews, investors gathering information about companies or potential projects—in short everyone for whom professional interviews are an integral part of their workday.

Simultaneously, a number of studies show that most people can improve their skill sets for the different interview phases. Even those who are already proficient will improve when they are given the added support of a method (Williamson et al. 2009). The techniques laid out in this book are designed to help you improve your ability to listen, transmit empathy, and ensure that the person with whom you are interacting feels that they are both seen and taken seriously. In order to achieve this, it is fundamental to ensure that you always go into an interview, conversation, or consultation with a clear understanding of your purpose. For police detectives, that purpose never involves judging, lecturing, advising, curing, or healing. It is a matter of acquiring and communicating the most accurate and reliable information possible. We can't see how the role of journalists is any different. The same can be said for HR personnel, asylum authorities, examiners, financial analysts, researchers, and others. Some professionals, whether they be doctors, lawyers, psychologists, clergymen, or child welfare officers, can also have objectives beyond that of the gathering of information, such as providing advice or making a diagnosis. Passing judgment or preaching, however, belong in the past. Taking a moment before an interview to ensure you are prepared to meet another human being, a human being who is just as valuable as a close family member, regardless of whatever the backstory might be, is a fundamental component of what we call mental preparation. Professional interviewers repeat this preparatory exercise before every interview, thereby maximizing their potential for communicating empathy. Communication is enhanced. Openness and honesty are prerequisites for good communication.

Empathy

If we are going to adhere to the humanist ideal of doing unto others as we would have them do unto us, this presupposes an ability to put ourselves in someone else's shoes. And to manage this, we must have *empathy*. Empathy can be defined in different ways. In their review of the concept of empathy, Cuff et al. list 43 different definitions. One of them is: "the ability to experience and understand what others feel without confusion between oneself and others" (2016). Several researchers emphasize that empathy is something more than an ability—that empathy is a process inherent to an interpersonal interaction. Psychologists describe different forms of empathy, both cognitive and emotional empathy. Because emotional empathy is more closely tied up with feelings, professional interviewers must learn how to manage it. Excessive emotion puts us at greater risk of falling into cognitive traps (Baron 2008) and also increases the risk of occupational burnout (Baker-Eck et al. 2020).

Cognitive empathy entails a more conscious approach, an active decision to show consideration. Deciding to show consideration is, however, not enough; the interviewer must identify when the need to communicate empathy arises and respond appropriately. This implies expressing empathy when the interviewee needs confirmation that you, as the interviewer, understand their situation, such as in situations when talking about a particular subject is clearly difficult for them. Achieving this requires an ability to understand what the other person is thinking and feeling. For exactly this reason, active listening is viewed as one of the most important elements of a professional interview.

Communicating empathy involves demonstrating an understanding of the other person's situation and state of mind, and showing an interest in them as a human being and in what they have to say.

In her doctoral research, psychologist Kristina K. Jakobsen (2019) investigated how the Norwegian police interviewed the young people who survived the Utøya terrorist attack in Norway in 2011. Through access to the recordings, the young people themselves, and the police detectives, Jakobsen acquired a strong set of data. Here, one of the challenges for the police detectives was, as always, to maintain "objectivity" and, at the same time, communicate empathy. Herein lies the professional interview's inherent, communicative dilemma: professional interviewers are supposed to be "objective" and "empathetic" at the same time.

It is not an easy endeavor, but Jakobsen concludes that the communication of cognitive empathy is sufficient. Even traumatized witnesses will experience a genuine sense of being taken care of without there being any need for the interviewer to activate and show emotion. Perhaps this was exactly what the neurologist and psychoanalyst Alberta Szalita (1976) meant when she described empathy as "consideration of another person's feelings and readiness to respond to his [or her] needs […] without making his [or her] burden one's own." To put oneself in the shoes of another, without absorbing their pain.

Empathy is advocated by many researchers of communication as a wholly necessary and critical component of good conversations. An integral aspect of empathy is ethical communication. What promotes and what hinders ethical communication? Research on police interviews show that the participation of victims, witnesses, and suspects alike in an interview situation is always influenced by the attitudes and conduct of the police. Professors of psychology Alice H. Eagly and social psychology Shelly Chaiken (1998, p. 1) define an attitude as "a psychological tendency that is expressed by evaluating a particular entity with some degree of favor or disfavor." If we apply the definition to an interview situation, it implies that our effectiveness will hinge on how the person with whom we are speaking perceives us. The other person will evaluate us in the course of a few seconds and, on the basis of that evaluation, react positively or negatively to what we say and do.

In his doctoral thesis, Swedish police officer Ulf Holmberg (2004) investigated the police interview experiences of convicted murderers and assailants. He said that the police used two different interview styles: a humane style and a domineering style. The domineering style was perceived as being impatient, stressful, condescending, and judgmental. The humane style was characterized by collaboration, facilitation, positivity, empathy, helpfulness, and an ambition to create a personal conversation. The humane style was associated with a feeling of being respected, while the domineering style was associated with a feeling of anxiety. Holmberg found a clear connection between interview style and the willingness on the part of the interviewee to acknowledge his or her crimes. Those who felt respected were more likely to admit to criminal actions. Holmberg's findings are substantiated by a series of studies from different parts of the world. When interviewees have an experience of being seen and respected, communication is established and the information flows. The myth of the hard-nosed, macho interrogator—often glorified in movies through the use of violence "in the best interests of the case"—has fortunately been dispelled through a number of empirical studies done in different parts of the world (Bull & Rachlew 2020).

Holmberg also investigated how victims of sexual assault or gross violence experienced being interviewed by the police. Once again, he found that the police interviewers were either domineering or humane. When victims were subjected to the domineering style, they froze and became frightened and stressed. They lost self-confidence and developed sleep disorders. When they felt they met with a humane interviewer, however, their experience was that of interacting with a fellow human being and of being respected, seen, and acknowledged. An atmosphere of kindness and collaboration was created. The conduct of the police again found expression in the outcome of the cases. When the victim's experience of the police was negative, they ended up withholding information. The majority of the cases in which information was withheld did not culminate in convictions. Either charges were not pressed, or the accused was not convicted.

"What was it you actually saw?"

Professor and journalist Bob Welch writes in his essay "A Matter of Trust" about the importance of an empathetic approach and active listening (2014). In an interview with a war veteran, he noticed that the veteran kept steering away from the subject of what had happened and what he had witnessed on the beach on D-Day in Normandy in 1944. Every time he approached the subject of the beach in his statement, he would suddenly change the subject. Welch tried patiently to guide him back to the critical moment. Finally, he asked:

"Fred, what was it you saw on the beach?

He gulped. His eyes glistened.

"... They were ... hanging from the trees."

"They" were the paratroopers from the 82nd and 101st Airborne Divisions, whose parachutes had become tangled in the tree branches as they descended. The Germans had used the men for target practice.

Welch writes: "You cannot force stories like that. You have to be patient, put yourself in the shoes of your source and try to understand. [...] Only then—on their terms, not your own—can you hope to hear the stories they need to be told."

An empathetic approach implies meeting the interviewee with an open mind, politeness, and respect. We simultaneously demonstrate an understanding of and interest in his story, opinions, thoughts, and feelings, by listening and following up on what he says. We allow time for reflection and the opportunity to communicate thoughts. We also attempt to put ourselves in the emotional world of the other person. To achieve this, we must listen and not interrupt. An empathetic approach also entails demonstrating that the other is an equal, with the right to self-determination and freedom of choice. The communication must allow for the possibility that the interviewee may be feeling stressed, angry, shameful, traumatized, or afraid. The objective is to create a situation in which the interviewee feels secure enough about the interviewer and the interview framework that he or she is able to share their entire story.

Communicating empathy does not mean that we must have *sympathy*. Empathy shows that we have understood the other person's feelings and that we acknowledge them. But we don't share the other person's feelings. Sympathy means to have compassion, to feel for the other person. Sharing another person's feelings beyond acknowledging them can interfere with objectivity when we are gathering information. Antipathy also involves strong emotions and in a corresponding fashion interferes with the aim of the professional interview.

Most readers will indeed concur if someone states that empathy is a prerequisite for creating trust in a professional interview. Sympathy and the consequences of sympathy, on the other hand, will potentially undermine trust. Imagine a case officer in a child welfare dispute who weeps with despair while on the witness stand because of the situation of one of the parties. This will quickly have an impact on the court's perception of how objectively the case has been handled, not to mention the trustworthiness of the case officer. If the case officer instead acknowledges that the situation is difficult for one of the parties, and expresses this, this will not undermine objectivity and trust in the same way.

It is important to communicate empathy in an authentic fashion. Only then does empathy have a function. But this can be difficult. In daily life, empathy quickly disappears when the person we are trying to understand behaves aggressively or has a hostile attitude. In a professional setting such as an interview, we must nonetheless uphold professional empathy. This does not mean we should be on the defensive. It means that we should acknowledge the situation of the other party and focus on the purpose of the interview: to obtain accurate and reliable information. In this way it becomes easier to understand the other person's behavior and show an interest in what that person has to say. The reason for this is simple: interviewees who experience a genuine interest and understanding of their situation on the part of the person in front of them will ultimately provide more information. Although the documentation for this is predominantly taken from studies of police interviews in the West, recent studies from other parts of the world have come to the same conclusion: empathy appears to stimulate communication in and across different cultures (Bull & Rachlew 2020).

After having studied more than a thousand hours of interviews of suspected terrorists in Great Britain, psychologist Laurence Alison and his colleagues concluded that there's no point in pretending to be empathetic (Alison et al. 2013). "You can't bullshit, you've got to mean it," the researchers concluded in an interview published in the *Guardian* (2017).

In the following sections we will describe some basic elements that must be included in your interviews if they are to be considered professional.

Active Listening

In a professional interview we either seek or share information. In order to retain what is said, we must listen actively. Listening is not the same thing as hearing.

> Hearing is something that we do passively. Listening, on the other hand, is an active, human process requiring attentiveness and concentration. (West et al. 1994)

Active listening is a skill implemented in an endeavor to understand and put what is said into a context. And like all other skills, active listening abilities can be improved with practice. To say, "Tomorrow I will be a better listener" is a bit like saying, "Tomorrow I will be a better football player." *Active* listening requires effort, commitment, and concentration. We listen with our ears, head, eyes, and feelings. The interviewee's ability to explain will only ever be as good as the professional's ability to listen.

The first thing we should think about is how to arrange the physical parameters to facilitate active listening. It goes without saying that it is difficult to listen if we aren't able to hear the other person, if there are disturbances, or if we are uncomfortable in other ways. Although the research on this point is far more limited than for more classical, eyewitness psychology issues, it seems clear that the physical layout of the interview space can have a positive or negative influence on communication. Dawson et al. (2017) found that test subjects who were interviewed in a relatively large room with comfortable chairs and using a nonconfrontational format provided significantly more information than test subjects in a smaller, relatively cramped interview room. A Japanese study showed that a confrontational format has a physical impact on the participants of a conversation (Osato & Ogawa 2003). They found that the pulse and stress rates of test subjects rose significantly when they were seated across from one another. Stress is known to have a negative impact on communication.

Environmental psychology—the study of transactions between individuals and their physical settings—deals with several important psychosocial issues, two of which are privacy and social interaction. Research confirms the Japanese study and highlights the value of 45-degree angles seating for conversations (Lattimore 2013). The angled arrangement serves as a negotiation between two competing sociopsychological needs. This is neatly explained by Judy Rollins (2009), a registered nurse with a PhD in health and community studies in her article about designs and policies on social interaction and privacy in hospitals. Rollins argues that while most human beings enjoy settings in which they can see and interact with another, humans also enjoy settings in which they can maintain some privacy from others.[1]

A face-to-face seating arrangement offers plenty of interaction, but little or no privacy. A back-to-back arrangement offers a high degree of privacy (you may even blow your nose unnoticed!) but provides limited interaction. A 45-degree seating arrangement allows not only for interaction but also

---

1. Arrangements stimulating interaction are sometimes referred to as sociofugal arrangements, while arrangements stimulating privacy are labeled sociopetal arrangements.

simultaneously for some degree of privacy—the optimal balance for a professional interview. We will address settings for professional interviews in further detail in the section "Physical Preparations" in Chapter 6 of Part 2.

When rapport is established and we start seeking information, it is more important to listen actively than to talk. Professor of psychology Ronald P. Fisher, one of the founders of cognitive interview techniques, takes this even further, stating that the normative ideal must be the *questionless* interview. This is easier said than done, but a good, empathetic introduction, followed by well-considered forms of encouragement, will potentially prompt the interviewee to share so much information that many subsequent questions will become superfluous.

A not uncommon misconception is that listening is too time-consuming. Professional interviewers know, however, that listening is extremely effective. But it requires, of course, good questioning techniques. We dedicate considerable attention to the subject of questioning techniques in the second part of the book.

Active listening entails releasing control of the conversation into the hands of the person providing information, while remaining actively present at all times. We attempt to understand what the other person is communicating and demonstrate through our body language that we are listening, that we are there for the other person—without staring. We receive and interpret information and view it in the context of the information we already have. We take note of any particular details or information we will want to follow up on later. After the person has finished their account, we can summarize briefly to ensure that we have understood everything. We will look at this in detail in the chapter "The First Free Recall."

Silence

For many people, including the authors of this book, the greatest adjustment in transitioning from experience-based interview methods to research-based methods involves learning to listen and employ silence during the interview. It may feel different or odd to allow silence in the interview situation. We don't mean an awkward silence, the kind you might experience when a conversation with a neighbor with whom you have nothing in common comes to a halt. The type of silence we are referring to is productive. The interviewee is given the time and opportunity to reflect and formulate his or her answers. Active listening and the use of silence is not necessarily more time-consuming, although at first, it might feel that way. It is in fact time well spent since an appropriate application of silence promotes communication and concentration. Silence also safeguards the integrity of the interviewee, irrespective of whether or not that person is trying to withhold information.

Active listening entails that we are for the most part silent. We give the interviewee control over his or her own story, without attempting to influence the telling. Another obvious advantage of silence is that it allows room for reflection. Remember what we explained in the chapter on psychology regarding factors that promote and impede memory enhancement. Time and silence are extremely beneficial when an interviewee is trying to retrieve memories, when the interviewer's task is to trigger as many senses as possible and subsequently, more details. Even though not everyone we interact with in a professional setting will be retrieving memories, silence and calm have a positive impact on our capacity for reflection. It gives the interviewee a better chance to formulate good answers on his or her own terms. In professional settings, the topic of the interview may be sensitive or difficult to talk about. In such situations, it can be crucial to give the interviewee the time and silence they need to explain at their own pace and in their own way. Silence can also foster an atmosphere in which interviewees understand that they are at liberty to decide for themselves whether or not they even want to continue talking.

Award-winning and world-renowned journalist Bob Woodward, famous for the disclosure of Watergate and many books about life inside the White House, holds that silence is the most effective measure a journalist can use. After a lecture in Oslo in 2019, he had the following to say about questions and silence: "The most powerful question, second only to the power of silence, is the question 'why.'"

In the publication ProPublica, Pulitzer Prize–winning journalist Ken Armstrong writes of a discovery he made when he went from writing for newspapers to creating podcasts/radio. At a journalism conference in Norway in the spring of 2019,[2] he said the following:

> As newspaper journalists we go into an interview with the goal of having the interviewee fill in the blanks in a story we have already written. In radio we ask questions to get the interviewee to talk. Ask open questions and then shut your mouth.

---

2. Ken Armstrong told Norwegian journalists about his work on the article series "An Unbelievable Story of Rape" at the SKUP conference in Tønsberg in 2019. For the full story, see https://www.themarshallproject.org/2015/12/16/an-unbelievable-story-of-rape.

In other situations, silence can be experienced as awkward. A study done by social scientists Namkje Koudenburg, Tom Postmes, and Erestine Gordijn (2011) showed that silence can be challenging, even after only four seconds:

> Four seconds appeared to be the ideal duration of silence with an eye to ensuring that participants did not notice the silence consciously, and still perceived the conversation as natural, but nevertheless felt that the conversation was significantly less pleasant.

Silence can be experienced as uncomfortable, both for the person interviewing and for the person being interviewed. With practice in the use of the investigative interview method, allowing silence becomes easier, as we come to understand that by employing silence in this way, the other person is given responsibility for breaking the silence and as a result will often share more information. It is important to remember that a professional interview is not an ordinary conversation. In a professional interview situation, silence is a tool we use to obtain relevant and reliable information. In a private conversation, we will often break the silence to prevent the situation from becoming awkward or to spare the other person discomfort. We must therefore mentally prepare ourselves for silence in our professional interviews. Besides, it is not necessarily the case that everyone experiences silence as uncomfortable. This will vary. Some of us appreciate silence, particularly when we need time to reconsider and want to respond at our own pace.

In order to ensure that silence does not become awkward and impede communication, it can be expedient to speak about silence before it is implemented. It should be included as part of the introductory information we provide about how the interview will be carried out. Such information and other similar forms of "communication about communication" are known as *metacommunication*, one of our most important tools as professional interviewers. An entire section is therefore dedicated to the subject of metacommunication toward the end of this chapter.

Body Language

Body language is also communication. Our physical demeanor can influence how what we say is understood. If somebody looks at you with a teasing smile and says, "You deserve a beating," your understanding of the message will be completely different from what it would have been had their eyes been flashing and fists clenched. In the latter situation you don't even need to hear that you "deserve" a beating, because you will feel threatened. The three most important words in the world—I love you—can also lose their impact if the body language of the person speaking the words expresses something else entirely. Body language can both enhance and alter the message of a conversation, and highlight an implied subtext, at least in daily life. In a professional interview, on the other hand, we cannot proceed according to the notion that clearly expressed information should be interpreted in light of body language. Body language can be manipulated and suppressed. It is culturally specific and can be affected by illness or injury. We also interpret body language subjectively, according to our own references. Our interpretation can be correct, or it can be wrong. It is merely an interpretation.

One example is eye contact. For most people from a Western culture, friendly eye contact is a sign that the other person is interested in what they have to say. It can be an expression of respect and recognition. In some cultures, however, eye contact can have the opposite significance. If you look directly into the eyes of someone who holds a higher rank in some kind of pecking order, it is considered disrespectful. In such a culture, looking older people in the eyes is also problematic. But even without a ranking system or culture, situations will arise in which an interviewee does not want or need to make eye contact. This can be the case when the interviewee is in the midst of an extensive, free recall or is speaking about a sensitive subject.

Everyone who takes part in a conversation will automatically register the body language of the other participants. We have already mentioned some of the potential pitfalls of instinctive responses when we are handling information. Such responses can easily throw us off-track. Neither it is possible to establish the quality of the information we receive based on an unconscious interpretation of body language. If we ask a question and notice the other person squirming in their seat, it need not mean that the question is difficult or that the person is lying. There can be many alternative explanations for squirming: the chair is uncomfortable, they have been sitting still for a long time, they need to use the bathroom, their parking meter is about to run out, they need to take medication, and so on. The point is that information must always be tested to determine its reliability. There are then two types of information we can test: what the interviewee says and what the interviewee does. Instead of interpreting the body language, we can explore the reason for their restlessness, simply by asking, "I have noticed that you are a little restless, can you tell me why?" We hereby also demonstrate empathy through our attentiveness to the possibility that the other person is perhaps not feeling well. Regardless of what this person's explanation for their restlessness might be, you can still make a note of how it *may* have significance for the quality of the information they have provided. It need not mean that the information is unreliable, but you can still follow up on the information you receive and test it thoroughly, either immediately or later. If we react to something about the body language of another person, we must handle it like all other information. We must test its reliability.

On the other hand, an awareness of own body language will strengthen communication. Greeting someone with a smile and a handshake establishes the foundation for a good conversation. Although we have highlighted some of the complexities of eye contact, it is nonetheless important to look at people in most conversations. By seeking eye contact we demonstrate that the other person has our attention. By showing respect, empathy, and presence, we acknowledge the other person as a human being and strengthen communication.

The importance of eye contact in an interaction is something most of us have experienced. Imagine a conversation in which the gaze of the other person wanders around the room, apparently in search of somebody more interesting to talk to. At best, the situation becomes uncomfortable; at worst communication breaks down completely. It need not even be other people who are the distraction. The countless digital screens of our era do not only steal time—they steal the gaze, concentration, and attention. Communication is quickly undermined if the gaze wanders to a mobile phone or laptop.

During a professional interview we must therefore be aware of how our own body language can influence others. It is relatively obvious that communication can be damaged if we roll our eyes, throw our arms up in frustration, or in other ways express feelings or opinions. These types of responses also corrupt the information. If we send out signals through our body language that communicates what we believe to be right or wrong, significant or insignificant, this can also have an impact on the interviewee's explanation.

When we meet somebody in a professional interview context and the conversation meanders or moves off-topic, our body language must remain positive and receptive. This strengthens communication. When the conversation gravitates toward the subject matter we are planning to explore in the interview, it is important to maintain neutral and empathetic body language that signals interest. Both positive and negative body language can influence the other party, and thereby influence the quality of the information we obtain. The person to whom we are speaking may often be uncertain about his or her response. If through our body language we indicate the type of answer we want, this will potentially influence not only the narrative but also memory. The other person can be more or less unconsciously influenced in a positive or negative sense through our body language. The big challenge for us when leading the interview is to balance a neutral approach with our role as an active and empathetic listener. It is never wrong to show that you are paying attention to what the other person is saying.

Imagine a victim of a violent crime who is describing a horrible incident. The police already have a suspect. When the victim is about to describe the appearance of the assailant, the detectives must be careful to maintain neutral body language. Otherwise, they risk confirming, and thereby reinforcing, the aspects of the description that coincide with the suspect and undermining details that do not. One of the reasons why the alleged serial killer Sture Bergwall (formerly known as Thomas Quick) was able to mislead the entire Swedish justice system with his false confessions, seven times in a row, was through such errors (Stridbeck 2020).

The detective must simultaneously show empathy and attend to the victim's needs during the interview. If this party has doubts about her description, she may read the detective's body language as a confirmation of the description she has given. This may in turn increase her certainty about the accuracy of her statement the next time she is going to describe the assailant. The wife of the Swedish prime minister Olof Palme, Lisbeth Palme, with time remembered more and more details about the appearance of her husband's killer, even though in the initial police interview she stated that she only caught a glimpse of him. Her certainty increased as the interviews proceeded, and finally, she identified the man who most resembled him in an identification parade. But there were a number of flaws in the way she was interviewed, and Christer Petterson was acquitted (Holgerson 1998).

Active Listening Challenges

Even if we concentrate, maintain neutral body language, remain silent, and otherwise do everything right, a number of other factors can still interfere with active listening.

Research on interpersonal communication has identified a number of variables that make listening difficult (West et al. 1994). Some of the variables are the responsibility of the interviewee and include a poor vocabulary, inadequate explanatory skills, or a limited cognitive capacity. These are variables we have no control over, but as professionals it is our responsibility to take such factors into consideration. Unlike the detectives studied by Geiselman and Fisher, professional interviewers use words and turns of phrase adapted to the person with whom they are speaking. Our professional language should not sound professional. It should be characterized by an everyday, easy-to-understand vocabulary. Avoid the use of technical terminology, jargon, and foreign words. If you have to use technical terms, you should at least take the time to explain them. If the person being interviewed uses unfamiliar names, words, concepts, or turns of phrase, you can ask for clarification. Once an explanation has been given, it is a good idea to use the interviewee's own words where this feels natural. You will both have a clear understanding of what you are talking about, and it will facilitate the interview process. For example, the restaurant Olympen in Oslo is sometimes referred to by the nickname "Lompa." If the interviewee uses this term, you can incorporate it into the interview as a matter of course. The word "dope" also means "fabulous" or "awesome" and is a word commonly used by many young people. It will almost always sound strange coming out of the mouth of an adult, and many adults won't even understand what it means. In such a case, you must request an explanation of the word. "You say that it was dope. What does the word mean?" After receiving an explanation, using the word may not feel as awkward. "What was it about the situation that was dope?" If using a word still feels unnatural, however, you are under no obligation to use it. The point is that this type of linguistic awareness demonstrates respect and empathy for the interviewee and, on the whole, will remove some of the asymmetry in the interview situation, because you are relinquishing control over language use.

External variables can also undermine active listening, such as noise, intrusions, attention grabbers (such as mobile phones, laptops, something taking place in the background), and poor seating options including too much distance between the interviewer and the interviewee. We can do many things to prevent these types of disturbances before the professional interview starts. We will return to this in the section "Physical Preparations."

Most of the things that interfere with active listening are nonetheless in the hands of the listener. In a way, this is a good thing because it means we can do something about it. But it also shows how difficult it is to be a good listener. Think of the effect on your ability to use active listening if you are tired or intoxicated; your listening skills will be less acute than if you are well-rested and sober. Similarly, if you experience something out of the ordinary before arriving to do the interview (like witnessing a car accident or learning that your partner wants to leave you), it can be difficult to refrain from thinking about it. Cognitive and emotional interference can undermine the quality of any professional interview. It can be difficult to listen actively if you have no interest in the speaker or what he/she is speaking about. Or worse, you may have had negative experiences with the person or persons you are about to meet. You can be prejudiced, fall into cognitive traps, or unconsciously employ other simplification processes. This cognitive "noise" disrupts active listening. Most of these challenges are things we can mentally prepare for and practice managing. The mental preparations are therefore an important part of the *planning and preparation phase.*

Interruptions

Interruptions impede active listening. The police have tended to interrupt during interviews. Ronald Fisher, Edward Geiselman, and D. S. Raymond (1987) are responsible for a classic study done in 1985, in which they analyzed eleven police interviews done by eight experienced detectives in Florida. The researchers found that on average, the detectives interrupted the interviewee every 7.5 seconds. The sample addressed by the study is small, but the results give pause, not least because a correlation was found in a similar study carried out on the British police from approximately the same time period (George 1991).

We all have a sense of how interruptions also break down communication. When this happens, important information can be lost. But we interrupt all the same, whether we are detectives, journalists, doctors, or directors, because we lack sufficient awareness of how interrupting compounds the risks of missing out on important information in the moment. We interrupt because we believe it will help us obtain more information. But even follow-up questions and clarifications may come across as interruptions. Research shows that the result of interruptions is *less* information, not more. An interruption undermines the concentration of all those taking part in an interview. The interviewee can lose both the thread of a difficult story and the motivation to provide details. She can also experience the interruption as disrespectful. She "learns" that long, detailed responses are not interesting. Her answers become shorter and information is lost. We may also lose the thread of a conversation by becoming overly fixated on our own questions and the answers these elicit. Witness psychologist Kristina Jakobsen (2010) writes:

> If the person being questioned receives a long series of closed questions, there will be a risk of him/her adapting his/her answers to conform with this style, giving only short answers to the interviewer's questions. [...] There is then a risk that the interviewee knows something which the interviewer doesn't ask about and about which the latter therefore gains no knowledge.

The failure to follow up on what is said can also be a kind of interruption. By failing to respond, we interrupt the interviewee's account and inadvertently demonstrate that it is not of particular interest. This can occur in two ways. If we move on to another topic before the interviewee has finished telling his story or without following up with a relevant question, we are showing little interest in what has been said. It is experienced as an interruption even though we don't actually interrupt the person while he is speaking. There is always something in a story we can pursue further, both to show the other person respect and thereby to strengthen communication moving forward, and because it can elicit even more details.

The second way is more subtle but just as damaging for communication. Special needs educators Åse Langballe, Kari Trøften Gamst, and Mari

Figure 8 The layers of a story. From CREATIV, based on Langballe et al. (2010).

Jacobsen (2010) write that a story consists of three layers (Figure 8). The external layer is *the context*—the story's framework, such as time, place, the weather, who was present, and so on. The middle layer is *the action*—the actual events, who did what, and so on. The innermost layer is *the feelings*—the experience of what took place.

In a professional interview, we should ask questions addressing the part of the story, or the layer, the interviewee is currently speaking about. Jumping back and forth between layers disrupts communication and access to memory. If the interviewee tells you about the fear she felt in a specific situation—the innermost layer—and you follow up with questions about what time it was—context—she might experience this as an interruption of her story. The risk is then that she will understand or "learn" that you aren't interested in her feelings, which are perhaps the most difficult things to talk about. The innermost layer of the story is thereby shut down. When we understand how important it is to retrieve all the elements of a memory, especially feelings, we realize that it is possible to miss out on wholly significant details from all three layers, if in some way we interrupt the speaker during the interview.

To prevent interruptions, we must improve our active listening skills. In a purely practical sense, it is as easy, and as difficult, as remaining silent. Let the other person explain themselves at their own pace. If information emerges that we want to explore, we should quickly assess whether it is necessary to ask a question to understand what the interviewee is currently saying. If not, we make a note of the question and refrain from interrupting.

Active listening is a difficult cognitive skill. There are also situations in which we should interrupt, ask questions, elicit an explanation. To avoid the potentially negative repercussions of this type of interruption and to prevent a breakdown in communication, it is important to prepare the interviewee for the possibility that such interruptions may occur. Preparations of this nature are a part of metacommunication before and during our professional interview.

Metacommunication

Metacommunication is communication about communication. In the context of the professional interview, metacommunication is information provided by the interviewer(s) about what will occur in the interview: what we will talk about and how we will talk about it. We use metacommunication to clarify what lies ahead and thereby manage the expectations for the interview. By providing this type of information, we limit interview asymmetry and strengthen communication. We also prevent communication breakdowns—situations in which communication becomes difficult or shuts down altogether, compromising the rapport with the interviewee. In the worst-case scenario, a communication breakdown can mean that the interview is over.

Each individual who takes part in a professional interview is unique, with unique expectations and needs. Some are anxious about the mere fact of being interviewed, or they can be nervous about the outcome. Others are feeling stressed because they have a vested interest in achieving a particular outcome. Some are perhaps dreading having to share information of a personal nature or secrets they are carrying. Regardless of the reason for this uneasiness, a respectful "prior conversation" will have a calming effect on most people. Even for individuals who are accustomed to taking part in professional interviews, it can be helpful to know how *this* particular interview will be carried out. Again, it is a matter of relinquishing some of the power in the interview situation and thereby preventing an unnecessary experience of a power imbalance—asymmetry.

Metacommunication also sends a signal that we know how to do our job, that we are well-prepared, and that we have respect for the person before us. This strengthens both professional trust and interpersonal communication. When we are able to put interviewees at ease through information sharing and the management of expectations, they will be better able to relax and focus their full capacity on providing information, rather than worrying about what will happen next. The professional interview can become more like an ordinary conversation, with all the benefits this entails.

Metacommunication promotes openness, self-assurance, professional trust, and equality of the participants in the interview situation. It prevents communication breakdowns and thereby fosters a better interview dynamic.

The first step of metacommunication entails providing information about *how* we will speak together. Here it is important to define the roles. It will give the persons taking part in the professional interview a sense of security to be informed of who they will be meeting, the reason they are there, and how they will behave during the interview. It is also useful to explain what will be expected of them, in other words, clarify their role. In situations involving more than one professional, it is especially important to clarify the roles of all involved parties. Being in the minority greatly intensifies the experience of asymmetry. The majority shouldn't come across as a troll with multiple heads. One person should take the lead and ask questions, opening up for questions from the other participants toward the end.

> Thank-you for taking the time to meet with us. We are looking forward to getting to know you. As you can see, there are three of us who are interested in talking to you this morning. Jens Pedersen is seated on my right. He works in the personnel department. On my left is Erving Johnson. He is a union representative and is here to ensure best practice. My name is Monica Jackson. I am the director of the department currently hiring a new staff member. I will be leading the interview and asking you some questions today. After I have finished with my questions, the others will ask questions if there are any relevant issues or concerns that haven't been addressed. What we will be doing today is listening to you and trying to get a sense of you as a person and your qualifications. You will have plenty of time to answer, so take all the time you need and try to answer each question as completely and with as much detail as you can. Before we start, do you have any questions for us?

Once the roles of each participant have been clarified, the person leading the interview should explain clearly how the participants will communicate during the interview. To prevent communication breakdowns, it is important to spend some time thinking about and preparing for any potential challenges. We have already covered the use of silence as a tool in professional interviews. Silence can elicit detailed information but can also cause discomfort. Interruptions can undermine communication but are sometimes necessary. To prevent silence and interruptions from undermining communication, we must be open and honest about our use of communication tools.

> After I have asked a question, you can take all the time you need to think about your answer. I will be silent and let you take your time. As the interview progresses, I may interrupt you now and then. If I should do so, it is not because I'm not interested in whatever it is you are saying. It may be because what you are talking about is beyond the scope of what we are supposed to cover today, or that we are running out of time and I want to hear your thoughts on other topics.

Sometimes it is necessary to repeat a question to elicit an answer to a specific issue. An interviewee may feel irritated by this. Asking or probing for details can also provoke feelings of discomfort or irritation. It is important to prevent this kind of frustration because it can have a negative impact on the communication.

> In the course of the interview, I might repeat questions or ask for more details. This will happen when I haven't fully understood what you have been saying or when I need more details in order to understand. I hope that's acceptable.

In some situations when the interviewee has a particular message he wants to communicate, he will often repeat that message rather than answering the questions. We can help prevent both the repetition of such messages and any irritation over repeated questions by being open and informative:

> I understand that you want to be sure to communicate certain pieces of information. You will have the opportunity to do so first. Then I will ask you some questions. If you keep repeating the same information instead of answering my questions, I may interrupt you and repeat my question.

The step-by-step method outlined in Part 2 of this book is designed to ensure that the interviewee will have the opportunity to explain themselves as freely as possible and without interruption. This can be an unusual experience for many people. It can be appropriate to explain this before we start the interview.

> When we start the interview, I will ask you to tell me as much as you can about what happened. The reason I do this is so you will be able to speak freely about everything that you feel is important, without my influencing anything you have to say. So, when we begin, I hope that you will tell me everything, including as many details as you can. After you've finished, I will probably have a few more questions for you.

As illustrated in the earlier examples, we can bring up other communication-related matters of relevance to the interview. For example, before an interview in an HR department about a deadlocked conflict in the workplace, it can make sense to agree that the interview will be conducted in a calm and restrained fashion.

The second part of metacommunication is the easiest part. It is a matter of explaining what we will talk about. For example, Elizabeth's parents are going to take part in a developmental interview with the class teacher. They have many questions: they are concerned about whether Elizabeth has been behaving appropriately, they are worried that something has happened at school that they don't know about, and of course they are wondering about whether she is keeping up with her schoolwork. They will find it easier to relax during the interview if they are met by a class teacher who shakes their hands, smiles, and gives them the following information:

> Today I was thinking we would talk about how Elizabeth interacts with the other children, about Elizabeth's homework routines, any challenges Elizabeth is experiencing with math and the school trip to the Science Museum. Finally, I have made sure we have plenty of time in case you have anything you want to address or ask me about. Before we get started, do you have any questions?

By using metacommunication before the interview begins, we help the parents to mentally prepare for what lies ahead. When the parents are informed of the talking points for the interview, they receive reassurance that Elizabeth is well-behaved, information about whether anything out of the ordinary has happened at school and whether she appears to be doing well on her schoolwork. Only two topics remain that may potentially have negative contents. The uncertainty is diminished. Now that the parents are informed of the topics that will be addressed during the interview, they will be more likely to speak about any difficulties their daughter is having with math and how they handle the homework situation at home. They also receive reassurance that they will have the opportunity to ask their own questions at the end of the interview, so they don't have to worry about there not being time for them to voice their concerns. If there should still be some matter that they are unable to put on hold, they also receive the opportunity to address this before the interview starts. If the parents seize this opportunity and bring up a complex issue during this preliminary phase, the teacher can consider asking whether they can wait until the end to address this topic. Then the issue has been flagged and won't interfere with the rest of the interview. Each of these measures is designed to clear away cognitive "noise" before the interview starts.

The use of metacommunication *during* an interview is addressed in the second phase of the method described in Part 2: "Engage and Explain— Establishing Rapport." There are at least two occasions when this can be prudent. One such occasion is when we employ one of the tools we have already presented during the introduction. In such a case, we refer to our introductory remarks.

I apologize for the interruption, but I did mention before we started that this might occur. I understand that you have some good suggestions for how you can help Elizabeth with her homework. We will follow up on this by email and in our next meeting. As you know, we only have until 4 p.m. To make sure we will have enough time to speak about the class trip to Science Museum, and so you will have the chance to ask any questions you might have in the end, would you mind if we moved on now?

The second situation in which we use metacommunication in the course of the interview is when we prevent communication breakdowns by framing a question. In this way we ensure that the interviewee does not feel threatened by the question. "It feels like I haven't really received an answer to what I am asking about. Let me ask the question again" (instead of saying, "Why don't you answer the question?"). By couching the question in a statement about our experience, we open up for the possibility that we may be wrong. It is possible that the other person has in fact attempted to answer to the best of his or her abilities, even though we haven't fully understood. If we are mistaken, the interviewee will then have the opportunity to clarify any misunderstandings without putting unnecessary strain on the communication.

In metacommunication it is also important to ensure that all parties are in agreement about communicating in the manner discussed. This can be done by quite simply asking, "How does that sound to you?" By doing this, the other party understands that they are playing a part in defining the ground rules. This helps counteract asymmetry in the interaction. If the other party disagrees, then you can find a solution together. When you reach an agreement, you form a kind of contract that can be referred to throughout the interview whenever necessary. "As stated at the beginning of the interview, I must interrupt you now. We have only a limited amount of time to cover all the topics we need to talk about, so I suggest we move on to the next topic." The risk of the communication breaking down is thereby substantially reduced.

The management of expectations through metacommunication can be illustrated by an example from daily life. When you are going to bring a child into a toy store, it pays to clarify expectations ahead of time. Before you enter the store, you make an agreement with the child that they will be allowed to choose one toy. If the child chooses two toys, you can refer to "the contract." "Do you remember what we talked about before we came in? That you would be allowed to choose one toy? Not two? So, you must choose one of the two toys and I will buy it for you." When done correctly, this will prevent the child from throwing a tantrum in the store. By explaining how we will communicate in a professional interview, we can prevent "a tantrum" in the conversation.

We have now completed Part 1 of the book, and it is our hope that the reader has gained a sense of the broad-reaching application and relevance of the methodology. Although all interviews are different, the comprehensive scope of the insights provided in Part 1 is intended to facilitate application of the method presented in Part 2, regardless of the type of professional interview you are going to lead or who you will be interviewing. The model we present in this book can be viewed as a large toolbox. Not all the tools are needed in all contexts, but there will always be tools we can use. The tools must be employed where suitable. But we believe that the comprehensiveness and flexibility of the model makes it suitable for most professional interviews.

Norway, 2011

In all criminal cases, detectives make a clear distinction between the person they are interviewing and the crimes he or she is suspected of having committed. This was the case even for the terrorist who committed the shocking acts in Oslo and Utøya Island on July 22 in which 77 people died.

The detectives tasked with interviewing the terror suspect know it is not their job to judge, moralize, preach, or advise. Their job is to investigate what has happened and why. The mindset of all three detectives is predominantly one of curiosity: What compels a young man to commit such horrific acts and how has he done it?

The detectives set aside sufficient time to plan and prepare for each interview with the terrorist. They must familiarize themselves with all available information about the matter under investigation and determine which subjects they need to know more about. Simultaneously, they must plan how they will ask the questions so they will receive reliable answers. The questions should also produce details they didn't even know they needed. They spend time preparing the physical parameters for the investigative interview. Transport, police escorts, security, refreshments, the interview room, appointments with other interview participants, and recording devices. The terrorist does not meet the interviewer who will carry out the interview until it starts. Hence, the interviewer is freed from other work duties that day and will spend this time preparing for the interview. The mental preparations must be extremely thorough in order to ensure successful management of the interview situation: the interviewing detective must treat the terror suspect with empathy and respect and be prepared to handle horrible details and any sense of personal outrage caused by the apparent meaninglessness of the criminal actions.

The investigative interview team knows that in order to receive a detailed and reliable explanation, they must establish professional trust. And they know that the physical and mental preparations and format for the interview are of decisive significance when it comes to engendering that trust.

The terrorist wants to explain himself. But the interview team is aware that this can change. For this reason, the fundamental principles for good communication embedded in the interview method are foremost in their awareness. In every interview of the suspect, they make sure to explain what will take place and remind him that he may be asked critical and detailed questions. The detectives explain their roles and what they expect of him. They also explain the roles of the other individuals the terrorist might encounter in the interview context.

The terrorist is cooperative and wants to demonstrate that he remembers many details. This becomes a challenge. The detectives must be all the more careful not to disclose information through the questions they ask or the way they ask questions.

When the interviews have been completed, the police know that there are no further terrorist cells waiting to be activated. The terrorist is not a member of a global network. He is still consumed by hatred, but he acted alone. The interviewing method kept him talking and he shared a complete account. Most of what he said corresponded with other evidence. The information is reliable.

The investigation, the interviews, and the trial against the terrorist not only put Norwegian society, the system, and public security to the test but were also an extreme test of the method that is the subject of this book. It is a method that, on the strength of the underlying research, ethics, and fundamental communication principles, is relevant in all professional interviews, from the questioning of terrorists to job interviews and doctor–patient consultations.

PART 2

5

THE METHOD

As we now begin the chapters outlining the method, it can be helpful to remember that the term *method* comes from the Greek word *methodos*, which means to follow a specific path toward a goal. Although current definitions and usage of the word may vary, almost all of them include the description of a path or a procedure leading toward a goal as a key feature. It is the procedure for a professional interview that we will now explain.

The method is based on the knowledge and research we introduced in Part 1 of this book.

For those who carry out professional interviews, the use of a method has many clear benefits. First, a method makes it easier to plan an interview. Second, it makes it possible to evaluate the entire process after the fact, both for the person in charge of the interview and for others who are involved the process. Without a method, it is difficult to identify what may have gone wrong, where this occurred, and why. The use of a method makes it easier and more interesting to discuss questions about interview technique or specific experiences, to identify what can be improved, and to address problems on the basis of a mutually recognized framework, terminology, and concept. The implementation of a practical and strongly evidence-based method will help develop and stimulate a professional community, which in turn will make the work of that community more interesting.

Introducing a theoretical method also makes it easier for new staff members to learn about investigative interviewing. Long-term experience is no longer required to become proficient. Of course, you will improve your skills and self-confidence through experience, but if you set your course in the wrong direction without training, correction, reflection, or critical thinking along the way, there is a real danger of that experience consolidating misunderstandings until in the end they are perceived as truths (Rachlew 2003). The potential for professionalization is considerable if you and your employer implement routines in keeping with the final phase of the method: the evaluation.

As we describe the method's dynamic and flexible framework below, our starting point is the different phases of the method in Figure 9.

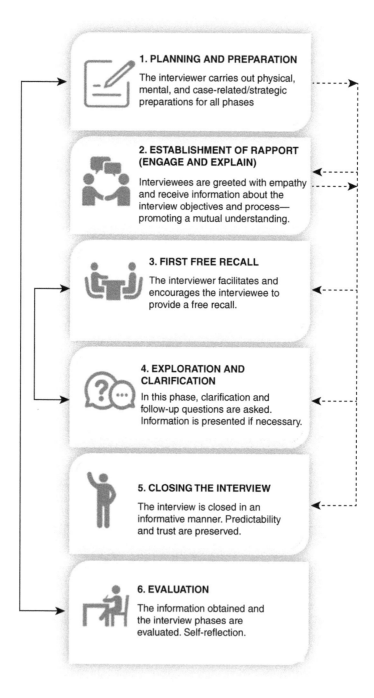

Figure 9 The interview phases, dynamic and flexible. *Source:* Author.

Dynamic and Flexible

Figure 9 illustrates the interconnectedness and flexibility of the method's phases. To be able to carry out professional interviews, the interviewer must understand that each phase is based on the other phases. Each phase is of critical importance for the subsequent phase. If an interviewer skips a phase, this must be a conscious choice based on the circumstances. If a phase is not completed or a mistake is made along the way, this can reduce the possibility of success with the next phase. The method's inherent potential for eliciting relevant, accurate, and reliable information is thereby compromised.

We will shortly explain how the *preparations* influence the entire process. If the interviewer does not succeed in *establishing rapport*, the possibilities for achieving a relevant, detailed, *free recall* are reduced. If free recall is not included, there is a risk of the *exploration* becoming piecemeal and awkward, and of missing relevant information that lies beyond the planned scope of the investigation.

Two fundamental elements are illustrated through the dotted lines of the figure. First, we must plan all the phases during our preparations. Second, the dotted lines indicate that the establishment of rapport and the upholding of contact through a rapport based on the principles of communication is a constant theme. Many of the communication principles for establishment of rapport will pertain throughout the entire interview.

At first glance, the method can appear to be a linear process moving in one direction and the interviewer's job is to work through the phases one by one, from the start to the finish line. This is not how a professional interview works. Communication can break down and then rapport must be reestablished. After the first free recall phase, we will normally enter an exploratory phase. Here central themes are introduced by another free recall session, which at this point will be more focused on the specific themes the interview is intended to illuminate. In the above model, the dynamic of free recall phases providing entryways to key themes is illustrated by the unbroken line between the two phases.

But if key themes are not identified during the planning and preparation phase, we risk overlooking them. An absence of active listening during free recall will also increase the risk of our missing out on important information that should be a theme during the exploratory phase. Perhaps key themes arise as we are concluding the interview. This provides an opening for another exploration, and the professional interviewer should then lead the interview back and repeat this phase to address the new content.

The flexibility of the method derives from the understanding that no two interactions or interviews are identical. Some are extensive and require days of preparations. Others are more peripheral or proforma in nature and require a minimum of preparations. A journalist in the crowd at a press con-ference must still make sure his or her microphone is on and functioning (phys-ical preparations). The journalist should also have an idea of what his one question will be about—and how it should best be formulated.

In many professions it happens that we interview the same person several times. The job applicant returns for an in-depth interview, our source may have more information, the patient or client may require follow-up, and so on. The way we close the first interview can have significance for the subse-quent encounter. Did the interviewee leave the interview with a positive or negative feeling? Did they feel respected and taken care of? The closing of the interview can have critical ramifications for the next interaction and the preparations for the second interview start during the evaluation of the first. During the evaluation we assess whether the objectives defined at the start of our preparations were met, what type of information we acquired, and how we carried out the interview process. The findings of the evaluation will influ-ence the planning of the subsequent interview. This is illustrated in Figure 9 by the arrows between planning and evaluation.

The different phases of the method have proven to provide an expedient structure for practitioners. The method was introduced in Great Britain 30 years ago. Today it constitutes the leading-edge framework for police interviews worldwide. The method's components are also well-suited for use as a framework and visualization during training and development. But practitioners also embrace it—for a number of reasons. They can visualize the interview through the structure. They can apply the structure during their preparations, and when it is internalized, it functions like a compass, helping the interviewer navigate throughout the interview process.

6

PLANNING AND PREPARATION

For practical reasons, we will break down the planning and preparation phase into three parts: *physical* preparations, *mental* preparations, and *case* preparations. After we have looked at the importance of good preparations and why time is a central factor in professional interviews, we will outline the most important elements of the different types of preparations that make up the planning and preparation phase.

Strictly speaking, carrying out an interview does not require more than showing up and doing your best. Carrying out the same process professionally, on the other hand, requires knowledge, skill, and effort. In this sense, a professional interview is no different from any other complex task. Identifying the relevant sides of a case, assuming the right mindset, and carrying out all the necessary preparations for a professional interview is extremely demanding and an acquired skill. The interview must be prepared.

Liberate Capacity

It is not unusual to hear that the secret to success lies in preparations. Whether you are building a house or planning a party, good preparations are important to ensure a successful outcome. That is also the case for professional interviews. Preparations are the foundation of the interview. The reader will notice that we dedicate considerable attention to preparations in this book. In the following we will explain why.

A basic condition for a successful professional interview is the establishment and upholding of good communication. The more we have prepared ourselves ahead of time, the less we need think about along the way. Preparations liberate cognitive capacity and increase our potential for active listening, and thereby facilitate good communication.

Freed-up capacity helps us at several levels. First, it increases our capacity for self-evaluation during the interview and for correcting and adjusting our approach if necessary. Skilled professional interviewers are able to manage this adjustment as they work. Those who don't will quickly fall behind. The consequential errors pile up, and due to our limited capacity, we risk landing in a situation in which we are "gasping for air." We become rigid and less professional. Available capacity allows us to be more attentive to the interviewee and makes it easier to absorb and process information. At the same time, it enhances our ability for handling any unexpected events that might arise.

Good preparations help us to meet another human being in a positive manner. When all the practical parameters of the interview are in place, and we know the types of information requirements we want to meet, it becomes easier to communicate without influencing the other party. Good preparations also mean that we know how we will ask questions in order to collect the information we need and even information we didn't realize would be of interest.

The success of any interaction between two people depends on both parties. Researchers from the University of Liverpool, who studied the police interviews of suspects in a large number of terrorism cases, looked at what caused terror suspects to divulge information during questioning. They found two factors of importance for achieving a positive outcome, in other words, important in terms of obtaining a lot of information: the suspects' motivation to provide an explanation and the extent to which the suspects understood the discrepancies between the information the police had, and what they themselves had said.

> In summary, factors predictive of success are often related to the suspect's intention to talk and experience of discrepancy. (Alison et al. 2013, p. 428)

What had a negative effect on the interview was the behavior of the detective.

> Even minimal expression of maladaptive interpersonal interrogator behavior increased maladaptive interviewee behavior as well as directly reducing yield. (Alison et al. 2013, p. 411)

Preparations reduce stress. When you are well-prepared, you are also less nervous. Arriving well-prepared gives you a sense of security and self-confidence that can be valuable, especially in difficult interview situations. The sense of security can rub off on the person you are interviewing. If your manner emanates confidence, you will be perceived as a professional. This inspires confidence and establishes professional trust.

The preparatory phase is not without its pitfalls. Tranøy (2017) defines a hypothesis as "a guess, a theory or explanation that appears reasonable based on the available knowledge and which one endeavors to confirm or disprove."[1]

---

1. Some will certainly contest this definition. It is nonetheless the definition we have chosen since we work according to an abductive logic. We are not working in a laboratory

In the course of our preparations, we may find a lot of information in support of a specific hypothesis.

Without a methodological approach to outlining the relevant and alternative hypotheses of a case, the preparations will potentially lead us into a one-track mindset that can make us biased. We thereby risk falling into the same cognitive traps the method is intended to prevent. When that happens, the danger of our unconsciously interpreting the information we receive through the prism of our preconceived notions also increases. This can lead us into a destructive spiral. Without methodological and critical thought, we risk acquiring a false sense of security. If "the case is clear" before the interview, there is little point in doing the interview at all. When we proceed on the basis of biases, we can easily forget to maintain the requisite impartiality and flexibility. Our attention is then unconsciously directed toward that which confirms our preconceived notions, and there is no room for curiosity or genuine inquiry. The interview will place too great an emphasis on what we believe and too little emphasis on new information. Or to put this differently: it will take a great deal to change our mind.

For this reason, the alternative hypotheses must be identified and listed— no matter how confident you feel.

Thorough preparations can also cause us to become fixated on adhering to a specific format, a meeting schedule or script. Preparations can undermine active listening and flexibility if we become more focused on our own questions than on others' answers.

Our preparations must therefore include mental exercises based on a method designed to promote an open mindset. How we can best achieve this is one of the central themes of the following as we cover physical, case-related, and mental preparations. However, before we start explaining the preparations, we must highlight the issue of time.

Time

Time affects all aspects of a professional interview and often in a negative sense. Time must therefore be managed throughout the entire process.

An obvious challenge is that preparations take time. When for the first time in history researchers gained access to recordings of police interrogations, they quickly discovered that many of the problems and errors of justice occurred quite simply because the detectives were not prepared (Baldwin

---

where we have control over all the variables. Instead, we endeavor to test the hypotheses until we are left with the most probable of these. Abductive logic and adherence to the best explanation will be described in further detail in the section "Case-Related Preparations."

1992). To questions from researchers about why they hadn't prepared for the interrogations, the detectives replied: "Do you think we have time for that kind of thing?" The discovery of the prevailing misconception that it is inefficient to prepare for an interview was a significant shortcoming that was met through the design of new interviewing methods. That is why the planning and preparation phase is set up as a separate phase in the interview model presented here. Today police detectives who are trained in the new methods understand that they don't have time *not* to prepare themselves.

The detectives' experience of not having time for preparations is not in any sense unique. Based on interviews with actors from a range of professions, we have understood that those who *don't* prepare themselves still claim that it's because they don't have time. Nobody has unlimited amounts of time at their disposal, and we all experience tight deadlines on occasion, but usually we can still find a little time. If we set the right priorities, we will find the time. If you don't have time, you should take the time anyway, even if it is just a few minutes, for preparations. Even a little planning is better than no planning.

In the Norwegian Police University College's lesson plan for investigative interview preparations, we find the English expression "Failing to plan—is planning to fail." Good police detectives now systematically integrate a planning and preparation phase as a given part of the interview process. They know what they are supposed to do, what preparations are required, and how they shall prepare, and they have their "blueprints" or checklists of items to be considered before every single interview. The checklist contains the legal frameworks for the interview, the physical preparations that must be carried out before the interview can begin, and some points related to mental preparations.

The checklists can be quickly adapted to each specific interview. Like surgeons, the detectives have also adopted an idea from civil aviation: Our work can have huge consequences for other people. We are morally bound to do what we can to reduce the margin of error. Short and adequate checklists produced by the practitioners themselves are not only an effective and helpful tool; they also reduce errors and save lives. In the award-winning book *The Checklist Manifesto*, Gawande (2009) explains why professionals should create checklists and outlines the best procedure for producing an effective checklist. The items on the list function like triggers—thoughts to be thought—and the method that the checklist is designed to quality assure must be familiar, comprehensible, and automatic. A pilot's checklists will not enable other people to fly, but for the pilot they are indispensable.

An important item on the checklists of professional interviewers is the very start of a professional interview. What will we say and do? An informative, accurate, and relevant introduction contributes to the creation of a strong, professional first impression. A good start puts us on track for achieving good communication.

Those who have experience with the interview method outlined in this book have also found that their preparations become more efficient with practice. The checklists are adjusted and revised in the evaluation phase, which also raises the level of professionalism. By dedicating sufficient time to preparations when you actually have the chance to do so, you will discover that you are actually practicing the process as you are producing it. Such a professional approach will increase your efficiency on occasions when you are short on time. As a result, you will get more out of any available time you have for preparations.

Spending a little extra time on preparations, and developing and adapting routines in non-stressful surroundings, will also come in handy when the pressure mounts due to factors other than a time shortage. An example of this would be when the police and prosecuting authority are working on an extraordinary case and the expectations of leadership or local government consciously or unconsciously create pressure: "We must solve this case." Or for doctors and health personnel: "Here there is no room for error." Or for journalists: "This story is so good that we have to run with it." Police detectives who have been in such situations state that having an established method and solid procedures produces stability. It's like having an anchor in a storm.

As we have seen, time is an important factor in any interview situation; this has been just a brief introduction. We will give more detailed advice on issues such as time management and the alleviation of time pressure in the following section on physical preparations and later in Chapter 7, "Engage and Explain—Establishing Rapport."

Physical Preparations

Physical preparations are intended to ensure that there is nothing in the environment that can have a disruptive impact on the interview. Creating a professional setting gives the interviewee a positive impression of you and the organization you represent. If we meet the expectations for a professional interview, this also contributes to establishing professional trust. If we surpass these expectations, our interviewees will feel especially valued and respected. The simplest manner of achieving this is to ask yourself: "What would I expect if I was coming to an interview?"

"Would I accept being kept waiting outside an office long after the agreed time for the interview? How would I react if the person I met was wearing dirty trousers and a torn T-shirt? What would I think if the meeting room was full of rubbish, or the person I was meeting spent 10 minutes running

> around looking for documents? How would it feel to communicate with three people, all of whom were asking me questions at the same time?"

The more you have prepared and put in place before the interview, the more you liberate cognitive capacity—brainpower—which you can then apply to the core tasks: explaining, listening, formulating, and asking good questions, thinking, and analyzing.

The Room

One of the first things we must prepare is the room or venue where the interview will take place. Most people understand that physical surroundings will have an impact on a meeting. In spite of this, a good deal is still left to chance. Far too often, and here the authors can identify, the "space" is decided hastily or as a matter of routine: "This is where we usually hold interviews." Then the interview begins, in a setting that is not necessarily the ideal site for communication. In this case, even minor measures can make a big difference.

In some professional interviews, the location is predetermined. You are in the police interview room, at the doctor's office, a radio station, a rape crisis center, the crime scene, a therapy office, or in a courtroom. But in many situations, you can decide for yourself the type of space you will use. Will you meet the interviewee at your place of work, at their place of work, in a meeting room, at an office, in a café, in a car, or outdoors? There can be a number of considerations that will determine the venue in the end. Sometimes you have the chance to find a place that promotes a feeling of security and calm; other times you must just make do with what is available. The point is that during physical preparations, professional interviewers do what they can to make the most of the physical surroundings. The goal is always to facilitate a secure and relaxed atmosphere without unnecessary disruptions, where the conversation can flow freely.

> The Norwegian television host Hans Olav Brenner demonstrated on the program "Stories from Our Country" that an old Volvo Amazon can work exceptionally well as a venue for good professional interviews. The traditional radio studio, on the other hand, which is designed and equipped for professional interviews, can be a poor site for good communication, at least for inexperienced sources. What normally greets you in such studios is a huge microphone, suspended from a crane-like structure. Both objects obstruct visibility and thereby contact with the host, who is also seated behind a similar structure. The technique trumps communication.

On television, on the other hand, small "clip mics" or virtually invisible
microphones are used, quite simply because large microphones, like those
used in radio, would be disruptive. Exactly. That is what they are.

Photo: NRK, "Historier fra vart land," 2011–14.

The radio studio for the populfar Norwegian program *Norgesglasset* (The Kilner Jar) in
2016. Source: Craft AB.

When someone enters your territory, it is important that the site you choose contributes to the fostering of professional trust. What does the room say about your professionalism? Does it look messy? Are the bookshelves filled with textbooks or flashy magazines and photographs from company parties? It can be wise to test the chair for the interviewee. Is the chair comfortable? What do you see from this angle? We should eliminate or do something about anything that could take the focus away from the interview. Is the light a source of irritation? Are there pictures or drawings in the room that are distracting? Is there a glass wall through which other people can be seen moving about in the background? If so, we can position the other person with their back to the glass wall. At the very least, we should remove everything that can influence information about the interview topic. We must do what is possible to prevent disturbances: put a sign on the door, turn off mobile phones, or at least mute the sound. The professional interviewer creates a venue in which there are conditions for good communication.

You should also think about where you situate yourself in relation to the interviewee. As stated previously (in the section "Active Listening" in the "Communication" chapter), we receive more information when we avoid seating arrangements that put us across from and face-to-face with the interviewee. Environmental psychology is an emerging field of science that deals with a range of important psychosocial issues, including social interaction and privacy. Several studies have disclosed that a face-to-face seating arrangement is less than ideal for the purposes of an interview. It might be perceived as too intrusive during

Figure 10 A typical Norwegian police interview room.

initial interactions. Two people who just met will be more relaxed if they are spared having to stare directly into each other's eyes. A 45-degree angle allows interaction and yet offers the necessary security and safety most of us require in a new experience (Lattimore 2013). When seated this way, the interviewee doesn't feel cornered by the interviewer and eye contact can be made easily if necessary.

As we can see in Figure 10, in the layout of the Norwegian investigative interview room, the chairs have been arranged with such considerations in mind. We see that there are comfortable chairs for both interview participants. The physical parameters are the same for both of them. Not only are there no objects between them that might disrupt communication, but there are also as few objects as possible in the space.

When we show pictures from Norwegian police interviews to colleagues from other parts of the world who have not yet been exposed to research-based knowledge about investigative interviewing, they will often express amazement about the way the interview rooms in Norway are set up. Two identical and comfortable chairs. A number of people state that "that is how we interview children who are victims of crimes" in "soft rooms."

We respond every time with a question of our own. Why do you interview children in "soft rooms"? Well, they reply, the comfortable room helps the child to relax, which makes it easier for them to talk to us. We then refer to the first lesson of the course. Here we are always in agreement about the purpose of the interview. It is, regardless of where in the world we ask the question, to obtain accurate and reliable information. Nobody—not even those whose interview method involves torture—disagree with this.

We then place the photograph of the Norwegian interview room on the screen. The class will then often fall silent. Some people are reflecting. Others experience such a powerful cognitive dissonance that they launch a verbal attack: "This would be dangerous in our country, the perpetrator would try to hurt us," as if the person they were interviewing had already been found guilty.

It is not only the Norwegian police who have understood that the layout of the interview room has an impact on communication. As Figure 11 illustrates, there are at least a few interviewers who have understood that a good interview room has a positive effect—no matter who is being interviewed.

To reduce asymmetry—the power imbalance—in the interview situation, we should arrange the physical parameters to ensure that they are as identical

Figure 11 The well-known interviewing style of Oprah Winfrey.

as possible for all participants. Sitting behind a desk and computer can undermine communication and increase asymmetry. Instead, you can pull the chair away from the desk. If possible, procure identical chairs and make sure you have nothing more to hide behind than the interviewee. This will promote the experience of an interaction between equals.

There are many examples of meetings in which many or all of the physical preparations are lacking. Imagine a parent–teacher conference at a school, where a parent is called in, whose role is that of the meeting's "interviewee." Many people are seated around the table, all of whom have unclear roles and duties. There are several from the school, an adviser from the Educational Psychological Services, a representative from the child welfare authorities, and a psychologist from the public Child and Adolescent Psychiatry services. The different individuals introduce themselves by name and title, but that is not enough information. What are the responsibilities of each individual? The person who will lead the meeting quickly loses control over the time and structure. People interrupt each other, their roles are not clear, the room is unsuitable, there is neither water nor coffee on the table, the parent didn't know there would be so many people in the room, several people have their phones on the table, others are looking down and typing on laptops. In short, there are many disturbances and unclear expectations. How will this lack of planning affect the professional interview and the information that emerges from it?

If many interviews are done at your place of work, the room in which these are held can perhaps be made a topic of discussion at the next departmental meeting. Is the room ideal? Is there something you can or should do to enhance communication, increase comfort, and create a better first impression?

Although we have argued for and described a one-to-one interview setting, we are aware that information gathering also happens in other settings. Some professions traditionally carry out their interviews with two or more interviewers or observers. Others may arrange meetings between parties of several people. Although we believe that interpersonal communication and rapport is best established in private settings, we recognize the argument that "two brains think better than one" and that professional interviews may indeed lead to successful outcomes with two or more interviewers. If your organization prefers multiple interviewers when interviewing one person, you may still consider an angled setting between the lead interviewer and the interviewee.

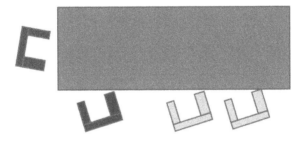

In some meetings, there may be cultural and/or professional expectations to engage with two or more representatives on both sides. In these settings, the lead interviewer should be seated in a central position, ensuring natural eye contact with the person expected to do most of the talking.

In both circumstances, a professionally planned and prepared interview will include an interview plan. By circling the interview plan among key stakeholders and encourage feedback, the need for additional interviewers may be reduced. In a setting with more than one interviewer and only one interviewee, you may consider an alternative setting—used by several police departments—in which the one-to-one interview is monitored live to a group of people situated outside the interview room. The group may consist of as many "brains" as required and will, through commercial communication platforms (two iPads or similar), assist the interviewer with relevant questions as the interview progresses. Either way, a few physical adjustments in the interview room can make a huge difference (Dawson et al. 2017). It is crucial to think about what you can do to minimize disturbances and increase professional trust.

Disturbances

Every interview and every meeting can be disturbed or interrupted. This need not mean that the interview is ruined. But should a disturbance occur at an inopportune moment, important information can be lost or withheld. If we are really unfortunate, the other person can lose the thread of their story or their motivation to elaborate may disappear. It has to be said that the greatest disturbance of our times is the mobile telephone. It rings, flashes, vibrates, and rudely demands our attention. Ideally, you should turn it off and put it away. You can consider asking the interviewee to do the same. If you must have your telephone on because you are expecting an important message or clarification, say this and explain the reason. In doing so, you prepare the interviewee for a potential interruption, and you can prevent that interruption from undermining communication. Also make sure that nobody comes storming into the room or interrupts the interview in other ways. A note on the door stating that an interview or meeting is in progress takes no time to organize and solves the problem. If you use a dedicated interview room, you could consider a permanent indication of the room's purpose (e.g., Interview Room) and that it is either occupied or vacant.

Computers and laptops can also constitute a challenge for communication. Hiding behind a computer does not promote communication. Eye contact is made difficult, and the computer becomes a barrier. Irritation over the sound of tapping on the keyboard can be a source of distraction that undermines communication. But at the same time, it can be important in some contexts to take precise notes, there and then, directly on a computer.

Picture a business meeting in which those who are asking the questions take notes on computers. The combined impact of the constant tapping from the computer and lack of eye contact culminates in the interviewee getting up and leaving what was an important meeting. We can just imagine the damage this does to the reputations of those who were left sitting in the room. In Part 1 of this book (in the chapter "Communication") we introduced the term *metacommunication*: communication about communication. It is a tool that stimulates communication in a number of situations, also here. If the participants of the business meeting had informed the other party about their need to take notes on their computers, the outcome of the meeting might have been quite different.

A Warm Welcome

Feeling welcome and taken care of from the first moment is important. If you don't personally greet the person you will be interviewing when they arrive, always make sure to have somebody waiting, who welcomes this person in a positive way. You, or the person receiving them, should accompany them to the interview room and stay with them until the interview begins. A meeting or an interview that begins with the person who was invited not feeling welcome can be ruined before it has even started. This must therefore also be planned. The same holds true for all physical preparations: incorporated routines reduce the time we need to get ready. What are your routines for receiving guests? Are they ideal or is there room for improvement?

Food and Drink

Offering food and drink is always a positive opening to an interview. It sets a tone of politeness and empathy. You show that you care about the other person. If the offering of food is not appropriate, such as in the case of brief interviews, at least offer water and coffee or tea. Make sure to have something to eat and drink yourself before starting an interview. Blood sugar levels have an impact on brain function. Low blood sugar weakens concentration, the ability to react and listen, and it also affects mood. If you expect the interview to take time and a meal break may be required, be sure to make the necessary arrangements for a meal and inquire about allergies. Leaving this to chance seems unprofessional and, in some situations, wastes valuable time. Suspend the interview if taking a meal break—it is difficult to eat while asking or answering questions or taking notes.

Breaks

Plan for regular breaks, outdoors in the fresh air if possible. It is easy to forget to take breaks, especially if you are deeply immersed in the interview. Plan for breaks but be flexible. The breaks should be taken at a natural point in the interview, or when absolutely necessary. During the introduction, mention that there will be breaks. Inform the participants that if they should need a break beyond those that have been scheduled, they can say so. Breaks can also ease the pressure in an interview. During the break you can have an informal conversation instead of talking about the case, allowing both of you to move a bit out of your roles as interviewer and interviewee. In this way you demonstrate that you see the other person as a human being, not merely as a source from whom you need information.

Equipment

As an interviewer you should organize and test any paperwork and equipment you want to have available in the interview room before the interview. You must ensure that you can navigate around the paperwork discreetly and efficiently. If you have both an interview plan and documentation you are going to use or show, then two separate folders may be helpful.

Make sure that any equipment (recording devices, presentations, etc.) you are planning to use is in working order. Do not assume that it is. Test all your equipment before the interview. Have extra batteries on hand, a power cord, backup. If your equipment malfunctions, this seems unprofessional and can create a distraction. Ensure that pens and paper are available for use if required, for example, where an interviewee's recall could be assisted by drawing a sketch or plan.

Everything you are going to use during the interview should be set up in the room or be just outside. It will take time and seem like you are unprepared if you have to go looking for what you need.

Documentation

Before the interview commences, you will naturally have had some thoughts about how the information that emerges will be documented. The final documentation of most professional interviews is usually in the form of a written account, memo, report, article, log, or journal. How we safeguard the information from the interview can have huge consequences for the final outcome. As mentioned in Part 1, the memory is both limited and selective. Many professional interviewers therefore take notes by hand or on a laptop to make sure they have recorded all the contents of the interview. But note-taking can also be selective and *cover only that part of the account that* we have understood *or focused on.* The *best* way to ensure all the information from an interview is secured is to record it.

In Norway, police interviews must be documented by audio or video recordings. This regulation is based on a number of considerations, several of which are equally valid for other professions. First, the recording preserves information in its original form. Should any doubts arise after the fact about what was said—by whom—and about the circumstances under which the words were spoken, these doubts can be dispelled by listening to the recording. In this context it is worth noting that when the recording scheme was tested, one of the most important findings (Ministry of Justice 2003) was that *when recordings are done, there is seldom any need to listen to them.* Both parties know that the recording exists, and therefore, nobody will make assertions about what was said in the interview that they know to be false.

Recordings have a number of benefits. During important interviews with a certain degree of complexity, the interviewer can postpone report writing until the interview is finished. Postponing report writing opens up for far better communication. The interviewer can make do with taking notes, and thereby be more present and liberate cognitive capacity. Active listening is raised to another level. It becomes easier to transmit empathy. Interruptions are significantly reduced, and the opportunities for considering how your own performance and the interview itself is going are significantly improved.

Recordings also open up a whole new realm of possibilities for evaluating the interview after the fact. You can evaluate yourself or introduce routines whereby colleagues evaluate each other. In this sense, the recording is, strictly speaking, a means of achieving your full potential as a professional interviewer. The recording can also be made available for research purposes and other forms of external evaluation.

In addition to your own professionalization, the recording represents a form of security for the interviewee. In some interview situations, it represents an important guarantee of legal protection.

For less-critical cases, the police still write their own reports, recording the interview "in the background." In this way the legal protection benefits of the recording are preserved, while the communicative benefits are diminished. This can be rectified by speaking together for a short period while taking notes, and then taking a short break to type the notes into a computer while the interviewee relaxes. When the notes are documented, the interview continues. This way the conversation will constantly be fresh in your mind. Although this has the disadvantage of the interviewee having to wait while the interviewer types up the statement, this doesn't seem to present a problem in practice. Often the interviewee is happy to have a cup of tea or coffee, check their phone, read a paper, and so on. Some also use the quietness to think about what you have been talking about and may come up with more details. This kind of approach would, for instance, be useful for a doctor who updates a journal while meeting with a patient.

If you have recorded an interview, you can listen carefully to the recording without disturbances after the interview has been concluded. You can put any feelings from the interview aside and listen without cognitive interference or stress. This will better enable you to assess the information that emerged in the interview. If you are going to submit something in writing after the interview, the report will potentially be more precise and more objective. Experience also shows that you can pick up on information that you missed while the interview was underway. The recording can on the whole lead to better evaluations and thereby better decisions.

Despite this, many professions have no tradition of using recordings. This can be related to capacity or access to equipment. It can also be due to the time required to transcribe the recording. There is an important reason why journalists have long sworn by the notepad. However, more and more journalists have in recent years switched to using the recording devices on their mobile phones, precisely for the above-mentioned reasons and benefits. This applies in particular to avoiding any uncertainty about quotes.

Such considerations will of course vary greatly according to the situation and profession. In some professional interviews, the interviewer fears the interviewee will have a negative reaction to being recorded and that the interview will consequently be over before it has begun. The police in Norway shared this natural skepticism. Several detectives held that witnesses and suspects would be reluctant to talk if they knew they were being recorded. This concern proved to be unfounded. Today nobody wants to return to the former practice of interviewing without recording (Sullivan et al. 2009; Riksadvokatens publikasjoner nr. 3/2015).

Regardless of the reason for not wanting to record an interview, an alternative is then to type or write by hand. The disadvantage of using a computer is, as stated earlier, that it can impede communication. The advantage is that those who are good typists are able to type more quickly than most people write by hand and can thereby take down virtually everything that is being said. The information is also easier to process afterward. The advantage of taking notes by hand is that it doesn't create the same barriers and doesn't make any noise. For certain professional interviews, it is also a commonly used method, so much so that the person being interviewed may even expect it. Taking notes by hand can also produce better results. Mueller and Oppenheimer (2014) compared students who took notes by hand with students who took notes directly on their computers. They found that the two groups retained equal amounts of factual information, but those who had taken notes by hand had a deeper understanding of the topic in question than those who had taken notes on a computer.

More Than One Interviewer?

Often more than one person is involved in a professional interview. It is then important to clarify roles. Who will do what? There are both benefits and drawbacks to including more than one person.

The largest benefit is that the many tasks can be divided up between several people. When several people are going to contribute, the most important task must be assigned first: Who will lead the interview? The person who has this responsibility must prepare the format and plan for the interview. After the plan and format are ready, the team should sit down and discuss, and possibly improve upon the format. When more than one person is involved, you should take advantage of the benefits this offers in the sense of two heads being better than one. A preparatory meeting ensures that everyone knows the objectives of the interview and how these can best be achieved. The meeting will provide an outline of what must be prepared and who will do what: who will greet the interviewee, who will take notes, and so on. In this way, the person leading the interview liberates capacity to do just that—lead the interview. Once the tasks have been delegated and the interview is underway, it is essential that nobody interrupt with questions from the sidelines. The interview leader takes the initiative and controls the process. It may be necessary to adjust the plan while the interview is in progress. Only the leader should be allowed to initiate a change of this nature. Of course, the other participants can propose a break during which the need for a new plan and strategy can be discussed. Interrupting halfway through the interview, changing the subject, or interjecting questions without this having been agreed upon in advance with the leader of the interview must be avoided at all costs. Professional interviewers ensure that the participants are given the chance to ask the interviewee questions at an appropriate juncture, such as before a new topic is introduced:

I don't have any more questions related to education. Before we move on to the next topic, do you have any questions for the candidate on this subject?

Unless such a professional approach is employed, the interview can quickly become chaotic and confusing, creating insecurity. The use of more than one person as an interviewer increases the risk of a power imbalance with all the inexpedient ramifications this involves. To prevent compounding asymmetry in the interview, all participants should be introduced by name and role. When it is clear who is leading the interview, the interviewee will find it easier to speak, and when everyone is informed of the roles of each participant, insecurity is mitigated, and the entire situation becomes less intimidating. Good planning will reduce the drawbacks and heighten the benefits inherent to a team interview approach.

Appearance

How are you dressed? What are the expectations of the person you will meet regarding who you are and how you come across? What kind of language do you use? What kind of impression do you make?

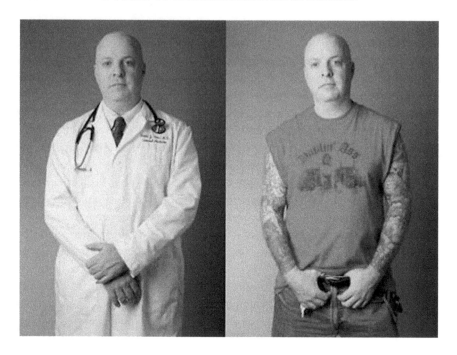

Figure 12 An illustration showing how differently we perceive a person based on how he/she dresses.

It is a widespread misconception that we communicate best with people by mirroring their appearance. The reality is that in an interview context, the interviewee will not necessarily expect to meet someone whose appearance resembles their own. To the contrary, they will have a set of expectations related to how someone in your profession and role should look. Please look at Figure 12 and think of how you would respond to how this physician is dressed. The extent to which we meet those expectations will unconsciously influence how the interviewee assesses our credibility and professionalism. Cognitive simplification processes, including personal schemata, influence the interviewee just as much as the interviewer. Although we should actually be allowed to dress in exactly the way we want, without being judged for this, it is a fact that the way we dress influences how we are perceived by others and, in the worst case, can create a poor first impression. We judge a book by its cover, whether we like to admit it or not.

When we meet someone, our first impression is formed in the course of the first few seconds. In fact, studies show that even after a few fractions of a second, the formation of that impression is already well underway (Willis & Todorov 2006). Fortunately, research indicates that it is possible to change the established impression, but it can be difficult. And after getting off on the wrong foot, the likelihood of having to "paddle upstream" is substantial (Brannon & Gawronski 2016).

Professional interviewers make sure to take advantage of the opportunity this represents: to create a good start and take this along into the interview. Be well-rested. Get a good night's sleep before any major interview, and arrive for the interview freshened up, wearing clean, comfortable clothing that is suitable for the occasion.

Time and Preparations

As mentioned by way of introduction, thorough preparations and good planning increase efficiency and alleviate time-related challenges. If the scheduled time for the interview is convenient for all participants and enough time has been allocated, we have already come a long way. Nevertheless, we can't always know in advance what "enough time" means. We can't control all the surrounding factors that will potentially influence time in an interview situation, and we can't continue indefinitely. Professional interviewers must usually function with an awareness of the time. The time aspect is therefore an important part of the physical preparations for most professional interviews. The impact of a time shortage and/or an overly optimistic time estimate can be extremely negative.

Scheduling the Time for the Interview

Deciding the right time for a professional interview depends on the subject of the interview. In an interview where we rely upon people's memories, it can be crucial to hold the interview as soon as possible after the event in question. As we explained in Part 1 (in the chapter "Psychology"), details can quickly disappear, and the memory is easily influenced. There can also be tactical considerations that will play a decisive role in determining the best time for the interview. Those who carry out investigations, such as an accident inquiry board, the police, the petroleum safety authority, and journalists, or someone looking into a whistleblowing case, must all evaluate the order of the sources they will be interviewing. Sometimes multiple sources must even be interviewed at the same time to eliminate the possibility of the sources comparing or adjusting their stories. Such considerations can also be invoked by the sources themselves: simultaneous interviews can help strengthen their credibility and the risk of sources comparing accounts is hereby eliminated.

In a given situation, the interviewer must also evaluate whether the interviewee is psychologically and physically in a condition to take part in an interview, such as in conjunction with the investigation of accidents or other traumatic events. Detectives, doctors, clergymen, support networks, psychologists, and journalists all carry out professional interviews in the wake of catastrophes and personal traumas. Is the purpose of the interview in this case to provide emotional support or to obtain accurate and reliable information?

If the purpose is to obtain information, we must consider allowing the source to be accompanied by a trusted companion. If there is no existing procedure for allowing companions, the person to be interviewed should be asked upon your initial contact whether they want the support of a companion during and after the interview. An ethical assessment must be made regarding whether the interviewee will be able to understand the purpose of the interview and any potential consequences it may have. A decision to postpone the interview for social and/or psychological reasons must be weighed against considerations such as the gravity of the case, the need to reduce social influence (for instance, that witnesses will confer with one another or be influenced by the media), and the fact that people forget quickly.

Regardless of the type of interview we are planning, it is important to schedule the interview at a time that is convenient for the other party. Otherwise, the person we are speaking with can become stressed and perhaps be more concerned about finishing than thinking carefully through the topic of the interview. Although as professionals we may have the power to decide when an interview will take place, it is wise to try and find a time that is also convenient for the interviewee. By doing so, we show respect and reduce interview asymmetry.

The Interviewer's Time

We must also consider our own time. Many of us may feel pressured to be efficient on the job and deliver results. Like all other forms of pressure, the experience of time pressure also reduces our ability to identify and assess relevant aspects or hypotheses that must be investigated and tested. If we schedule insufficient time for the interview, we risk not meeting our objective. In the worst-case scenario, we will have to spend time scheduling and carrying out yet another interview. If so, this is poor time management. If possible, it is always best to schedule an interview at a time when you will have no commitments immediately afterward. Should it take longer than planned to achieve the objective of the interview, you will not be worried about making another appointment. A shortage of time for one or both parties will often lead to stress for both. Stress is of course something professional interviewers must know how to handle, but nonetheless we should do what we can to avoid it.

Respect for the Other Person's Time

In addition to the fact that the scheduled time for the interview should be convenient for both parties, it is important to always arrive punctually. We have all experienced how irritating it can be to have to wait for someone who is late for an appointment. If we are delayed in arriving or in another manner not prepared—and don't call or message to inform the other party—we send an implicit signal that our time is more important than that of the other person. This can be perceived as arrogance. The trust and respect you require diminishes with every passing minute after the scheduled time for your appointment.

Imagine that you are someone who has agreed to be interviewed and are now late for the appointment. You don't even have time to drop your children off at daycare, so you have arranged for a neighbor to do it. You rush to your meeting only to learn when you arrive at the reception that the person you were supposed to meet is not there and neither is he answering his phone. You are left waiting in the reception area, without any information, until the other person finally shows up, 20 minutes late. Whether you were waiting for a doctor, job recruiter, detective, lawyer, journalist, teacher, or the asylum authorities is irrelevant. It is irritating.

Imagine then arriving on time and the person you are meeting, or a colleague, greets you in the reception area as you walk through the door. This person shakes your hand and asks if you would like a cup of coffee. It is freshly brewed. You understand in this case that time has been set aside for you. You feel that you matter. You are respected.

However, we don't always have the opportunity to wait in the reception area for a guest. But we can all send word that we have been delayed or, in the worst-case scenario, that we can't make it at all. And we can send word as soon as possible. Arriving on time shows respect. It promotes a calm establishment of rapport and the ideal start for a professional interview.

Shortage of Time

A shortage of time affects both parties in an interview, regardless of who is experiencing the time crunch. A shortage of time and being in a hurry are enemies of the interview. As stated earlier, the method is flexible and designed for both brief meetings lasting a few minutes and interviews that continue for several hours. If it is the other person who is pressed for time and in a hurry to finish, there is a risk that she won't invest the time and energy required to adequately reflect upon her answers. Stress steals cognitive capacity and the answers become brief. If as professionals we don't realize that the other person doesn't have time to give the interview their full attention, this can also produce frustration, which in turn has an impact on the communication. Either way, the outcome is that we obtain less information.

For the interviewer, a shortage of time will be negatively self-reinforcing. A destructive spiral. The value of the time we have left is diminished when we are stressed about running out of time. The stress takes up space and reduces our available working capacity. In interviews under the pressure of a time shortage, we can become obsessed with getting through all of our questions. Then the focus shifts away from listening to asking questions, and we become essentially incapable of catching everything that is said. The quality of active listening is undermined, which in turn affects the interviewee's ability and motivation to explain.

When you are struggling, the interviewee will unconsciously attempt to help you. They will notice if you glance at your watch or if you open your mouth to ask the next question before they have finished answering. Glancing at your watch can also be interpreted as a signal that they or whatever it is they are talking about is not of interest. Their answers then become increasingly brief, containing less and less information. Time pressure can also (i) make it more difficult for you to identify alternatives, (ii) cause you to ask closed questions in order to elicit the answers you feel you must have, and (iii) lead you into cognitive traps more easily. A shortage of time thereby produces a situation in which the final valuable remainder of available time is poorly exploited. The result is that you obtain less relevant and less reliable information. Haste makes waste.

What Can We Do?

Before scheduling an interview, it is helpful to prepare the case thoroughly (see the next chapter). Through case-related preparations, we gain a clear grasp of what we know as well as the information we are lacking. We will be able to define the purpose of the entire interview and isolate a specific theme. This will provide us with a realistic idea of the amount of time we will need for the interview. We will also have clarified key themes and the most important questions with an eye to achieving the purpose of the interview. We can then prioritize topics and eliminate less-significant topics in advance. Here as well, our preparations make us more effective.

Good preparations notwithstanding, time pressure can still arise during the interview. But when we are conscious of the topics of priority, this enables us to be more flexible during the interview. If we see that time is running out, we know what to make a priority and what we can put on hold, because the case has been adequately prepared. In this way we increase the chance that the topics we give priority, both the questions and answers, are of high quality.

Another time management measure involves clarifying any time-related concerns with the interviewee at the start of the interview. We will address this in further detail when we explain the phase "Engage and Explain—Establishing Rapport" in Chapter 7.

How Can We Best Manage Our Time?

In many fields where professional interviews are used, effective time management is crucial. The alternative is quite simply unprofessional. But it is difficult to keep an eye on the time without simultaneously giving the impression that you are in a hurry or not interested. As explained earlier, the act of glancing at your watch can suggest to others that you are in a hurry and cause them to shorten their replies. If interviewees experience a lack of interest on your part, this can negatively affect their motivation to provide interesting answers.

The best solution is to have a clock in the interview room that is placed in a location where you can see it without anyone noticing. If you nonetheless have to look at your watch, you can do some metacommunication about this beforehand or during the interview to prevent the misconception that you are not interested or are short on time. "I am just going to check how much time we have left to make sure that we will be able to cover everything you have to contribute." This is openness and honesty in practice. It also demonstrates professionalism and shows that you care about the interviewee's contribution. All of this will reinforce the ongoing communication.

The physical preparations share a common feature. If you are well prepared, they won't take up space in the interview. If the physical parameters are not in place, they will occupy a lot of space. The attention that should have been focused on the core issues is instead applied to extraneous details and can lead to irritation and stress for both you and the interviewee.

Once all the logistics and other physical preparations are out of the way, we can apply our full mental capacity to the interview, but the final prerequisite is that we know what we are going to talk about.

Case-Related Preparations

When we are going to do a professional interview, we should have a clear idea of what we are going to talk about. To put this more succinctly, we must specify the purpose of the interview. This is accomplished by viewing the interview as one part of a larger whole. For the police, an interview is an important part of the investigation. For a social scientist, the interview is one of a number of tools utilized to investigate a larger phenomenon. In a child welfare case, interviews must be held with legal guardians, teachers, family members, and children to supplement home visits and the review of journals and documents. A headhunter who is trying to find the best-qualified candidate will, through several rounds of interviews, reference checks and maybe own inquiries, produce a list of the most promising applicants. These are just a few examples. Most professional interviews are one part of a larger process.

We will therefore first look more closely at how the professional interview fits in as one of several sources of information. We will demonstrate how case-related preparations help us to specify the purpose of the individual interview in a way that doesn't lock us into the kind of intuitive thinking that unconsciously strives to draw conclusions before the interview starts. Finally, we will show how the purpose (why we are speaking with exactly this person) defines the contents of the interview.

Gathering Information

Because professional interviews are usually one part of a larger process—an inquiry, a case, an investigation, or a study—the case-related preparations for the interview must of necessity be linked to and underpin the process as a whole.

To structure their investigations, the police in Norway introduced an investigative model, developed by Ivar Fahsing as part of his doctoral research on the decision-making processes of police detectives in Norway and Great Britain (Fahsing 2016). The investigative model first and foremost helps us to identify and account for the questions raised by a case, but it also serves the function of a mental and practical tool during interview preparations. By following the model, we ensure that the purpose of the interview itself is linked directly to the purpose of the investigation and the specific information requirements.

The cognitive traps we introduced in Part 1 are not only a challenge during the interview; they are also a challenge during our preparations. That is why the investigative model is based on the same knowledge about unconscious, cognitive simplification processes, on the one hand, and the logical strategies best suited to reduce the detrimental effects of these, on the other. The point is simply that if our fact-finding processes are curbed by tunnel vision, our interviews will be characterized by the same—and vice versa.

Fahsing calls the model *The 6 Cs Generic Investigative Cycle*. Like the CREATIVE interview model, which also has six phases, this model sharpens the awareness of the investigator. The model also serves as a guide for the listing and testing of relevant hypotheses (see Figure 13).

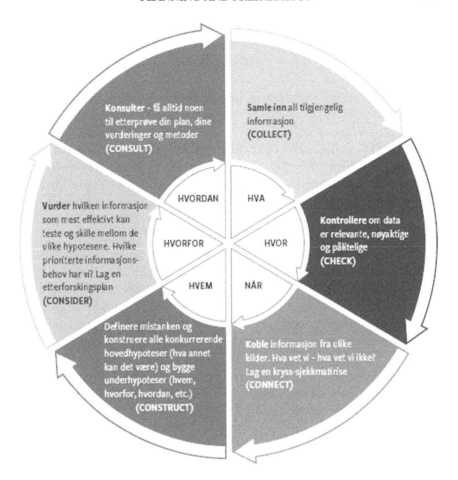

Figure 13 The 6 Cs generic investigative cycle, according to Fahsing (2016).

The model is named after the first letter of the terms representing each step: collect, check, connect, construct, consider, and consult. In contexts other than police work, the process can be best described as a fact-finding process. The process is illustrated by the "pie pieces" seen in the model. The questions the investigation aims to answer are in the center. The model offers a generic description of a wide range of investigative tasks and illustrates a cyclic nature of the problem-solving process (Fahsing 2016). The process of hypothesis refinement, information gathering, and retesting should ideally be done in cycles as long as there is relevant information available, until sufficient light has been shed upon the case at hand (Cook 2019).

In a laboratory, scientists endeavor to achieve the utmost control over variables when doing experiments. There they can propose, test, and eliminate hypotheses until they are left with the only possible answer, using what is known as *deductive logic*. It is usually impossible to achieve corresponding control over all the variables in investigations that are done outside the scientist's laboratory. The different sources of error we have already discussed also imply a reduced degree of precision. *Abductive logic* is hypothesis-driven and functions on the basis of an acceptance of such uncertainty rather than its attempted elimination. This best describes the logic of the process in our case. By following abductive logic in our processes, we try to test all plausible hypotheses before finally drawing *a conclusion about the best explanation*. From a philosophical perspective, Simon (2012) and Fahsing (2016) emphasize that when investigating facts, we should never lose sight of doubt.

Information can be used to disprove—rule out—some hypotheses, but usually not enough to leave us with just one. Often the best we can do is amass a preponderance of evidence for one hypothesis, which gives us the opportunity to draw a conclusion about the best explanation. The goal must be to gather a sufficient amount of relevant and reliable information so the preponderance of evidence in support of one hypothesis makes the relevance of other hypotheses purely theoretical.

The requirement for accuracy varies from one profession to the next. Police detectives must continuously strive to meet the legal standards of proof: the main hypothesis (the charges) must be proven beyond any and all reasonable doubt. If the courts discover that the police have overlooked or haven't adequately investigated a plausible hypothesis, reasonable doubt will quickly sneak in—and thereby the possibility of the accused party's innocence. Other professions have their own specific requirements for how thoroughly a given hypothesis must be tested in order to provide the basis for a conclusion, but nobody is served by erroneous inferences and the logic remains the same. Doctors, child welfare officers, investigative committees, journalists, directors, and analysts who overlook a plausible alternative hypothesis increase the probability of erroneous inferences, which in some situations can have dire consequences.

In the following we will explain the six phases (the 6 Cs) of fact investigation and the expediency of the model in planning a professional interview that directly corresponds with the relevant questions of the investigation according to the principles of abductive logic.

Collect

When the police have just been assigned a new case, a journalist a new story, or a doctor a new patient, the first step of their investigation will be to gather all the relevant and available information from the usual sources. The scope will be determined by what they know will be relevant information for this type of case in general and as far as they know for this case in particular. Here knowledge about the phenomenon (the field under investigation), experience from similar type of cases, checklists, and curiosity will be a big help in disclosing sources of information.

The number of sources we have access to when preparing a case or an interview will of course vary. Different professions have different sources. The access to sources also varies according to when in the investigative process the interview takes place.

Much like when a doctor meets with a new patient for the first time, the police have a limited number of sources during their initial interview of a homeowner who has reported a break-in. Like a surgeon who has spent months doing research, tests, and procedures, after months of investigation, a detective will also have many more sources of information—sources that in both cases must be addressed during preparations. In somewhat simpler terms, we can perhaps say that the more we dig, the more sources of information we will find. But where shall we dig? And what must we do to ensure that we are not digging in the wrong place? The next step in the model helps us to move forward.

Check

When information comes into our hands, we must immediately establish whether it is relevant and reliable. For example, when the Occupational Safety and Health Administration investigates a restaurant's employee timesheets, only the events within the timeframe during which the current owner has been in charge will be relevant. Old timesheets can be put away. Once having established the information of relevance, we must assess its reliability. What is the source and how has the information been obtained? If we are considering presenting financial information in an interview, a bank statement will generally be considered more reliable than any information we might find in the media. Finally, we check whether the information is detailed enough to enable us to proceed or if we must search for more details.

In short, we must check the information as best we can to determine its significance and the role it will play in combination with the other information we have gathered. This may sound simple and obvious, but when the pressure is on and we can discern the contours of an attractive solution, our subconscious doesn't want information that will potentially complicate the process. This was shown in the theory from decision-making psychology we introduced in Part 1. By an attractive solution, we mean, for example, a solution that will offer recognition, status, or other kinds of rewards.

Connect

The more information we have, the greater is the need to structure it and see it in context. We make such connections in part automatically and unconsciously, but in a professional setting, this is not adequate. Connections must be made in a structured and conscious manner. If not, we risk allowing Kahneman's System 1 to get its way, and the danger of walking into cognitive traps increases. When we form connections between pieces of information, we can discern common features and correlations. Who knows who, are there recurring locations, which events happened at the same time, or is there any causality between events? If we don't make connections between the pieces of information and instead handle information from different sources separately, in isolation, and in different formats, it is naturally much more difficult to see any connections. This is just as true for the detective who has information from a phone tap, a stake-out, video surveillance tapes, and interviews as it is for the stockbroker who has information from quarterly reports, market surveys, meetings, and audits.

Construct

When we have to the best of our abilities collected, checked, and connected the available information, hopefully we have, metaphorically speaking, placed the available pieces of the puzzle in the right places. And if we have enough pieces, we can get a sense of the full picture. But there will still be missing pieces. Then we need to ask ourselves: What may have happened? What can the causes be? What could happen? A typically human error is the omission of the "may/can/could," jumping instead straight to premature conclusions about "what *has* happened." A key aspect of this phase of the investigation in general—and the preparation for the interview in particular—is the list of alternative hypotheses. A good thought process in this context requires that we list all the plausible hypotheses about how the full picture might look, based on the elements we are able to discern, without favoring our most natural or immediate inclinations.

Formerly the police did not have a method that challenged immediate and subjective assumptions. Today, detectives are "forced" to construct alternatives as a means of preserving objectivity. What else could have happened, based on the information we have? The answers to the two questions "What may have happened" and "What else could have happened?" generate the central hypotheses in an investigation.

Regardless of how much information we have and how detailed it is, we can eventually begin to list the plausible hypotheses for the other questions we need answered: who, what, when, where, why, and how. These questions are collectively referred to as the 5Ws+H and are particularly effective in probing for further detail after open questions and prompts have been used. They will be explained in detail later. This thought process helps us to illuminate the relevant sides of the case and approach the ideal standard for objectivity.

Imagine the following: A homeowner comes home and finds a broken window. She also discovers that her husband's watches are missing. That is not a lot of information, but it is enough to enable the case investigator to generate some key hypotheses in answer to the question "What happened?" An obvious hypothesis is that there has been a burglary. But it could also be an attempt at insurance fraud, or someone with legal access to the house may have simulated a burglary and stolen the watches. Perhaps there is no connection at all between the broken window and the missing watches. The damage to the window could have come about as an act of vandalism, an accident, or through natural causes. The watches could be misplaced, lent to someone else or in use.

The police are summoned; they collect information at the scene based on the list of hypotheses and find a fingerprint on the broken windowpane, the fingerprint of a man, as it turns out, previously convicted of breaking and entering. Let's call him "John." The development of the case strengthens the hypothesis that a break-in has taken place. The most probable hypothesis for "Who did it?" is naturally John. But if we drop setting up alternative hypotheses, things can slide off-track. The police must still remain open to the possibility that it is in fact not John who has committed the burglary. Could John be a close friend or a relative of the person who reported the break-in? Perhaps he attended a party at the house? Or has he done carpentry, cleaning, or moving work for the owner or a company hired by the owner? Is John a co-conspirator in an insurance swindle? Has John been an employee of the factory that made the window? Has John broken into the same house before? It might be that even though John's fingerprints are found on the window, he is still innocent of the crime under investigation. This possibility must define the parameters and focus of the ongoing investigation and therefore also the preparations for the interviews with John, the owner of the house, neighbors, and other relevant sources.

An obvious advantage of connecting the interviews so closely and systematically to the investigation as a whole is that the preparations for every single interview will proceed more quickly and be more precisely targeted. The entire process is managed by objectives: We know which hypotheses must be illuminated and why. After having listed the relevant hypotheses of the case, the time has come to test them.

Consider

The purpose of this phase is to gain an overview of *what* information is needed in order to test the hypotheses and *how* we will search for it. It is wise to write this down in the form of a checklist of work tasks to be done.

This system helps us to maintain an overview and remember what we have to do, and reminds us of the purpose of each individual work task. By connecting the work tasks to our established hypotheses, we gain an overview of the decisions we have made, why, and when. The method thereby makes it easier for us (and others) to understand, carry out, consult on, and where necessary reexamine the investigative process.

The next step is to prioritize the work tasks. In this context, the available time, supposed significance, resources, and order are of central importance. We know that people quickly forget things. The memory is easily compromised. Other sources of information can be erased (such as electronic traces) or can disappear (damage). Some work tasks must be made a priority because we can't move forward with our investigation until they are done. Other work tasks are less important and can wait. If we are working on a team, the work tasks must be delegated as quickly as possible. If an investment fund is considering the acquisition of a company, a questionnaire filled out by the clients of the company can be relevant. This is a task that can be completed while the analyst collects and structures information from other sources. When we have a snapshot of all the work tasks, we avoid the risk of having to do the same task several times. We become more efficient. For example, in a hiring process, an overview of the references for relevant applicants can disclose that several applicants have listed the same reference. Then you are spared having to call the same reference more than once.

If it is not already clear or obvious, this phase will help identify relevant sources who should be questioned. For example, if we are going to test the alternative hypothesis that John could be a family friend, we will quickly find the necessary sources. It is here that the professional interview comes in—as an information-gathering tool. When we decide to carry out an interview, we must have simultaneously identified one or more specific objectives for the interview with an eye to the primary goal of acquiring information that will enable us to test at least one of the relevant hypotheses of the case. Usually, one source will be able to fill several information needs and contribute to the testing of more than one hypothesis. This is also why an interview is typically the most commonly applied method for collecting information in an investigation of facts. It is a good rule of thumb to have one or more defined objectives when we start the case-related preparations and embark on the task of setting up a specific plan for the interview.

Consult

When dealing with high-pressure, high-profile, and/or high-priority cases, it pays to have a third party evaluate your hypotheses and planned work tasks. Another pair of eyes can assess whether you have included all the relevant hypotheses, remembered to list all the sources of information that can test the hypotheses, and prioritized the work tasks correctly. Consulting with others will improve the quality and objectivity of your investigations.

Collect

Then the process starts all over again. We will again collect relevant information. The difference from the first round of collection is that now we will work in a more targeted and efficient manner. We will have a better grasp of the information we are looking for, where we will look for it, and how. We will to a lesser degree collect general information, in other words, information that we know from experience will be needed for this type of case. In the subsequent rounds of the ongoing fact investigation process, the collection of information increasingly narrows in on the information we need in order to test the hypotheses for the specific case we are working on. Experience and phenomenon-specific expertise will still be helpful in finding sources of information, but now the process will be managed to a greater extent by the objectives. And it will consequently be more efficient.

The new information must then of course be checked and connected to the information we have already collected. Then we will see if any of the hypotheses are refuted, strengthened, or weakened. Perhaps new hypotheses will even emerge. We must continue to test the remaining hypotheses. The investigation of facts continues in this way—through the 6 Cs, again and again—until we have ended up with the most probable hypothesis.

The model is a theory-based, structured, work method for factual investigations. Using the model does not mean that practical experience is irrelevant. When applied correctly, experience-based knowledge can help us to form relevant hypotheses about the focus of an investigation. Experience from similar cases gives us an idea about the kinds of sources that can provide us with relevant information and how we can obtain information from these sources. Experience will also potentially give our investigations a broader scope and more pieces to the incomplete puzzle. But as pointed out in a critique of the former Norwegian police interrogation practice,

> experience is all well and good, but if the course is set in the wrong direction, without training, correction, reflection or critical thinking along the way, there is a real danger that the experience can consolidate misunderstandings so in the end they appear to be truths. (Rachlew 2003)

Classic pitfalls will be reduced by adherence to the model and consulting with and seeking advice and constructive feedback from others.

The model can appear comprehensive and detailed. It might also appear suitable for only police investigation purposes or for large-scale investigations. It is true that the need for a clear process is greater when there is a lot of information to be processed. Still, we can quickly work our way through the phases of the process, even for the smallest of cases.

We actually go through similar processes—consciously or unconsciously—several times a day as we are processing more or less trivial information: We observe an incident (collect), such as a mother trying to control her son through the use of physical force. We might observe carefully (check), to determine whether the mother is tugging unnecessarily at his arm or if the son is really out of control. Unconsciously, we place what we see into the cognitive schemata we have for this type of situation (connect). Is she just a frazzled single mother, or is it a matter of culture and child rearing? Have we witnessed this type of behavior before? Then we form an opinion about what has happened (construct). It is probably just a difficult little boy, and the mother is doing her best. Usually, we will choose to believe the first and most likely explanation. If we were to collect more information (consider) after having formed an opinion about the situation, that information will appear superficial. Even if the first assessment is often correct, we risk walking into a cognitive trap and unconsciously interpreting any new information as a confirmation of that which we already believe has taken place.

If what we experience attracts attention—because the mother's treatment of her child was unusually rough-handed—we will proceed more methodically (follow the model) in seeking to deduce what is taking place. Then we will evaluate the information with greater impartiality (consider). Maybe the boy took sweets off the shelf and is misbehaving, which confirms that the mother is trying to manage a challenging situation. But what is the nature of the interaction between the mother and the child? The boy's eyes are shining more with fear than obstinacy and automatically we look to see if the child has any physical injuries. If we talk to others about the experience, their impressions will potentially strengthen or alter our perception (consult). We ask the man behind the cash register, and he says he was thinking about calling Child Protective Services earlier. It was more serious than we initially thought.

We need the support of a method to avoid blunders. As professionals we can't trust our unconscious thought processes and collect and process information haphazardly. The model enables you to systematically approach your work with greater awareness. It makes you more professional because it promotes good thought processes in both the general investigation phases and the case-specific preparations for interviews.

We will now redirect our focus to the collection of information—the professional interview—at all times keeping in mind the model for factual investigations. The information constitutes the "blood vessels" of the investigation. Without information, the investigation stalls, and should errors sneak in during the collection phase (unreliable information), the investigation becomes "contaminated." The potential sources of error and pitfalls are many, but the direct connection between collection and the investigation's relevant hypotheses helps us to define and understand the objective or purpose of the interview, and the objective of every topic you plan to illuminate. Yes, the purpose of every question you are planning to ask. This approach also makes it easier for you to coach yourself. Do the questions I am planning to ask correspond with the information needs raised by the case?

The Need for a Strategy

In addition to a method that helps us identify the information needed (what we want to know) and how we in purely practical terms will carry out the interview (the phases), we also need a strategy for how we will handle critical information during the course of the interview. When we use the word "strategy," we mean a plan for obtaining a specific goal, which includes tactics for how that plan will be executed. What information will we withhold? And not least, when is the right time to present critical information to the interviewee?

When the research-based interview methods were introduced to the Norwegian police around the start of the new millennium and the confession-focused techniques were taken to task, an experienced and critical detective stood up in the lecture hall and protested:

"Being a policeman must still be allowed!"

Ethics, empathy, active listening, communication, open questions, and others were relatively strange terms and far afield from the techniques he had learned.

"Of course, you're allowed to be a policeman," we, the instructors, replied and followed up by asking what the detective thought "being a policeman" during an interrogation meant.

"Using tactics, playing your cards right," the detective replied.

When the same detective was asked to explain what "using tactics" meant and how to play your cards right, a problem arose. He could neither describe nor explain these things. It wasn't his fault. The Norwegian police had no strategic method or approach to the interrogation.

The understanding was that strategy and tactical approaches were cultivated and acquired through experience. But even the most experienced detectives could not manage to explain the components of their strategy. It was a less-than-effective system in an organization where the new recruits were all lined up and eager to learn.

Through the introduction of the new interview methods, a strategic model was also introduced. This model is a formula for the presentation of *critical information* during an interview. The reason we are introducing this way of thinking here—in the chapter about the preparatory phase—is related to the fact that a successful presentation of critical information requires preparation. The timing of the presentation can be decisive to both the reliability and the credibility of the information we collect. We therefore need a strategy that will help us find the right moment—a strategy that helps us to "play our cards right" when necessary.

Critical Information

Handling critical information is important in many different types of professional interviews because such information typically holds the potential to undermine or support key hypotheses that must be investigated in conjunction with the case. By critical information we mean information that can be difficult for the other person to address during a professional interview. This can be information indicating that something doesn't add up, that the person in question may have made a mistake, withheld information, or tried to cover something up. It can also be information that the other person isn't trying to hide from us, but which we possess and must address with that person, regardless of how difficult this might be.

In police investigations, such critical information is referred to as evidence or potential evidence. If handled correctly in the tactical sense, the information can lead to the conviction of guilty parties or acquittal of innocent suspects. If handled incorrectly, the guilty party can go free and innocent parties be convicted. DNA, fingerprints, and key surveillance tape footage are three examples of critical information in the context of a police investigation.

For the Internal Revenue Services, an example of critical information would be a bank statement showing that the taxpayer has failed to report financial transactions. For Child Protective Services, it could be information about a boy who is struggling at school and always comes to school with new bruises on his body. A financial analyst has discovered that the volume of goods in stock of a company in which they are considering investing appears alarmingly high. Is the company unable to sell its products? A recruiting firm sees that a job applicant has not listed a single reference from his last place of employment. Did something happen that they should know about before hiring this person? A journalist finds a document indicating that several years ago someone sounded the alarm about the scandal she is investigating. Critical evidence can also be something a child has told others at school, and which a teacher, social, or health-care worker must address with the parents.

The interviewee may be prepared to speak about the critical information, but this is not always the case. Critical information can fall into our hands without their knowledge. A child may have confided in a teacher at school about violence or other critical matters at home.

On other occasions it might be that the person we are going to interview doesn't know that the information even exists. One example would be that of financial analysts who use questionnaires for customer surveys in their work of assessing a company. The survey can disclose critical information of a problematic nature for the company and which the company itself knows nothing about. Through anonymous sources, a journalist may have gained access to a critical email containing information about a politician, information to which only a small number of people from the party leadership have been made privy.

In all cases, it can be difficult for the interviewee to address the critical information, perhaps because the information will potentially put him or her in a bad light. It could be information that indicates that this person has made a mistake, withheld information, or tried to cover something up. As is the case in criminal proceedings, critical information can in other contexts also rectify an unfortunate impression, such as by clearing up a misunderstanding or suspicion.

Irrespective of the profession or situation in question, when a case, investigation, inquiry, or process discloses critical information, the need for a well-founded strategy to handle the information becomes all the more important and especially when the critical information should potentially be presented during an interview with the involved or implicated party.

In the fictional case mentioned earlier about the suspected burglar John, the police's forensic investigations found his fingerprints on the broken window. The information is without doubt critical in nature and can potentially be submitted as evidence in a trial. What John says when being questioned about the fingerprints can determine whether this critical information supports the hypothesis of guilt or of innocence. Should it turn out that John is in fact a good friend of the person who owned the house that was broken into, this will of course weaken the hypothesis of guilt. A simple explanation has been given for what the detective thought might be incriminating evidence. We will return to the criminal case against John to illustrate how the strategy we explain next can help us carry out a tactically correct investigative interview.

Critical Information and the Construction of Hypotheses

What each of the previous examples have in common is that they are situations in which we, as professional interviewers, must create a plan for if, when, and how we will present the critical information during the interview.

In keeping with the underlying logic of the investigative model (the 6 Cs), we must check the reliability of the information before making connections and subsequently make a list of alternative hypotheses to be tested. To illustrate how this can work, we use the fictional case of a boy, "Jonas," who is reported to Child Protective Services as having unexplained bruises. While Child Protective Services must allow for the possibility that Jonas's bruises were caused by physical abuse, they will ask themselves, "What could have happened?" and listing the alternative hypotheses ("What *else* could have happened?"), they will find alternative explanations: the boy is highly active, loves to climb trees and jump out of them, and so on. Maybe he plays a sport that causes many minor injuries such as BMX-cycling, karate, or skateboarding. The bruises could also have a medical explanation such as osteoporosis or hemophilia. And the bruises can be due to something random—bad luck, nothing more. Listing all the plausible hypotheses for the other 5Ws+H questions is also useful. For example, by asking "Who?" and "How?" Jonas may have been physically abused by others, without his parents finding out about it, such as if the abuser has manipulated the boy into saying he fell (again).

Before the interview with the parents starts, the person leading the professional interview must have identified and written down all plausible explanations—in other words, alternative hypotheses that can explain the boy's bruises. A written list of alternative hypotheses helps the fact finder avoid or counteract cognitive traps (Ask 2006). Furthermore, those who support, evaluate, or check the work of frontline investigators will be able to quickly ascertain whether the relevant aspects of the case have been illuminated or, in the opposite case, establish that there is insufficient breadth and/or a unilateral focus on one hypothesis. If Jonas is not a victim of child abuse, there must be an alternative explanation. This is when the tactical management of the information Child Protective Services possesses becomes relevant. Which hypotheses must be tested during the interviews with the parents, before presenting the critical information about the boy's bruises?

It is essential not to introduce the critical information before all the plausible alternative hypotheses have been tested. Child Protective Services must of course be honest and inform the parents that they have received a child protection alert, but the presentation of the critical information—the details about the bruises—must be postponed until the alternative hypotheses have been tested. In an interview without such a plan where the information about the bruises is presented by way of introduction, we deprive the interviewee of the opportunity to offer his or her explanation freely, on a voluntary basis. Presenting critical information too soon will simultaneously make it easy for the interviewee to present a false but plausible alternative explanation.

There are a number of good reasons why the presentation of critical information must be postponed. Combined, these reasons constitute the foundation of the strategy being taught to police detectives of today. The strategic presentation of critical information in given situations may seem more relevant for some professions than others. However, as illustrated in the next section, when and how to present critical information may indeed be a useful technique to be aware of for anyone who conducts interviews as part of their everyday work.

In his annual report to the UN General Assembly, the special rapporteur on torture describes the strategy and recommends that the United Nations ratify the logic, so it can be held up as "best practice" for all states (Méndez 2016, art. 54):

> As a matter of best practice, interviewers are encouraged to proceed, when necessary, with probing questions designed to elicit information that will test all possible alternative explanations identified during the preparation of the interview. Strategic probing and disclosure of potential evidence

> allows officers to explore the interviewee's account in depth before pro-
> ceeding to the next topic, helping to ensure that the presumption of inno-
> cence is respected while strengthening the case against a guilty suspect by
> preventing the subsequent fabrication of an alibi.

An Open Mind

From a decision-making psychology perspective, the strategy encourages us
to consider alternatives. It compels us to search for information in support of
explanations beyond the first that comes to mind. Testing the alternative hypotheses—in other words, exploring whether there could be other explanations—
counteracts tunnel vision and stimulates an open mind in the interviewer. Using
the previous Jonas case study as an example, we search for information that can
provide a natural or innocent explanation for the bruises. If we can't find such
an explanation, the hypothesis of physical abuse is strengthened.

Before we continue the explanation of how an interview should be prepared and the strategy planned, it can be helpful to imagine a corresponding
situation from your own daily life. Imagine that you are working on a case,
inquiry, or investigation and your organization has received critical information of relevance that must be investigated and where an interview is a natural
source of information.

A job recruiter has been informed by a former employer that a candidate is
lazy and unstructured; a journalist has information about a politician who has
decided to allocate funds to an enterprise in which he personally owns shares;
a doctor has information about how a patient has previously abused the same
medication for which she is now requesting a prescription; a caseworker at
social services has information revealing that a client who has applied for welfare benefits has a new, expensive car; a child welfare officer has received information from a neighbor about recurring domestic disturbances, including the
sound of children screaming in pain.

The process starts with a suspicion, conjecture, or concern that must be
investigated. To maintain objectivity, the alternative hypotheses are just as
important as those that seem obvious. Earlier we have explained the inner
connection between hypotheses that must be tested in order to shed light on
the case as a whole and how the hypotheses come to define the preparations
for the interviews in particular.

Let us illustrate the thought process using the case against John.

John has a prior conviction for a burglary. His fingerprints were found on
a broken window. The owner of the house reported the case as a break-in.

John doesn't know that the police have found the fingerprints, but he has been informed that he is under suspicion for the burglary and that the police want to talk with him in conjunction with the case.

If John hasn't committed the burglary, there must be another explanation for why his fingerprints were found on the window. The alternative hypotheses must be listed during the preparations for the interview and subsequently tested during the interview. They include the following:

- John is a friend of the house owner and has visited the house on a number of occasions.
- John knows the daughter or others in the household.
- John has done work on or in the house for the owner.
- John has worked in the company that made or delivered the window.

We have purposely left out (at least) one alternative hypothesis—in other words, a possible, alternative explanation for how John's fingerprints ended up on the broken window. We have done so to illustrate a key point and will return to this shortly.

Based on the alternative hypotheses, we can now determine the right moment for presenting the critical information about the fingerprint to John.

By preparing questions designed to elicit information that will test the hypotheses, we operationalize the principle that in a criminal law context is called the presumption of innocence, or innocent until proven guilty. In practical terms, this means that the police will search for information indicating that John is innocent—despite the presence of the fingerprint on the windowpane. If we apply the principle to other professions, it represents a right held by all those summoned to take part in professional interviews, a right to be met by an interviewer with an open mind who has not formed an opinion in advance—regardless of the amount of critical information the interviewer might have acquired. When the person being interviewed is allowed to explain freely about topics of relevance without our introducing the information we already have, we ensure that the interviewee is given a true opportunity to introduce the critical information—before being confronted with it. The risk of influence is reduced, which strengthens the reliability of the information collected.

This strategy also contains an ethical dimension. If the interviewer does not have a clear idea about how any critical information should be handled, there is a risk of presenting it too soon. This will then deprive the interviewee of the opportunity to establish his or her credibility; the interviewer creates a situation in which the interviewee risks being subsequently accused of having fabricated or adapted his or her statement based on information provided by the interviewer.

If John had done some work on the house, premature presentation of the critical information in his case could have transpired as follows:

DETECTIVE: How do you explain the fact that we found your fingerprints on the broken window?
JOHN: I don't know. Where did you say this was?
DETECTIVE: This address on Maple Street.
JOHN (TAKES A MOMENT TO THINK):   'Yes, I've been there. With a friend of mine who did a job there a long time ago.'
DETECTIVE: 'Well, you perhaps should have mentioned that before. Now it sounds suspiciously like a justification.'
JOHN: 'Yeah … but you didn't ask me if I had been there before.'

Postponing the presentation of critical information gives the innocent parents of the boy with the bruises the chance to talk about their hyperactive child. The owner of the company in which we are considering investing has the opportunity to talk about his sales strategy for the upcoming quarter, which has entailed stockpiling goods over the course of the winter in preparation for the rise in demand—and therefore also the rise in price—anticipated in the spring. The job applicant explains that he was obliged to leave his former job because he stood up for the employees and demanded the overtime wages they were entitled to by law and was then frozen out by the director. A social welfare client speaks about how his need for welfare benefits arose after his brother, who was drowning in debt, died, leaving him a leasing agreement for a car that the client is unable to get out of. And John might have mentioned that he had been to the house before.

By postponing the presentation of critical information, we see that we can elicit answers during the free recall phase, which renders the critical information less critical. There can be a simple explanation that emerges in a manner that strengthens both the reliability and the credibility of the innocent party's account. On the other hand, if none of the alternative hypotheses that are tested during the interview can explain the critical information, its validity is strengthened.

By testing the alternative hypotheses, a person intending to cover up, justify, or evade responsibility will run into difficulties. A premature presentation of the critical information will in fact make it easier for the interviewee to present a false but plausible alternative explanation. By waiting to present the critical information until such time when all the alternative explanations have been tested, it becomes difficult to fabricate an alternative explanation, exactly because the alternatives have already been tested and eliminated through answers to our open questions.

It is therefore important to know the right moment for presenting the critical information so as to avoid influencing the reliability of the information we obtain. By postponing presentation, the credibility of those with nothing to hide is also strengthened, while the strategy makes it more difficult for those presenting false information to appear credible.

Let's return to the case against John, who is suspected of burglary. Imagine that he is guilty and wants to evade criminal liability. Because we have prepared a list of the alternative hypotheses and proceeded according to a plan containing interview questions suitable for shedding light on these, John has now explained that he doesn't know anyone who lives in the house, he has never been inside the house—neither in his free time nor in connection with work. Neither has he ever worked at a factory or in a transport company that could explain the presence of the fingerprints on the broken windowpane. Once all the alternative hypotheses have been tested (in this case, disproven), the moment has come to present the critical information. Matter-of-factly, calmly, and with nonconfrontational curiosity. There may still be explanations for the fingerprints that we have failed to consider. At the same time, this type of procedure can strengthen communication:

> Ok, John. You have told us that you don't know the owner of the house; you don't know anyone who lives there; you have never been inside or near the house, neither socially nor professionally; you have never worked in a window factory or a transport company that might have done work at that address. We have found your fingerprints on the broken windowpane where the break-in occurred. In order to understand the connection, I must ask you to explain why your fingerprints were found on the broken window.

It we have tested all the alternative hypotheses, it will be difficult for the guilty party to present a credible, alternative explanation. The hypothesis of guilt is strengthened. John can of course amend his story and say he forgot something and that he now wants to change his statement. He may be telling the truth, but normally such a revised statement will damage the credibility of the suspect. Regardless, we will be ready to test the reliability of the explanation now being presented.

We mentioned earlier that we consciously left out one alternative hypothesis. We did so to illustrate the strategy's tactical and logical structure. Which hypothesis did the detective who was going to interview John forget to include in his preparations and has therefore not explored? Can you come up with an alternative explanation? Assume that John was guilty and that the interviewer has now presented the critical information about the fingerprint as described earlier. John is still interested in evading criminal liability. What explanation can he invent while at the same time retaining enough credibility to introduce doubt about his guilt?

Because the detective (we) forgot to list all the alternative hypotheses that could be relevant to the theme of "John's connection to the scene," John can now explain that he must have touched the window from the outside on some other occasion. Perhaps he explains that he was invited to a party in the neighborhood a couple of weeks ago. He got the address wrong, so he walked into the backyards of a number of houses and peeked into the windows before he realized that he was on the wrong side of town. He therefore gave up and went home instead. This "tall tale" can be difficult to test because the story gives a more or less plausible explanation for the fingerprint. The story can be difficult to refute (disprove) and therefore creates reasonable doubt. If this explanation had been included as an alternative hypothesis during the preparations and tested through open questions before presenting the information about the fingerprints, it would have been more difficult for John to dig his way out.

The procedure we have described is effective because the credibility of interviewees who intend to withhold critical information, escape liability, and so on, is undermined. At the same time, the procedure is ethical, and solid from a decision-making psychology perspective. It encourages us to list and test alternative explanations. Imagine if John were innocent and the detectives sufficiently creative in their case-related preparations. Then in response to the question of whether he had been in the area where the burglary was committed, John would probably have told us about the party he was supposed to attend in the neighborhood and the evening where he got the address wrong and looked in the windows of several houses before going home. John's somewhat unlikely story would have emerged without the critical information being presented to him. It would then have strengthened (the compromised) credibility of the innocent John in the context of the case, in which several random coincidences put him under suspicion.

Information that emerges before critical information is presented will normally be more reliable because the information emerges with a minimum of influence on the part of the interviewer. At the same time, the explanation appears more credible because it is less likely to have been adapted to the facts of the case.

So far, we have covered two of the essential elements needed to prepare for professional interviews—physical preparations and case-related preparations. Now we come to the third element—mental preparations. These may not take as long as the other types but are just as essential. If you skip this final part of the planning and preparation phase of the method, it can be difficult to make the most of both your own potential and that of the interview itself.

Mental Preparations

Significant mental effort is needed to interview people with respect, honesty, and empathy, without judging, criticizing, or lecturing. We must therefore prepare ourselves mentally for the interpersonal communication that will soon take place: Am I ready to listen actively; be silent; not interrupt; follow up with open, relevant questions; and adhere to the structure of the interview? Time spent on preparing mentally for the interview helps us get into a mindset where we are ready for anything.

In 2020, Ray Bull and Asbjørn Rachlew presented an updated review of what characterizes good investigative interviews, where they summarize previous research. The list reminds us that a professional interview is created by people who

- keep an open mind, without prejudice
- are accommodating and considerate
- are curious and listen actively
- are not judgmental, condescending, or false
- are structured and flexible

This list can easily be converted into a checklist that would be natural to have on hand during mental preparations, but the research projects from which it emerged emphasize that the elements on the "checklist" are just as important during the interview.

Interviewers who manage to adhere to the basic principles for good interpersonal communication increase the probability that the interviewee will choose to share relevant information. Studies from different parts of the world indicate that the principles appear to be universally valid, regardless of whether the person with whom we are speaking is a terror suspect (Alison et al. 2013) or a victim of terrorism (Jakobsen 2019). Along the same lines, research shows that violent-crime suspects experience the interviewer's interpersonal attitude in the same way as do people who have been victims of violent crimes (Holmberg & Christianson 2002).

In a study of police interviews of terror suspects, Alison et al. (2013) found parallels between research on police questioning and research exploring psychologists' therapy sessions with patients. Interpersonal communication focusing on confirmation of the other person, understanding, and adapted empathy increases the quality and strength of the relationship of people in an interaction (Horvath & Bedi 2002). Feeling understood and accepted can make it easier to take part in a conversation (Bohart et al. 2002). Whether the interaction takes place in an office, a health clinic, or a police station is irrelevant. The fundamental, social-psychological processes of the interpersonal encounter are the same.

The professional's behavior influences then both the other person's motivation to talk and how the other person communicates. One interesting observation made by Alison et al. is that interviewees will see right through interviewers who try to motivate them to speak or collaborate using instrumental interview techniques or "tricks." The respect must be genuine. It is not possible to pretend you are interested. If your interest is instrumental and stems exclusively from a wish to get something in return for your efforts, you risk being perceived as false. Then you will find yourself in a hopeless situation.

Personal Motivation

Physical and case-related preparations are behind you. The question is now whether there is something about you—or the situation—to suggest that you are not ready to carry out the actual interview.

> How are you feeling on the day? Are you ill or have you experienced something that can cause cognitive noise? Did you get a good night's sleep? Sleep deprivation influences our cognitive capacity in a negative sense. It may have been a long day and now you are going to carry out "yet another interview." Maybe it is your fifth student conference, consultation, witness deposition, or job interview? Maybe "you know" what the other person is going to say? Maybe you believe the interview is purely a formality or, in the worst case, that the entire matter is trivial? Why are we even doing this?

If your lack of motivation is due to your mental or physical state on this particular day, a short, mental exercise can quickly put you back on the professional track:

> Even though I don't feel that this case is especially serious/important/ inspiring, I must remember that this particular interview might mean a great deal to the person with whom I will be speaking. It can be an important, yes, even a decisive day in the other person's life.

Are you experiencing mental "interference," thoughts, or emotions that can make it difficult to uphold the principles for a good interview? On the whole, will you be able to stay open minded, curious, empathetic, unbiased, and flexible in this meeting?

> Are you ready to meet the interviewee? Have you thought through the situation? Are you ready to practice active listening and collect as much information as possible? Have you thought about the life situation of the interviewee?

Mental preparations are also about being prepared for the opposite case: Perhaps the interviewee will not find the interview to be of interest? Strictly speaking, we don't know what we will encounter and must be prepared for every contingency. Are you ready to listen to stories and details that in a private context would provoke sympathy and tears? Maybe you will be meeting someone who ordinarily would cause a negative reaction in you, a person who in a private context would trigger negative reactions and emotions: irritation, frustration, or anger? In either case, you are the professional, and if you are going to succeed, you must handle the situation professionally, every single time. You need to mentally prepare to maintain impartiality at all times and not to prejudge on the basis of something about the other person (e.g., what they're wearing, how they speak, how they act). The interview methodology described here cannot eliminate bias. However, with knowledge and awareness, and by following the procedures described here, professionals may reduce the negative effects. Furthermore, envisioning different types of potential scenarios will increase your capacity and potential for managing the unexpected.

Active Listening

As we wrote in Part 1, listening is completely different from hearing. We must therefore be mentally prepared for the demanding task of listening. We must show interest in both the person and in what they have to say. Interested listening leads to more interested speech. And the opposite holds true: if we demonstrate a lack of interest and engagement, the speaker will become less interested in sharing their story. Then the story also becomes less interesting. This vicious circle can only be prevented or broken by our interest and curiosity. We must, in short, prepare ourselves to be curious and interested.

It is not certain that members of the royal family are equally interested in everything and everyone they meet when they travel around to perform all manner of presentations and company visits, but when they arrive prepared, it becomes simpler to show, even emanate interest. In a corresponding manner, we must be mentally prepared to be interested in what we are told. No matter what the subject matter might be, we can ask a follow-up question. In that way we acknowledge both the people with whom we are speaking and what they are telling us. We are all different, but to be seen and experience acknowledgment of who we are and what we represent is something everyone appreciates. Active listening is a central component of all phases of a professional interview. It is an acquired skill. Techniques we can use to stimulate active listening will be described when we address the subsequent phases of the interview, but the point here is that listening is difficult. This is the case, among other reasons, because when we listen to someone speak, this naturally triggers associations, and as a matter of course we also start making assessments. It can therefore be wise to include a reminder to yourself of the significance of listening. It is easy to forget and requires practice. Make your mental preparations a part of your practice sessions.

Flexibility

As highlighted earlier, we must prepare ourselves for the unexpected. One of the reasons for this is that our own reactions can influence the person with whom we are speaking. Being mentally prepared for "everything"—including the unexpected—increases our capacity to handle it. At the same time, the risk of unwanted influence is reduced.

The contents of an interview will never be exactly the way you have imagined in your preparations. Although we have planned what we will talk about, we will be at the mercy of how the other party responds. The interviewee can suddenly say something that changes the conditions for the entire interview. Then we must be mentally prepared to adjust our plan and strategy in order to follow up on what is happening in the interview.

Preparing the necessary flexibility need not take a lot of time. It is basically about asking yourself a final question right before the interview starts: What do I do if the interview moves in a completely different direction from what I have envisioned? Without this type of mental exercise, your thorough preparations can become your worst enemy. If you haven't thought through how you will behave in the event of an irregularity, you risk becoming hung up on your own outline, agenda, or script. This can quickly undermine active listening. We become essentially more interested in our own questions than the other person's answers.

Self-Assessment

On the other hand, the person who is prepared for the eventuality of a discrepancy between plan and implementation will also be mentally prepared for the possibility of a need for a break at some point in the interview. This won't necessarily mean a break where participants leave the room, but a break in the interaction, when you as the professional allow silence in the room for a moment or two, while you reassess your plan. The psychologist Ray Bull has done research on police questioning for almost fifty years. During an interview in 2001, Bull was asked to name a feature that distinguishes professional from less-professional interviewers. After a break of a few seconds of silence—not an awkward silence, because it was clear he was thinking—the psychologist replied that professional interviewers dare to include silence as a part of the interview, and they do so without creating an awkward atmosphere. His experience was that the most proficient interviewers employ silence to double-check and adjust their own plan when required.

The inner control was not just about the case-related preparations, the plan, or the need for an adjustment. The self-monitoring was just as focused on the basic principles for good interviews. Professional interviewers find moments when it is natural to take a breather, when they will stop and check in with themselves about whether their conduct is that of an interested and non-judgmental person. Am I being accommodating, curious, and attentive? Do I still have an open mind and am I asking open questions? Or have I slipped into a style that any adult without training or a methodological approach would have managed just as well?

It can be just as important to prepare yourself mentally for handling the silence that can follow after you have asked a question. In ordinary social situations, we will often help others to answer a question, such as by offering a possible answer. In a professional interview we must avoid influencing the response. We must trust the question we have asked and remain silent until the other person replies. It sounds simple, but it is difficult and requires awareness, preferably as a part of your mental preparations.

Reaching a level of sufficient cognitive capacity that will enable you to monitor yourself while you are working requires self-assurance and skill. It is not easy, but research shows that to a large degree it is a matter of how the professional interviewer initiates contact and establishes his or her role. Basic principles, insights, and objectives must be implemented in practice, every single time. Now and then you may experience that you are faced with an "easy" interview. Preparing yourself methodically can seem a bit artificial, a bit "overkill." But you have in fact received a brilliant opportunity to practice the ideal procedure. Through a systematic and professional approach to the task, you improve the quality of your work, so it becomes increasingly second nature, which will come in handy when the pressure mounts and you are facing the most important interview of your career. High performers, commonly referred to as professionals, such as elite athletes or celebrity speakers, say that they motivate and convince themselves that they are facing their most important match or speaking engagement, every single time.

Your next professional interview is your most important. Not just for the person you will meet but also for yourself. If you approach all future interviews with the same attitude, we are convinced that in addition to personal development, you will also experience greater job satisfaction.

Feeling confident about your own preparations will help you in the next phase of the conversation—establishment of rapport. But without the skills required to help the other person feel secure in the situation, it becomes difficult to realize the potential of researchers' recommendations for the optimal collection of relevant, accurate, and reliable information.

7

ENGAGE AND EXPLAIN—
ESTABLISHING RAPPORT

A professional interview can be characterized by asymmetric communication, uncertainty, pressure, and stress. How we handle these challenges as professional interviewers contributes to determining the outcome of the interview. Our actions determine not only the quantity and reliability of the information we collect, and consequently the conclusions that are drawn, but also the trust in you, your organization, and your profession.

The First Impression

The establishment of rapport starts from the first moment of contact, whether this takes place over the phone, by email, or in the form of a personal meeting. As explained in Chapter 6 ("Physical Preparations" section), the first impression is formed quickly and can be of decisive significance for the subsequent communication. Although the interviewee receives information throughout the interaction that may change or contradict the first impression, he or she makes a judgment of the interviewer(s), which to a large extent is based on the first impression (Olcaysoy Okten 2018).

Human beings' tendency to classify and judge one another at first glance can work both ways: a good first impression will potentially have a positive effect on the interview. The challenge is of course that the person who starts off on the wrong foot may find themselves struggling to establish a rapport. There is little we can do about another person's prejudices and personal cognitive schemata. The first impression, on the other hand, is something we can influence. Professional interviewers will do what they can to conduct themselves in a manner that promotes confidence and trust from the moment of the initial contact.

It is worth remembering that the initial contact is often made before the interview. The first impression of your organization or company is often made over the phone or through an email. How long they have to wait for a reply and how the reply is formulated play a part in determining how the person with whom you will be speaking perceives your organization. There is a risk of setting yourself up for an uphill battle before even meeting the other person. You should therefore exercise awareness starting from the moment of your initial contact.

In short, the establishment of rapport starts before the interview takes place and illustrates an important point: the phases in a professional interview are mutually dependent.

Expectations

Everyone we meet will "see" us through their personal cognitive schemata. Researchers often describe personal schemata as "the glasses through which we see the other." We don't notice that we are wearing these "glasses," but they help us form an impression of the person in front of us and do so quickly and efficiently. These schemata evolve and change throughout our lifetimes. I see a police detective and, based on my former experiences, my attitudes, values, and knowledge, conclude that she is nice/authoritarian/corrupt/professional. This man is an executive, he is proficient/power crazed/insensitive/decisive. The classification takes place automatically.

Even though we do what we can to make a positive impression—of ourselves, our role, or our company or profession, there is little we can do to correct or influence the perceptions of others *before* we meet them. The mental preparations we have outlined in Chapter 6 will nonetheless improve your chances of making a good first impression. The preparations are designed to establish a rapport in which the interviewee feels seen and respected for who they are, and not on the basis of a particular role or category (client, patient, suspect, unemployed, competitor, etc.).

The interpersonal communication that is established has an evident ethical dimension that we must never lose sight of. In Part 1 we discussed Immanuel Kant's categorical imperative. His formulation of humanity applies to all the phases of the interview: "We should never act in such a way that we treat humanity, whether in ourselves or in others, as a means only but always as an end in itself" (Stanford Encyclopedia of Philosophy 2016). As professionals we must always view the interviewee as an end in and of themselves and never as the means to our end of making a diagnosis, solving a case, earning money, or concluding a process.

Information

The recommended procedure for establishing rapport is based to a large extent on the themes introduced in the beginning of this book: psychology, communication, and ethics. A good rule of thumb is to ask yourself: "How would I want to be met?" The answer to the question will provide a good guideline for how you should meet others. But everyone is different, and nobody is just like you.

Simultaneously, research shows that most people have some basic needs. Not knowing what lies ahead creates the feeling being out of control, which however natural is uncomfortable. This type of discomfort occupies cognitive capacity at the expense of presence and effective communication. As professional interviewers, one of our most important tasks is to reduce the uncertainty of the person we are interviewing—and to do so as quickly as possible. Creating predictability is a key objective of rapport establishment.

Receiving relevant and clarifying information about what will take place reduces uncertainty and promotes an impression of the professional party as a person who really cares and shows consideration for the situation of the interviewee. The initial contact gives us an opportunity to communicate empathy in a natural and credible manner, so it will also be experienced as authentic and sincere (Jakobsen 2019). We must grasp that opportunity, not solely because we are ethically obliged to give information but also because an empathetic first impression increases the likelihood that the interview will surmount any challenges and resistance that may arise. It becomes easier for the interviewee to speak about difficult subjects with someone who is, after all, a stranger, if that stranger shows consideration from the first moment.

The Content of Rapport Establishment

To reduce uncertainty and create predictability, professional interviewers must preface the interview by giving three types of information before the collection of information begins: First, we must introduce ourselves and explain our role. Second, we must provide information about the more practical aspects of the interview: for example, water, the lavatory, coffee, time, breaks. Third, we must give information about the parameters for the interview, such as what we will talk about and how.

To understand why specifically the communication of information is such an essential component of professional interviews, it can be helpful to remember that knowledge is power. In Part 1 we discussed power balance and asymmetry. When in your role as an interviewer you share knowledge and speak about the interview parameters, you reduce the experience of asymmetry and its inexpedient repercussions. We share knowledge (about what will happen) and therefore also some of the power in the interview situation. It is particularly important to do this when meeting people who are not used to taking part in professional interviews. The need for security and predictability can vary considerably, depending on how accustomed the interviewee is to being interviewed, but the recommended procedure remains the same. Also experienced interviewees will have a need for information. They may have had negative experiences or feel insecure about this interview in particular and/or the interview frameworks. We create trust by speaking to the interviewee empathetically and in a manner appropriate to the context.

Presentation

The first thing we do is of course to introduce ourselves: name, place of work, and job function or title. In private contexts it can be appropriate to conclude with "looking forward to speaking with you, … nice to meet you" or other phrases of this nature. This is, however, not always appropriate in professional settings.

A truly embarrassing moment arose at the homicide division of the Oslo police force a few years back when one of the authors of this book was standing next to a colleague who was waiting to receive the bereaved in a murder case. The detective started out well, but he was probably nervous and forgot the setting. As he reached out his hand, he bowed politely and said:

"Hi. My name is Peter Applegate. A pleasure to meet you."

The intention was good but completely missed the mark. The detective should have introduced himself differently, perhaps as follows, and calmly:

"Hi. My name is Peter Applegate. I am a detective here at the Violent Crimes Division. I will be talking to you about this unfortunate matter. First and foremost, I want to offer my condolences. We have mobilized all available resources and are taking this case very seriously. Thank you for taking the time to come down here at this difficult time. We will talk in an office just down the hall. There is a lavatory on the way. Would you like to freshen up before we get started?"

Based on our experience, it can be wise to introduce yourself by name once more, as soon as you enter the room where the interview will take place, perhaps immediately after the two of you have sat down. Many people will be nervous in this situation and not retain the name the first time it is said. At the same time, we can use the occasion to introduce metacommunication as one means of providing information about what is going to happen:

> "There's water here, just help yourself. As I said when we met, my name is Peter Applegate. Feel free to call me Peter. What would you like me to call you?
>
> "Thank you, Jens. First, I want to explain how I have planned to do this interview. I cannot know how you are feeling right now … but I am, to the extent this is possible, apprised of the situation and will do everything I can to be considerate. I have planned to carry out the interview by …"
>
> If there are other people present during the interview, such as an interpreter, lawyer, or companion, after introducing yourself and your role, it is important that you immediately share corresponding information about the names and roles of any third parties and clarify any expectations regarding their functions.

For interviews requiring the use of an interpreter, it is the interviewer's task to inform the interviewee of the role of the interpreter, such as the following:

- The interpreter is neutral.
- The interpreter will translate everything that is said.
- The interpreter will speak in the first person.
- The interpreter is bound by professional secrecy.
- The interpreter will shred his or her notes after the interview.

Practical Parameters

The practical parameters will differ from one interview to the next and can influence communication. To make sure the parameters do not infringe on the capacity of the interviewee, we should inform the latter about the framework for the interview. One piece of information that is useful for both parties is to clarify and confirm the duration of the interview.

Although we have scheduled the date, time, and duration of the interview, unexpected events may have led to us having less time than planned. Before we start, it is therefore a good idea to ask the person or persons taking part in the interview if the scheduled amount of time is still convenient. If something has happened to create an element of uncertainty regarding the time frame, it is helpful to clear this up before starting. When we can ensure that the interview will not run beyond the scheduled time frame, the interviewee will no longer be as concerned about the time. We clear away any related "cognitive noise," and the interviewee(s) will be better able to be present during the interview. When we take this into consideration, we show empathy in practice.

Clarifying the time-related factors also helps the professional to organize the interview. Should it turn out that the interviewee actually has less time than we believed, we have the chance from the beginning to revise our plan for the interview should this be necessary in order to achieve our aim.

In addition to clarifying the use of time, it can be fitting to inform the interviewee about breaks, food, drink, confidentiality, and other parameters or relevant factors. If we are going to use equipment during the interview, we can explain the use and benefits of this, such as an audio recorder. Then we can also explain how the results of the interview will be documented—whether this will be in the form of a memo, report, minutes, and so on.

The Parameters for the Interview

After having introduced yourself and clarified the physical parameters, the time has come to inform the interviewee about how you have planned to carry out the interview itself. For example:

> First I want to inform you of the formal parameters for this interview (rights/confidentiality/informed consent). Subsequently, I will give you the floor, so to speak, so you will have the chance to talk to me about whatever it is that you feel is most important here. My job is then to listen.

After that I have some questions that I have prepared. The number of questions will depend a bit on what you tell me first. It can often be the case that the more you explain, the fewer questions I will have. If you have any questions, at any time, please don't hesitate to ask them.

It can often be appropriate to open up for questions right away: "Do you have any questions before we start?" Other times it can be more expedient to wait with opening up for questions until after the formal parameters for the interview have been presented.

The interviewee is to be immediately informed of any rights he or she has before the collection of information begins. For the police and a number of other professions, the formal parameters can include fundamental human rights, such as the right to a lawyer. In other cases, the formal parameters can be related to matters such as confidentiality, anonymity, informed consent, or reporting.

The first thing to be clarified is why the interview is being held. Often this is obvious, but not always. This introduction is essentially about ensuring that all parties have a common understanding of why the meeting is taking place. If it is obvious, the introduction will regardless provide a nice point of entry into the case and subject matter: "We have invited you to the studio because you are the Minister of Education and Research and a resolution has now been passed regarding ...," "You have applied for the position of senior adviser and in that context we would like ...," "We are considering making an investment in your company and would therefore ...," "You contacted us because you want to explain/would like to investigate/explore ..."

Regardless of whatever other formal parameters might apply (confidentiality, free will, informed consent, etc.), the interview's formal parameters give you an excellent opportunity to show empathy in that you are demonstrating that you take the interviewee and their rights seriously. An important measure in keeping with the methodology in such cases is to confirm that the other person has understood their rights. In addition to ensuring that the interviewee understands the formal parameters, you hereby open up for a dialogue and empathetic communication.

Skipping the formal clarification can under certain circumstances have serious consequences. Other times it can cause irritation or misunderstandings. Either way, it is a poor start.

The authors of this book are contacted by journalists from time to time. Although we are experienced in our work, the reason a journalist contacts us can become a source of pressure. It can be a matter of a difficult case. Everyone has a need for predictability and the worst conceivable start is when the journalist skips the informative introduction that is a critical element in the establishment of rapport. All journalists introduce themselves. They are also good at stating who they work for, but many will forget to inform interviewees about the parameters for the interview. This is irritating and unprofessional.

"Hi, my name is Peder Aas and I am a journalist for the Norwegian Broadcasting Corporation. I am working on a story about the false confessions of the serial killer Thomas Quick. Do you have a few minutes ...?"

"Err ... Yes ..."

"Terrific—and thank you. As a researcher in the field, what do you think about ..."

The journalist is trying to be polite, but completely violates several principles, including those pertaining to establishment of rapport and the fostering of a sense of security and predictability in the interview situation. It is also unethical to start collecting information without informing the other party about the parameters for the interview. As an interviewee, I don't know for sure whether I am about to be interviewed and, if so, what I will be interviewed about, whether my answers will appear in print, if I will have the chance to read the article, if the interview is being recorded, or whether the entire interaction will be a more informal conversation to provide the journalist with background information or help in his ongoing investigation.

An experienced interviewee will perhaps have the courage to interrupt, and in a state of (more or less) irritation, ask the journalist to explain the parameters for the conversation. Less-experienced interviewees will potentially feel blindsided and answer the questions, without really understanding what it is they are being asked about.

The asymmetry in such a case is substantial, and the bar for interrupting a journalist, doctor, or future employer can be experienced as being so high that interviewees "give in" and keep their insecurities to themselves. The chance of a good interview is reduced considerably. If the same journalist or a colleague from the same newspaper were to call again later, it is absolutely not certain that the interviewee will be interested in responding. The entire experience is uncomfortable, and for a person, organization, and profession dependent on trust in every sense, a negative experience may harm their reputation. The negative experience may be shared with the interviewee's family, friends, and colleagues. One slip can cause negative ripple effects, causing damage to reputation far beyond the interview room.

In Part 1 we addressed the balance of power and asymmetry. When as an interviewer you share knowledge and explain the parameters of the interview, you reduce the unfortunate ramifications and the experience of asymmetry. You share knowledge (about what will happen) and therefore also some of the power in the interview situation. Regardless of whom we meet for a professional interview, information about what is in store promotes a sense of security and predictability and inspires trust.

After we have created a shared understanding of the parameters, it is important to open up for questions. There can be some issue that the other person has not understood or something he or she is wondering about that we haven't considered. By encouraging the interviewee to share their thoughts at this point, we reduce asymmetry, show empathy, and eliminate cognitive noise that can interfere with good communication. Maybe the interviewee is thinking about something that is easily cleared up, but without such clarification, the matter will occupy their thoughts and disrupt communication.

"Did you receive the results of the tests?," "Have you spoken with the sources/the others?," "When will this be published?," etc.

Encouraging the interviewee to offer input or ask questions does not only prevent unnecessary disturbances. It also opens up for dialogue and creates an atmosphere where it is understood that active participation in the interaction is accepted. It is not unusual to be nervous when summoned for an interview. A natural and early involvement will help alleviate this and facilitate the process of developing a good rapport.

If you know that in the course of the interview you will have to use technical terminology, these terms should be explained at this time, before you start using them. However, as a rule of thumb, technical terms or jargon should be avoided if the interviewee can't be expected to be familiar with this type of language.

Metacommunication

A key part of clarifying the parameters for the interview is "communication about communication," or metacommunication (see Part 1). The communication should take place in a manner that fosters understanding and not cause the interviewee to feel that the parameters are being crammed down their throat. It is important that we reach an agreement about the parameters, that we form a kind of meta-contract—the experience of a contract for the parameters of the interview and how we will communicate. If disagreements or uncertainty arise, we should take the time to reach a mutual understanding. As the professional party, it is both natural and expedient to start out by providing information and subsequently involving the interviewee. This is how parameters are mutually established.

The meta-contract creates predictability and security, and should communication challenges arise during the interview, the contract can be referred to as a means of resolving these.

Metacommunication must naturally be adapted to each person we meet and each individual interview. An interviewer who rattles off a prepared "list" of bullet points without having made the necessary adaptations or established a rapport will quickly be perceived as instrumental, not particularly empathetic, and in the worst case, false. The most skilled interviewers adhere to the recommended structure because they understand and know from experience that it alleviates feelings of unpredictability, nervousness, and uncertainty. The structure is second nature to them and is thereby also experienced by the other party as natural. Interviewers who have learned their script by heart are those who come across as the most natural and credible. A bit strange maybe, but that is how it is (Gallo 2014). The foundation of all metacommunication is the recognition of the other person's needs.

In many interviews it can be appropriate to explain that we may interrupt, be silent, or repeat a question. Informing the interviewee about this (or other matters) and creating an understanding of what the interview will entail promotes a sense of predictability and a meta-contract that enhances communication. Should the communication become impeded at some point due to repeated questions, we can refer to what we spoke about earlier. Other times it can be more important to inform the interviewee that we will be introducing topics that may be difficult to talk about, and for that reason our questions may come across as criticism:

> As I mentioned earlier, it is my task to illuminate the different aspects of the case. If you feel that the questions I am asking sound like criticism, that does not necessarily mean that I don't believe you. I am quite simply obliged to investigate all potential explanations. For example, if I have information that seems to contradict what you are saying, I will need to ask you to explain this discrepancy.

Let's return to the case of Jonas. Child Protective Services have called the parents in for a conversation after having received a notification from the school about Jonas's behavioral problems and suspicious bruises on his body. Here it can be expedient to warn the parents that it may be necessary to ask questions that will potentially make them feel uncomfortable. If Child Protective Services prepares a strategic process for handling the critical information, such as to withhold the information about the bruises until all alternative hypotheses (explanations) have been tested, the interviewer should metacommunicate about the procedure:

> As we explained over the phone, Child Protective Services has received a child protection alert from the school about your son Jonas. The school teachers feel he is more reserved than usual, and they are concerned that he may be having a hard time. Before we address the details of the alert, we would like you to tell us how you think Jonas is doing. In this context we have some questions of a general nature. We have scheduled plenty of time and an important part of our job now is to listen to you. Eventually we may need to follow up with more specific questions. You may experience some of these questions as criticism but bear in mind that it is our job to ask these questions because we are bound to explore all aspects of the case. The goal for all of us is to ensure Jonas's well-being.

The reader will remember the model presenting the interview phases (Figure 9), and in particular the dotted lines, illustrating the flexibility and connection between all the phases of the model, such as how in the preparation phase we should plan all the phases. It is possible to predict a number of challenges that may arise, and we take these into consideration in our planning. The strategic presentation of critical information raises a challenge related to the main components of metacommunication: information transparency and openness.

When the delayed disclosure of critical information is necessary, it is natural and understandable that the interviewee will wonder about what kind of information we already possess. In our explanation of the case-related preparations, we emphasized the importance of having a good, thoroughly considered plan for what information we can and should share, in order to mitigate any problems related to asymmetric communication and to establish rapport. The plan should also include critical information to be strategically disclosed at a particular stage in the interview. The interview situation can become uncomfortable and even provoke unprofessional altercations if we are not prepared for legitimate questions from the person we will be interviewing.

When the moment to present the critical information in the exploratory phase comes (in the case of Jonas, the bruises), we must be prepared for the possibility that our questions may provoke discomfort. It can then be a good idea to refer to the introductory part of the interview—the meta-contract—when we inform them that we might be asking some questions that can be interpreted or experienced as criticism.

First of all, the procedure helps to create predictability. Second, we will be able to use the meta-contract to resolve any communication breakdowns by referring to the agreement formed during establishment of rapport and "what we spoke about earlier." It is of equal importance that the procedure includes a form of openness about any critical information we must withhold for ethical and strategic reasons, until such time when the alternative explanations for the information have been tested.

Once we have reestablished a shared understanding of the parameters for metacommunication, it is important to open up for questions. There may be something the other person has not understood or something he or she is wondering about that we haven't considered. By opening up for this possibility, we reduce the asymmetry, show empathy, and remove cognitive noise that can obstruct good communication. Maybe the person we are going to speak with is sitting there thinking about something we hadn't planned to mention. Their thoughts may be occupied with worries about parking, the pickup of children from day care, and so on.

When people are called in to a meeting or an interview, it is not uncommon for them to feel nervous. The natural and early involvement that occurs through creation of the meta-contract will help to alleviate nervousness, and the chances of getting the interview process underway smoothly and quickly increase. We therefore create a space in which the person we interview feels comfortable asking questions. If the interviewee has formal rights or obligations, we reinforce the meta-contract by ensuring they have understood the formal parameters for the interview.

Managing Time Shortage and Spin

In many professions, the reality is that there isn't time to carry out professional interviews as one might wish. This can unfortunately affect communication. Then we must take steps to obtain the most relevant and reliable information possible in what little time we have available. A doctor has only a limited amount of time for each patient, and a television host doing a live broadcast has perhaps two minutes for questions for the prime minister. A teacher has to speak with six parents in the course of a single afternoon, a financial analyst has 60 minutes—not 61—for an all-important meeting with a director. In all of these cases, it is of course important for each of these professionals to be well-prepared so they know what they will talk about and which topics are the most significant. We can also prepare the establishment of rapport, so it helps us focus the available time on what is relevant during the interview itself. We can use our information about how we will speak together and what we will speak about, to achieve maximum efficiency.

In some interviews we meet people who have a prepared message they want to get across. They must of course have the opportunity to do so, but we don't need to hear it more than once. After they have delivered the message they feel is of importance, we must make sure that we also receive answers to our own questions. If not, it will become difficult to preserve the defined purpose of the interview, which usually involves addressing the information the interviewee wanted to share in further detail, along with the topics we want to speak about. Some interviewees may use a filibuster strategy: they fill the allotted time by speaking about their own concerns, so they are thereby spared having to answer difficult questions. The interviewee tries to spin his answer in such a way that it resembles the prepared message as much as possible. Most of us have witnessed situations in which the person answering questions has a vested interest in promoting his own agenda, his own take on the issues, and for that reason spins it, in this manner.

Those who have come prepared to employ such a strategy will do their utmost to build a bridge from every question we ask that leads back to their prepared message. One example here is a politician who exploits every opportunity to promote the party's platform or numbers without answering the question he or she has been asked. Another example would be a business magnate who uses every interview as an opportunity to speak about his impressive profit margins instead of answering critical questions about the figures behind those results.

In the establishment of rapport, we can counteract problems caused by such time thieves by explaining how we will speak together and what we will be talking about:

This case raises several important issues that affect many people. Our job is to shed light on all relevant aspects of the case and I am interested in what you perceive as being the most important. So, I will probably have some follow-up questions. If I feel that you are repeating yourself or not responding to the questions I ask, I might interrupt you because I have several questions about matters on which you can contribute valuable insights. If there are questions you don't want to answer, it is better to say so. How does that sound to you? Do you have any questions about the interview process?

Some professional interviews can be about the presentation of results, reports, or other information. Other interviews can be a continuation of previous interviews. If we are well-prepared and have familiarized ourselves thoroughly with the materials forming the basis for the interview, we can use the opportunity found in the establishment of rapport to inform the other person(s) about this. This creates a sense of security, and the interviewee is spared having to spend unnecessary time giving us information we already have. Instead, both parties can spend the time exploring the material in depth.

Asking relevant questions frees up time. When we demonstrate that we are informed about the subject of the interview, this also builds professional trust. A doctor could have a legitimate need to establish clear parameters before a patient talks about her ailments, especially if the doctor already knows the patient. When establishing rapport, the doctor can explain that he has reviewed the patient record and demonstrate this by summarizing what is already known. The patient then does not have to waste time explaining her entire medical history. A financial analyst who will be meeting a director to talk about the latest quarterly report is well advised to study the report thoroughly before the meeting. During rapport establishment he can explain his preparations and show that he is familiar with the contents of the report. This frees up time to explore in greater depth issues of relevance to both parties, and the 60 scheduled minutes are spent more efficiently.

The management of expectations through metacommunication does not only raise questions pertaining to the subject matter of the interview. Conflicts of interest may also arise. If the interviewer establishes parameters that are too narrow, there is a risk of missing out on essential information. A balance must be found through professional and ethical reflection. The number of patients a general practitioner should consult per day is not something about which we can have a qualified opinion or the number of clients a lawyer can represent at the same time. Each profession knows best where the limits should be.

We don't know how many incorrect diagnoses are made as a direct result of doctors whose management of expectations is so narrow and specific that the patient is barely heard. We do know from experience that it happens. All professions experience time pressure, and some certainly more than others.

The proper amount of time to be spent on the professional establishment of rapport in general and the clarification of expectations in particular varies considerably, not only from one profession to the next but also from one interview to the next. A judge who is going to question eight witnesses in one day normally has less time per witness than a police detective. The procedure must be adapted to the situation. Everyone understands this, also those called in as witnesses. However, a conventional reading-out of formalities takes about one minute, whereas the establishment of rapport can be achieved in three minutes. Three optimally utilized minutes are sufficient to preserve the fundamental principles we are describing here. The cost of two minutes does not mean that the judge will be less efficient. On the contrary, by establishing rapport, the judge will increase the likelihood of obtaining an account of higher quality and more details in a shorter time.

Television news anchors who have 30 seconds of broadcast time know that rapport establishment and the clarification of expectations must be done in advance. The principles and the methodological approach are equally relevant.

This brings us to the next topic that professional interviewers must address, typically during the "informal" establishment of rapport before the interview officially begins.

Informal Conversations

The Norwegian police have received a great deal of criticism for that which in internal correspondence and documents is referred to as "informal conversations." Up to the year 2000, it was accepted and recommended practice for a detective to establish an informal rapport before an interrogation, in the context of which the suspect was to be encouraged to make a specific statement in the upcoming interrogation. The purpose was to lay the groundwork for a confession. The use of such informal conversations was brought to light when the interrogations of Birgitte Teng's cousin were reviewed. The abuse of this type of rapport establishment led to the director of public prosecutions in Norway putting an end to the practice. In his circular from 1999, he wrote that "any informal conversations shall be brief—the case is not to be discussed and there is to be no doubt about what is the interrogation and what is an informal chat" (Riksadvokaten 1999).

The practice was the subject of serious public debate when the manipulative techniques were exposed in a published research report for the first time (Rachlew 2003). Today such an approach would be considered an illegal police interview by the Norwegian Supreme Court (Rt. 2003, p. 549) and is defined as a clear violation of the police's own standards (Rachlew & Fahsing 2015).

The phenomenon of informal conversations is also well-known in journalism. In the so-called Bar Vulkan story from 2019, Norway's largest national daily newspaper *VG* was convicted on several counts in violation of the Ethical Code of Practice for the Norwegian press (mentioned in Part 1). The story was about a high-profile politician who was filmed while dancing with a young woman at a bar. The politician had resigned only a few months before following several reported violations on his part of the party's rules against sexual harassment. When the video from Bar Vulkan fell into the hands of the newspaper, the story was presented as a new whistleblowing case. The press coverage was massive. *VG* wrote that the woman felt things got "a bit out of hand," so she left. It turned out that this was not correct. The woman did not in any sense feel that she had been compromised by the politician.

The most serious violations of the Ethical Code of Practice in this case involved how quotes from an "informal conversation" between the journalist and the woman were used as key information and published. The woman maintained that the quote was not only incorrect but in fact expressed the opposite of what she meant. And on top of everything, she had felt pressured by both the journalist and the editor.

VG later printed an apology for the story and agreed that they had committed a number of press ethics violations. The newspaper also changed several of its procedures for journalistic working methods. In the new traffic rules for the newspaper, about the use of sources, it reads: "VG always has a responsibility for ensuring communication of the true meaning of sources' comments. In keeping with proper VG practice and journalistic method, we will ask *open questions* and demonstrate a genuine interest in eliciting the source's version of a story" (emphasis added).

There are several examples of news articles based on information that surfaced before or after the interview itself, typically documented because the recording equipment was already on or still recording. Well-known examples include the former Swedish minister of industry Bjørn Rosengren, who said, "Norway is the last Soviet state," and the former British prime minister Gordon Brown, who spoke in defamatory terms in front of television cameras about a voter he had just met. Both felt betrayed by the journalists involved. Publishing such materials can be a violation of the ethical guidelines for clarifying the terms of an interview in advance. Simultaneously, the editors defended the decision to publish such materials by claiming that what was said before or after the interview stood in stark contrast to what was said in the interview itself. The logic is thereby that the article discloses what the interviewee *actually* means or is justified because the words were spoken by a person in power, and the public has a right to be informed. In either case, it is reasonable to expect that the trust in journalists will be undermined. The ethical framework of the investigative interview method, on the other hand, stipulates that such techniques must never be employed as a conscious strategy.

A clear indication that journalists don't distinguish adequately between informal conversation and interviews is that most communication advisers would remind their clients that they should view every conversation with a journalist as an interview, from the moment you answer the phone or open the door until the conversation is over, unless another agreement has been made.

In the textbook *Intervjuteknikk for journalister* (Interviewing Techniques for Journalists) (Handgaard 2008), the author addresses how to plan an interview. He touches on different types of briefings and informal conversations, in which the goal is to gain trust: "Listen actively and show an interest in what the interviewee is saying, speak freely and at length on the interviewee's terms, about the traffic, neighborhood, weather or workplace."

Professional interviewers will always explicitly inform the interviewee that the interview has started or whether the conversation is to be viewed as "off the record" background information. Taking advantage of "informal conversations" to shed light on a story, regardless of the interviewer's profession, violates the fundamental principle of honesty and ethical practice in communication. (The collection of information while undercover is another type of activity and is not relevant here.)

When we look at statements from the Norwegian Supreme Court, the Office of the Public Prosecutor, the earlier cited work on interviewing techniques for journalists, and on the whole, other theories and advice from communication advisers, a clear image emerges of what does and does not constitute an informal conversation. Small talk about subjects unrelated to the matter under investigation are not unethical or negative, insofar as this constitutes a part of the establishment of rapport with all the positive ramifications this entails. But if the "informal" setting is abused through a covert, camouflaged, or manipulative attempt to "get into the head" of the person we are talking to or make them "lower their guard," not only is the interviewee's integrity compromised—in some situations, the trust in our own organization and profession will also be damaged.

To summarize: Introduce yourself, your organization, and the parameters of the interview. The first impression you make can prove critical to the quality and outcome of the interview and therefore also the quality of the information collected. Share all relevant information about what will take place. Metacommunication of this nature creates predictability and establishes a sense of security and professional trust. The chance of success is strengthened by the mental preparations you have made before the meeting in the planning and preparations phase in which you think about the situation of the interviewee. You should have mentally prepared yourself to meet the other as a unique individual and in such a way that he or she relates to you as a human being rather than on the basis of your role.

These preparations will have strengthened your ability to transmit empathy when you meet. Instrumental compassion that is intended to advance a hidden agenda is unethical and will often be understood as such and, if so, with the worst imaginable results. Even if your approach is characterized by an informative and empathetic attitude, your efforts to engage the interviewee and acknowledge their response will also constitute key elements in the establishment of rapport.

The person you are interviewing may have questions about what will happen during the interview. A listening and welcoming response mitigates uncertainty. Don't move on, in other words. Don't start collecting information before the meta-contract has been formed, which entails that there is a shared understanding regarding how you will communicate and what you will talk about. Once rapport has been established, you increase the possibilities of eliciting a relevant, accurate, and reliable explanation.

8

THE FIRST FREE RECALL

Interviewers with little or no knowledge of professional interviewing techniques will generally assume that it is at this moment, when the first free recall begins, that the interview starts. As should be clear by now, this is incorrect. Without preparations and rapport building, it becomes difficult to make the most of the free recall's full potential. But *recall* itself starts here. In this part of the information collection process, the interviewee is to be given a genuine opportunity to tell her version—what she feels is relevant. In this way, we can collect a lot of information without exerting influence through questions, we can obtain information we didn't know we were interested in, and we counteract the asymmetry of the interview by relinquishing control—we hand over some of the power.

It is a common misconception that an interview that begins with free recall will take too long. It is true that a free recall segment that is not introduced correctly can take time, but with a carefully planned introduction, the free recall will in fact save you time. Those who see the connection between the phases and do the groundwork in preparation for free recall will discover that it will produce a lot of the information you are actually looking for. The term "free recall" does not imply that this phase of the interview is not structured or managed. The point is that the flow of prompted information is relevant, sufficiently detailed, and otherwise uncorrupted by any influence on our part.

This phase can be compared to a farmer who needs water for his farm. For years he has walked to the brook carrying a 10-liter bucket, filled it up, and walked home. One bucket at a time. It was time-consuming and hard work. The water was often spilled on the bumpy road home. In the language describing the method for the investigative interview, we can say that the farmer's strategy contains many sources of error. But then he came up with a new method. The farmer laid a pipeline a little way up the river. The water now flows freely all the way into his house. Several hundred liters a minute. Just like the information that emerges during free recall. The flow of information moves more quickly, even though it took some time to install the pipeline. In a professional interview, we install the pipeline through good preparations, the establishment of rapport, and a thorough introduction to the free recall phase. He who tries and succeeds is thereby spared having to collect one bucket at a time of relevant information through many individual questions.

We often use the following exercise to illustrate how effective free recall can be.

The course participants are divided up into groups of three. Participant no. 1 is to be a witness and describe a person he or she knows well, but whom participant no. 2 doesn't know, such as a neighbor. Participant no. 2 is given five minutes to ask participant no. 1 questions with the objective of collecting as much information as possible about the neighbor's appearance. Five minutes. Not a second more. What neither participant no. 1 nor no. 2 know is that participant no. 3 (who they believe is just keeping time) has been instructed to keep track of the number of questions the interviewer (no. 2) asks the witness (no. 1) in the course of the five minutes.

All detectives know that the interview is a central part of their work. How skilled are they when competing with their colleagues on the use of interview techniques?

As far as we know, the record in Norway for the greatest number of questions in a five-minute period is 30, and that record was set by an experienced detective from a special investigative unit. We have also experienced around forty questions, a record set by a high-ranking police officer in one of the largest cities in the world. Forty questions in five minutes! Many of the questions were leading and as such not suited for collecting reliable information. We would remind the reader of the discrepancies between the testimonies of test subjects in Elisabeth Loftus's "car crash" study, discrepancies that arose simply because the interviewer changed a single word in the question.

A professional interviewer would address this challenge by using the memory enhancement techniques developed by Geiselman and Fisher in the late 1980s (cognitive interview techniques). By employing this research-based method, test subject no. 2 (the interviewer) helps the witness mentally return to a moment in the past, encourages the witness to picture the neighbor in question, and instructs the witness to take all the time he needs. The interviewer instructs the witness to mention all the details he can recall and to leave nothing out. Yes, the neighbor must be described in such detail that if this person were to come walking down the street together with 100 other people, the interviewer would be able to pick the neighbor out of the crowd.

"Do you understand the level of detail I want from your description?"

"Yes."

"Great. Now you have about four minutes to describe your neighbor. I will not interrupt you. Picture your neighbor and describe her in as much detail as possible."

Instead of asking 20, 30, or even 40 questions, the professional interviewer encourages the witness to describe the neighbor in as much detail as possible. Then the interviewer's task is to listen. If you try the exercise, you will witness what we experience every time. The interviewer who stops talking and listens for four minutes will collect the most information. The witness has the time and opportunity to "warm up" the network structures of her memory. The information about the neighbor is stored in different places in the witness's memory. Giving the witness time to concentrate also provides her with the opportunity to generate associations and hereby make the most of the potential of the memory's network structure.

As shown in the chapter "Psychology," under the subject of *false memories*, the interviewer influences the information elicited through his questions. A well-introduced free recall reduces the need for follow-up questions. Because our influence on the information is minimized, the information is more reliable, and by virtue of its reliability also more valuable.

A well-introduced free recall is like a Kinder Surprise Egg (where a chocolate egg surrounds a yellow plastic capsule with a small toy inside). Like the egg, free recall also gives us three things in one—we obtain a lot of relevant information, it is more reliable, and we have obtained it in an effective manner.

Unnecessary Questions

Analyses of police interviews of witnesses, plaintiffs, and suspects have disclosed substantial room for improvement in the formulation of questions. In the next chapter, "Exploration and Clarification," we will elaborate on the differences between good, bad, and potentially dangerous questions. A question can be considered dangerous if it risks contaminating the information collected. In the context of how we can best encourage free recall, the subject of this chapter, we will limit ourselves to listing all forms of questions in one category, quite simply because at this stage of the interview, all forms of questions are essentially viewed as unnecessary questions.

Specifically, we can say that unnecessary questions are those that could have been avoided.

The introduction to *the first free recall* is to be concluded by encouraging the interviewee to tell us everything of relevance within the framework for the interview outlined during the rapport establishment phase. Subsequent to this, our task is predominantly to listen. It sounds simple. But it requires in fact more knowledge, structure, discipline, and skills than traditional question-and-answer interviews, interviews that could be described as adhering to a form of ping-pong dynamic.

Without training, knowledge, reflection, or correction, it is the ping-pong dynamic that comes most naturally to most of us. We are socialized to believe that this is the most effective way to collect information. That is not strange, in that in many cases, it is true: "How much does it cost?" "Did you brush your teeth?" "What time is it?" "Have you done your homework?" This is how information is exchanged. Quickly, simply, and easily. Should we feel a need to know more, we ask again: "What homework were you assigned today?" Follow-up: "Was it difficult?" The quickest route to the answer we are seeking involves asking different types of leading questions. "Are you okay?" "Yes, just fine, thanks. And you, are you doing okay?"

If a neighbor or colleague actually goes to the trouble of explaining how they are doing, we will often start to feel uncomfortable in the situation, because we actually don't have a great need for information. We are just trying to be nice. The same holds true for the colleague who has just come home from vacation: "Did you have a nice time in Mallorca?" A quick confirmation is usually all we need to hear. A 15-minute account of how fantastic life is in the Spanish holiday paradise becomes inappropriate and awkward.

The dynamic is different in conversations that are deeper or more personal in nature. What is interesting about these types of interactions is that those who are good listeners are those who are showered with praise and enthusiasm. "He is such a good listener. I fell head over heels." Active listening is not restricted to couples. Your best friend is usually someone who listens when you need them to.

Without training, methodology, or reflection, research shows that most police detectives—even though curiosity is a part of their job description—will resort to the quick and easy version, the ping-pong dynamic. Question and answer, question and answer comes naturally. And this is true even though 50 years of cognitive psychology research has proven that the listening approach holds the greatest potential when the objective is to obtain relevant, accurate, and reliable information.

It is not only the police who fail to exploit the potential found in free recall. Actually, to the contrary. In Annika Melinder's studies of psychologists' interviews of children, the psychologists didn't fare any better than the police detectives (Melinder 2004). In some of the greatest legal scandals of our time, psychiatrists and psychologists have served as advisers for police interrogators (Alison 1998; Riksadvokatens publikasjoner nr. 3/2015; Fallon 2019). Neither are legal professionals and journalists any better equipped than the police in this sense. Job recruiters, child welfare employees, the school system administrators, and asylum authorities probably wish that good listening skills were taught as a given part of their professional training, skills that could then be honed by their motivation or enhanced through experience. The limited research that has been done on interviewing practice outside the context of law enforcement indicates that without a methodology and proper training, most people will adhere to a question-and-answer strategy. Slipping into a deep conversation mode with strangers seems counterintuitive. The clear message of the research would be to relinquish more control to the interviewee. To use the language of TV-hosts: Ensure that the guest becomes the star of the show.

For decades, the Canadian journalist John Sawatsky has taught an inter-view technique that resembles the CREATIVE method, particularly with regard to the use of the free recall and exploration phases. His cool and humorous statement about interview quality illustrates the proximity to our method: "When you speak more than the interviewee, it is a clear sign that the interview is not particularly good" (Sawatsky 1999).

In that we also know that the interviewee's memory will be influenced and altered by our questions, it becomes evident that we must do what we can to reduce the number of questions to a minimum. Eyewitness psychology lit-erature compares the memory to freshly fallen snow. Through the metaphor we can imagine that a recently experienced and untouched memory is like a blanket of pristine new snow. Every question asked leaves behind an impres-sion in the memory, like a footprint in the snow, and like the footprint, the impression becomes a part of the memory image as a whole.

During forensic investigations of a crime scene, the police are extremely careful about preventing contamination. Contamination of physical evidence such as blood, saliva, skin cells, and so on must be avoided at all costs. The police's crime scene tape illustrates this. Forensic scientists have developed a series of methods and procedures to prevent contamination of physical evi-dence, such as hair nets, face masks, gloves, and suits, all to preserve the integ-rity of the evidence.

So how do we work behind the crime scene tape in a professional inter-view, when the evidence we are collecting is oral? This evidence is every bit as important and vulnerable to contamination (influence). How can we ask questions protected by gloves, face masks, and hazmat suits?

The Hierarchy of Reliability

Figure 14, the hierarchy of reliability, is inspired by the research findings of one of Europe's leading experts in eyewitness psychology (Milne 2006). The figure, which resembles a funnel, summarizes much of the available research done on the impact of different types of questions on the quality of the answers. The connection between the type of question and the quality of the answers is presented according to two dimensions: the degree of detail (amount) and reliability (influence).

Figure 14 illustrates the eyewitness psychologists' findings, specifically that the quality of the information collected increases when the interviewee is encouraged—and given the chance—to explain freely and without intervention on the interviewer's part. Free recall enhances both dimensions: it provides the most reliable information (minimum of influence) and the greatest amount of detail, illustrated here by the color gray at the very top of the funnel.

This does not mean of course that the information we obtain through free recall is always reliable. But the information is ranked as having greater reliability because numerous studies have confirmed that in free recall the influence is reduced to a minimum. The quality of the information in any answer depends on how much or little we have influenced the explanation with our questions.

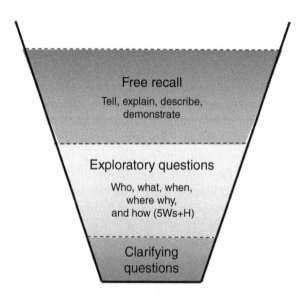

Figure 14 The hierarchy of reliability (inspired by Milne 2006).

A person who wants to tell the truth may still provide unreliable information. The person may also have been mistaken in their observations or interpreted something incorrectly. In Part 1 we have described several potential sources of error. The point here is to ensure that the interview and the questions we ask do not become a source of error in their own right.

During the first free recall, we facilitate the collection of information of the quality while we stay in the uppermost field in the hierarchy of reliability. The goal is to collect information in a way that minimizes our "footprint." What typically distinguishes professional interviewers from others is exactly their ability to prompt free recall in such a way that so much relevant information is provided that the need to ask exploratory questions is reduced to a minimum. When we later test the reliability of the information, we will benefit from the fact that we have influenced the interviewee's statement as little as possible through our questions.

In the next chapter, "Exploration and Clarification," we will address in greater detail the exploratory questions, 5Ws+H questions, and more closed and clarifying questions. As illustrated, these questions take us further down the hierarchy of reliability, because while such questions elicit less information, they also influence that information more.

Prompts

The difference between open and closed questions has with time become more or less common knowledge. But research on this subject is generating new knowledge and concepts all the time. The collection of evidence in professional interviews does not start with a question, but with a prompt. The chance of success is the greatest if we *prompt* free recall.

The interviewee receives a brief set of instructions and is subsequently encouraged to *give an account, explain, describe,* or *demonstrate*. The order we present in the following is not random, and the procedure has been developed based on research findings on the makeup and structure of the memory (see Part 1).

Instruction

We start the collection of information by encouraging the interviewee to tell their story. We do this simply, for example, as follows:

"I would like you to tell me everything you remember from the accident, in as much detail and as accurately as you can."

Without any form of instruction ahead of time, the prompt to start talking will not have the optimal effect. There is not really anything wrong with this prompt. It offers an open and neutral entryway to the subject we want to illuminate. But without more informative, memory-enhancing instructions in advance, explaining among other things the amount of detail you are looking for, you risk receiving a sparsely detailed and abridged explanation. You may then be obliged to abandon the first free recall without having capitalized on its potential and move into the exploration by asking follow-up questions. Without an adapted and clear introduction *before* prompting the interviewee to start speaking, there is a risk that the interviewee will not understand that they are supposed to switch into "deep conversation mode." The subconscious suggests a short and simple response. That is the most common and safest interpretation.

The more questions you have "on the list," the greater the need for instruction before the first free recall segment. When we have successfully introduced the free recall to the interviewee, we can sit back a bit, listen actively, and collect the most reliable form of information while simultaneously crossing one question after the next off the list. The information needs we have identified are filled by the interviewee, without any influence on our part. We are like the farmer: we install the pipeline. A good introduction establishes both the context and the quality of the information that emerges.

A successful introduction might result in the following:

The *job applicant* speaks about her motivation, what she can contribute, and why she believes she will succeed, along with detailed descriptions of previous experience and relevant training and education.

The *patient* opens up and speaks about underlying problems because the attending physician has succeeded in establishing a kind of rapport where it feels safe to open up.

The *politician* speaks about a difficult ethical dilemma because he experiences sincere empathy and a professional approach, and thereby trusts that the issue under investigation will be handled properly.

Research shows that our greatest possibility for success lies in following these five points:

1. *Inform the interviewee of the need for details.* The interviewee needs help to understand that we actually want an explanation that is so detailed that in other contexts it would not seem normal. Make it clear to the interviewee that you want the full story, with all the details, as if they were having a deep conversation with a sympathetic friend. A recommended procedure is to explain that it is your job to illuminate all relevant aspects of the case, but because you don't know all the details and extenuating circumstances, you now need help to understand—absolutely everything.

2. *Inform the interviewee that details must not be omitted.* In our daily lives we are not accustomed to including fine-grained details. We include what we believe is relevant, quick, and effective, enough so that the person we are talking to gets the point. A professional interview is different; the details

are often important. Research shows that instructing the person with whom we are speaking not to omit any details is effective. It prompts a more extensive free recall. It can be a matter of details the interviewee does not think are relevant, but which can be important for us. We explain that we would like to have all the details and that it is our job to determine what is relevant. Based on what we know about the structure and makeup of the memory, we can also explain to them that telling us one detail can cause them to remember others.

3. *Inform the interviewee that they have plenty of time.* Because it feels abnormal and strange to "run off at the mouth" with a stranger, we must help the interviewee to understand that details and specificity are not merely okay; they are what we want. We therefore remind the interviewee that we have plenty of time. This information must of course be adapted to the parameters for the interview. But even in a live television interview with a five-minute time frame, the host's assurances that time is not an issue foster good communication. "Relax. We have plenty of time." Even if the time frame is tight, this statement will not automatically make the guest talk up a storm. The guest is still aware that they are in a studio and that there is a time limit for the broadcast. But it can engender a sense of security and thereby better answers. If the setting is wholly different and the interviewee is reporting a rape, it is easy to accept that there are no time limits.

Nobody has unlimited amounts of time at their disposal. But before we become concerned about the free recall segment continuing indefinitely, it is important to remember that it is unusual for someone to continue an ongoing free recall for more than 10–15 minutes. In reality, thousands of professional interviews are done every day, where there is no time limit for the amount of detail in the first free recall, but where that portion of the interview is still not particularly long. The fact is rather that the majority of those who employ the method will be very satisfied if they manage to prompt a relevant, free recall lasting more than 10 minutes.

In practice this means that as professional interviewers, as *a basic principle*, we should always assure the person with whom we are speaking that we have plenty of time and encourage him or her *to take all the time they need to tell us everything.*

We will explain next the best way to introduce the first free recall when time is short. The procedure is similar to the management of expectations during *rapport establishment.*

4. *Inform the interviewee that we will listen.* Informing the other person that we will be assuming the role of the listener makes it easier for the interviewee to assume the role of the "deep narrator." Listening also implies silence

on the part of the interviewer, which the interviewee may experience as out of the ordinary. It is therefore also a good idea to inform the interviewee that the interviewer will be quiet in order to give them the chance to think and answer at their own pace. As stated earlier, the interview situation is unnatural, but with an empathetic establishment of rapport and instruction as outlined earlier, we will have a better chance of achieving our objective: An interviewee who feels secure about giving a detailed response when prompted *to tell, explain, describe, or demonstrate* everything she knows about the case, process, or topic for which we are seeking information.

In addition to informing the interviewee that we want to listen to what they have to say, it is recommended to inform the interviewee if we will be taking notes so as to ensure an accurate report and/or so we can ask follow-up questions afterward. As explained earlier, it can feel strange (and therefore disruptive) that the person with whom you are speaking is taking notes.

5. *Ask the person to mentally return to the situation.* Extensive research has shown that when we want to gather information from the episodic memory about a particular situation or event, context-specific mental reinstatement enhances recall. This holds true when the details of the matter under investigation are extremely important and we know that the interviewee will be asked to retrieve information from her episodic memory. Mental reinstatement is a recognized memory enhancement technique, but very few interviewees will employ it unless they are encouraged and receive guidance on how to do so. When it is natural and expedient, we must encourage and help the interviewee mentally to return to the place and time when information *encoding* took place (such as the scene of an accident or a meeting about which we want to know absolutely everything).

The contents of the introduction to free recall are of course important, but so too is the form. In other words, how we say what we say and how we behave. In order to succeed with mental reinstatement and help the interviewee to activate the memory's associative network, they must feel secure and relaxed. As explained in Part 1, it is fully possible to retrieve memories we wouldn't normally have access to. This requires peace and quiet, and concentration, which is then also one of the reasons why the establishment of rapport has such a central function in the method we are describing. Stress and nervousness occupy cognitive capacity and impair recall. The goal is to create as calm a situation as possible, so the person who is going to give a statement has the chance to associate freely. This requires concentration of the kind most of us need when trying to remember the contents of the syllabus during an exam. It is very demanding and is not common in the context of ordinary conversations. In addition to promoting a sense of security and calm, we must therefore help the interviewee enter this unusual state of mind. We do this through instructions. To ensure that this person understands the entire introduction, we should talk and behave calmly. We must metacommunicate, explain what we are about to do. We have already informed the person of the need for details, that we have plenty of time, and so on.

Memory Enhancement in Practice

Tell the interviewee that the goal is now to remember as much as possible. In order to avoid putting unnecessary pressure on the interviewee, make it clear that it is fine if they can't remember everything, but that you want to elicit as many memories as possible. A portion of the metacommunication must address how this part of the interview requires concentration, like an exam. The recommended procedure is to ask the person to imagine the surroundings, the buildings, the people, and the weather (the external context) and how they felt when the information was encoded: their mood, feelings, and state of mind (inner context). Because it is the sense impressions that are stored in the memory, researchers recommend that interviewees be prompted to think about exactly what they smelled, tasted, saw, heard, felt, and so on when mentally reinstating the encoded context.

The goal is for the introduction to trigger one or more pathways to the long-term memory. Each individual sense and emotion can trigger impressions from the other senses. Our task as interviewers is to spark associations but not lead or disturb them. The person who is mentally reinstating a past event will find associations best on their own. Combined, the associations will fill several of the missing gaps in the jigsaw puzzle constituting a memory.

Emotions and odor are the strongest memory triggers or pointers. Many of us have certainly experienced how a scent can incite strong memories, such as the aroma of Christmas cookies. Sounds can trigger corresponding memories, for example, when we hear a song that reminds us of a specific time or event. The point is that sense impressions can awaken memories through unconscious associations. This is what we will utilize in the interview situation.

The mental reinstatement must be done calmly and slowly:

Picture the surroundings ... the people/the buildings around you/the room you were in. ... What was the weather like? ... The temperature? ... What did you see? ... Could you smell anything? ... How did you feel? ...

The interviewee has now projected themselves mentally back to the situation in question and can "see" the surroundings. Then and only then has the time come to encourage him or her to explain, describe, or relate in detail what happened:

> When you are ready, I would like you to tell me everything that happened. Don't leave out any details.

For interviewers who are unaccustomed to using the recognized interview techniques we are describing here (cognitive interviewing techniques), it can feel odd to encourage the interviewee to "sniff your way back." But it works. As explained in Part 1, research shows that the cognitive interview techniques elicit 40 percent more information than interviews using traditional question-and-answer techniques. The same research shows that if we carry out the procedure described here, the interviewee will understand and follow the instructions without experiencing any embarrassment. Some will close their eyes, and they must feel free to do so. Others will look at the ceiling or stare at a point on the wall. Eye contact in this phase is not recommended. It feels like a teacher standing behind you during an exam and looking over your shoulder as you write. It is disruptive.

At this point, it is important to listen. Asking the interviewee at this moment if they would like a glass of water before they begin will destroy everything. The order in which the instructions are given is not random. Mental reinstatement requires concentration and must be the final instruction given.

The person who begins free recall will not necessarily choose to start at the point the interviewer thinks is natural. Our wishes and needs for an organized, chronological presentation must be put aside to allow for the potential found in allowing the interviewee's associative explanation to unfold freely. Memories are not stored in one location. One detail produces associations of other details. That is why it might seem as if the person doing free recall is jumping back and forth in their story. The most important thing is that they keep talking and keep recalling details. We can gather all the threads at the end.

The order in which you inform the interviewee of the first four instructions as described above (1–5) is not important, but if the nature of the case stipulates a mental reinstatement, it is crucial that this be the last item you mention as an interviewer, just before prompting the interviewee to speak. Some cases where this could prove relevant would be an in-depth television interview about an accident, an interview with a potential carrier in conjunction with a virus-tracking initiative, or when receiving a child's description of a serious incident.

It goes without saying, perhaps, but we will repeat it to avoid any misunderstandings: the memory enhancement techniques are used only when the objective is to retrieve as many detailed memories as possible about a specific event in the past. The techniques would be unsuitable, and indeed unnecessary, for an interview about a company's most recent quarterly figures or when an architect is trying to understand a principal's current needs and expectations.

Painful Details

If the person you are going to speak with has something difficult to tell you, it can be a good idea to explain that you have training in listening to the type of story the interviewee is going to share, that you are prepared to absorb all manner of information, and that you are used to addressing painful details. That it is your job. In situations where the contents of an answer can be dramatic or overwhelming, such as in the case of traumatic events, accidents, or other tragedies, we must take into account that the interviewee may be consciously or unconsciously withholding information, because she wants to "spare us" the most horrific aspects of the experiences.

Volume 2 of *Det kliniske intervjuet* (The Clinical Interview) includes a chapter about interviewing children traumatized by war. Here the well-known Norwegian psychologists Atle Dyregrov and Magne Raundalen (2002) give examples of rapport establishment, metacommunication, and an introduction to free recall/the interview, which are similar to what we present here in our method. In one of the examples, the psychologist states:

> My name is Magne. I am a psychologist. I know how to talk to children about sad things and about war. I know you have experienced horrible things. Your mother has told me this. [...] In order to understand how you feel, I will be asking you questions about your experiences in the war before you came to Norway. [...] You have to remember that no matter how awful what you have to tell me might be, I am prepared to hear about it.

Fifteen-year-old Benjamin Hermansen was attacked and stabbed to death outside his home in the neighborhood of Holmlia in Oslo, Norway, in the winter of 2001. One of Benjamin's best friends witnessed the murder. The following is an excerpt from the interview of this friend, as the interviewer introduces the free recall phase:

> I am accustomed to hearing stories about serious incidents. My job is to listen and take notes. Then I will ask you some questions afterward. Please tell me everything. Even the smallest of details can be significant. Don't leave anything out. Use all your senses. How did you feel at the time, did you hear anything, smell anything? Put yourself mentally back in the events of Friday evening.
>
> (Silence)
>
> The friend:
>
> "Friday evening. Around 11:15 p.m. Benjamin calls me ..."

The witness started in the present tense. This was a sign that the introduction had worked and that the witness had managed to mentally reinstate the Friday evening in question. The witness decided to start his statement before the murder. He was of course not interrupted. The introduction led to a lengthy, free recall of the murder and the painful details.

If it becomes too painful, of course, we do not just carry on. Take a break or stop. Professional interviewers do not compel anyone to keep talking, through neither pressure nor manipulation in the form of instrumental compassion, or other such tactics. We already covered the reasons for this in Part 1 when we addressed ethical perspectives. Interviewing trauma survivors is a specialized field with its own domain of expertise. In keeping with the ethos of investigative interviewing outlined in this book, the fundamental principles of this field should be covered. For an in-depth explanation of how the trauma perspective can best be preserved during investigations in which also the requirement for an objective investigation must be upheld, we recommend Jakobsen, Langballe, and Schultz (2017) and Jakobsen (2021) and their evaluations of the police interviews of the survivors of the Utøya domestic terrorist attack in 2011.

Varied and Adapted, but Always Open and Neutral

The introductory prompts for free recall are neutral, and a conscious use of such prompts implies that the words give no hint of the kind of information we are looking for. In this way we reduce the risk of influencing the answer by our perceptions and opinions, or what we might *think* is important or *believe* has taken place. Introducing a free recall in this way helps us to maintain an open mind and avoid cognitive traps. *Tell me about what happened in as much detail and as accurately as you can.* The prompt can always be used. The memory-enhancing components (1–5) are tools that can be used when suitable.

In some interviews, we meet people who have a limited vocabulary or other issues that make it difficult for them to speak. In such cases it is better to encourage them to demonstrate. Imagine a conversation between a child and an employee of Child Protective Services: "Show me exactly what the adults did." This can also be helpful in interviews when someone is going to describe an action.

Some actions will be easier to demonstrate than explain.

Most people would find it a challenge to explain how to ride a bike. It is also difficult for a soccer player to explain how to score a goal. Or to describe a practical process. When the Occupational Safety and Health Administration is investigating an occupational accident, it can be helpful to encourage the witness to demonstrate rather than describe: "Show me step by step how you operate the cardboard baler."

Another memory enhancement tool, which can also function well as a communication-stimulating technique, is to encourage the interviewee to draw. Drawing or illustrating with a pen and paper can be helpful in the context of both free recall and the subsequent exploration. Drawing can help the interviewee to focus and picture what they are talking about. They will then often recall more details. A drawing can also make it simpler for the interviewer to understand the contents of the free recall. Professional interviewers who have experience in using the method will often have a pen and paper on hand. Like the instruction to demonstrate, drawing is also recommended for people with a limited vocabulary, such as children. It often feels natural to explain and draw simultaneously.

Narrow or Broad? The Interviewer's Inherent Dilemma

There are clear parallels between the introduction to the first free recall and the management of expectations during the establishment of rapport. Both are central components of metacommunication. In both cases it is about communicating what we want the other person to talk about and how.

Based on the interview objective and the established parameters, we introduce the free recall in conjunction with the clarification of expectations during establishment of rapport. This procedure upholds the need for predictability and simultaneously ensures that the interviewee understands how much time they have and the level of detail they should provide.

The response to the prompt to describe accurately and including all details can be extensive. If we succeed with rapport establishment and the introduction to free recall, we can receive all manner of information about the subject under investigation—without having to ask a series of follow-up questions. When we use *tell, explain, describe,* or *demonstrate,* we can also receive information we didn't even know we were looking for.

The job recruiter had not planned to ask the applicant about any potential work conflicts at his last job. There was nothing in the case file to suggest the need for a question of this nature. But because the applicant felt secure in the situation and was encouraged to give a detailed description of his own career, the applicant included information about a conflict that arose with a former employer. Freely and of own volition, the applicant spoke about an episode in which he demanded better safety gear on behalf of the staff. This culminated in an ugly conflict with the management, a piece of information that could be of critical significance in the assessment of subsequent reference checks and a topic perhaps worth investigating further.

In order for the explanation to meet our defined objectives in an effective manner, we must inform the interviewee of the parameters for what is to be explained. Regardless of whether we want the free recall to be as long as possible or no longer than 45 seconds, we must make sure that the prompt has a defined focus and clear external frameworks. The prompt must leave no doubt in the interviewee's mind about what it is we want the free recall to address.

The challenge in both cases is that through our attempts to define the focus and external frameworks, we risk imposing so many limitations that we miss out on essential information, including information we didn't know we were interested in. Considerations for time, efficiency, and relevance, on the one hand, weighed against considerations for shedding light on all aspects of the case in its entirety, can be described and sometimes experienced as a dilemma.

Doctors who see multiple patients in the course of the same day must, like all professional interviewers, consider establishing a focus and external frameworks—or parameters—for the patient's free recall of ailments and relevant medical history.

A television host in the studio must set even narrower parameters. When the host has only three minutes, ninety or forty-five seconds to make an introduction, it must be clearly targeted.

An examiner who is going to commence his first interview with a director in a large and broad-ranging corruption case has much more time. This is inherent to the nature of the task. But if the examiner's prompt does not specify a clear focus and external framework, she also risks not receiving enough relevant information from the director's free recall. The director has his own perception of the case, although this will not necessarily correspond with the examiner's information needs. The interviewer can of course interrupt and/or try again, but this does not make for a good start. The risk is then greater of sliding into an exploratory phase where all topics remain unanswered.

It is possible to regroup, stay calm, and guide the interview toward topics we have defined as relevant. But meanwhile, time is passing and if a feeling of pressure arises, the interviewer will be more likely to fall into a ping-pong dynamic of questions and answers. It is easy to lose one's professionalism and revert to what comes most naturally.

Introducing a relevant, free recall is demanding and must be planned if the interview is to achieve its information-collecting potential. In this sense the doctor, television host, and examiner all face the same challenge. They are all well served by thinking through how the introduction to the free recall should be formulated, as early as during the planning and preparation phase. As stated earlier, it will then be helpful to have a clear idea of the purpose of the interview.

After the Introduction

During the introduction to the free recall segment, we are the active party. When the interviewee starts telling their story, the control is transferred and the interviewee becomes the active party and to a large extent decides what comes next. When the interviewee begins the free recall, we must demonstrate through our body language that we are interested in what is being said, while we allow the interviewee the time to think in peace. We can signal that we have relinquished control into their hands by leaning a bit back in our chair and waiting attentively, without further intervention. Now it is up to the interviewee to set the pace. Since we should preferably remain silent and not interrupt, small nods and short verbal confirmations indicating that we are listening (mmm, yes, okay) will constitute the extent of our contribution to and support of the free recall.

As stated, eye contact can be disruptive when the interviewee is deeply immersed in free recall of an encoded situation. Eye contact can also be experienced as disruptive when something is difficult to talk about or remember and the interviewee needs a break or silence to think. In this case, repeated attempts to make eye contact are experienced as pressure. Instead, you can focus on your outline or notes, yet always remain attentive and prepared to meet the gaze of the interviewee, should he or she seek eye contact. Someone who is speaking while in a state of deep concentration will typically have a need for confirmation now and then—to make sure you are listening, that you understand, that you are there. And you are. You meet their gaze and confirm this.

Active Listening in Practice

Active listening entails being able to tolerate silence. This is not just because we don't want to interrupt the explanation, with all the pitfalls this can entail, but also because silence can lead to a more detailed explanation that is less tainted and influenced by extraneous input. Especially during free recall, it is important to exercise discipline with regard to allowing silence to prevail in the situation. This is challenging, not just because it is difficult to remain silent during a conversation but also because it can be complicated to understand the full picture simply by listening. Now and then we must therefore interject a clarifying question. It is not unusual for a free recall narrative to be sprinkled with personal pronouns, such as "he," "she," and "it." To stay with the plot and context, we must from time to time ask questions. A single word cue can be sufficient: "She …?" "Yes, correct. Lena, she left the room, too …" The same applies to places, referred to using words like "there" and "here." "There …?" "Yes, at the office, and there was …" Then we return to a listening mode.

During the first free recall phase, we might be tempted to ask follow-up questions about the contents. Sometimes a simple follow-up question, asked at the wrong time, in the wrong way, is all it takes to interrupt the flow of free recall. At worst, it can lead to a breakdown in communication or loss of information. In Part 1, in the section about the memory's structure, we have explained why such questions should be avoided. A better strategy is to make a note of the question and save it for the phase following the free recall—the *exploration*. Such patience is often rewarded when the very issue we want to ask about is cleared up at some later point during free recall. The chance of such a reward increases if we allow the interviewee to "dance around" during free recall, allowing his or her own associative memory to take the lead.

Still, if asked at the right moment, in the right way, a question need not be experienced as an interruption, but instead further stimulate the free recall. In this way, recall is improved and becomes more detailed.

In a radio interview about bullying, a young girl said the following:

There was some emotional bullying, talking behind people's backs, sending notes, which can seem pretty innocent, but which actually wasn't at all, it was […] it was like they couldn't stop themselves from blurting out things that really hurt, they would say things like …

(silence)

"Things like what?"

What emerged in response to the question were many new, painful details and examples. The interviewer in this example was an active listener. The girl just needed a little help when it came to talking about her most difficult experiences. In this case the question is not an interruption, but rather an enhancement of free recall.

There are a number of ways to enhance free recall while it is ongoing. Although the golden rule is to listen and allow the other person to speak freely and without interruption, the interviewer can help the interviewee by selecting a key word or phrase from their explanation, if the interviewee should lose the thread or for any other reason the free recall should come to a halt. "You were frightened. Tell me more about that."

Taking note of or noticing key words ("frightened") while you are listening to free recall will come in very handy in the next phase when we will explore the key themes in further depth. "You said that you were frightened. Tell me more about that?" Then we can follow up on this later. "Why was that?" "How so?" "In what way?"

Summarize

To make sure that we have understood what is being said, it can be expedient to summarize before moving on to the exploration phase. To do so we must of course listen actively to the entire free recall and take notes throughout. A correct summary shows that we have in fact been listening, which is in turn a sign of genuine interest, empathy, and respect for the other. When we know that we are going to summarize the contents of the free recall, this makes us more alert. Because the information that emerges during free recall will provide the basis for the rest of the interview, a precise summary will also be useful in the subsequent interview phases. A summary creates a space in which we ensure that we have understood the information and cleared up any misunderstandings.

During or after the summary, the interviewee may have remembered more information and we may have come up with further questions. We take these questions with us into the next phase—the exploration. A final benefit of the summary is that it connects the interviewee to the explanation. If some information should later emerge that contradicts the explanation, which has been summarized and confirmed, it becomes more difficult for the interviewee to claim that we have misunderstood.

* * *

The introduction to the free recall phase is so fundamental that it should be planned. How broad or targeted should the introduction be? How do you want to stimulate and "fine-tune" the interviewee to ensure they provide the right amount of detail? An empathetic and informative establishment of rapport increases the chance that the interviewee will open up and tell their story. When the details are important, we must help the interviewee to understand that we want all of them. Based on the amount of desired detail and the time available, you must assess whether the use of memory enhancement techniques would be expedient. In keeping with the hierarchy of reliability, we subsequently introduce the recall phase as *tell, explain, describe,* or *demonstrate,* combined with *as much accuracy, detail, and precision as possible.* In this phase it is crucial to listen actively, refrain from interrupting, transmit empathy, and in this way prevent communication breakdowns. When the free recall segment has ended, and we have summarized the contents, we move on to the next phase, which is exploration and clarification.

9

EXPLORATION AND CLARIFICATION

We have prompted free recall, listened actively, and asked simple, clarifying questions where necessary, but for the most part, the interviewee has been in control and taken the initiative. The interviewee has assumed ownership of their own story. In the next phase of the CREATIVE model, the exploration and clarification phase, it is our turn to direct the interview toward the topics we identified during our preparations and topics that have become relevant during the first free recall segment.

Structure the Interview

Normally we begin by introducing topics that emerged during free recall as they will be fresh in the mind of the interviewee. We do so by introducing one topic at a time. Finishing one topic before moving on to the next makes it easier for the interviewee to concentrate and enhances their memory. Clues in the brain's network structure are activated and kept warm. Interviewers who jump back and forth between different topics, however, generate the opposite effect. Unlike the free recall phase, where the interviewee is encouraged to associate freely, and because of which they will frequently change the subject as they follow the lead of the memory's associative network, during this phase of the interview, a shift in focus will be experienced as disruptive when it is initiated by the other person.

This does not mean that in the exploration phase we ignore knowledge about the memory. Every topic is to be introduced in the same way as it was during the free recall phase. If the details of a given topic are of central importance and our aim is to retrieve information from a memory, it can be pertinent to initiate another mental reinstatement, in this case about the topic in question.

You said that you walked into a room where there was a table. Now I would like you to describe this room in as much detail as possible. Just like earlier, I want you to try to think back, but now to the moment when you walked into the room. ... Picture the surroundings ... the door ... the walls ... what was the lighting like ...? Did you hear anything? Did you notice any odors?

When you are ready, I would like you to describe the room and everything that was in it in as much detail as possible.

It is not often we that we will proceed as thoroughly and with as much detail as this when we want information about a subject. Sometimes it isn't necessary; other times we don't have time. It is far more common to introduce topics about which we want further elaboration by using a short and concise prompt: "Please describe the pain in your back in more detail" or "Please tell me more about the reasons you left your last job."

The memory is best enhanced, and our influence minimized, if we start at the very top of the hierarchy of reliability (Figure 14) every time we introduce a new topic. In a targeted interview, on the other hand, when we have perhaps only 45 seconds at our disposal, the interviewer must introduce the first free recall in terms of the specific topic identified by the preparations as most significant. "The government has decided to close the schools. How did you come to that decision?"

Regardless of the parameters for the interview, the next step will be to follow up with an exploration of the topic until it has been sufficiently illuminated. We are hereby descending on the hierarchy of reliability and "exhausting the topic" with open or exploratory 5Ws+H questions. In a short, targeted interview, this method can also be used:

You say that it was with a heavy heart that you decided to close the schools. Can you expand on that?

Or

When you say, "with a heavy heart," what do you mean by that?

We finish by summarizing and where relevant asking a closed but nonetheless expedient, clarifying question:

I understand now that it was a difficult decision to make, but does it have the support of all the parties in government?

Now we have reached the bottom level of the "funnel" in this short and targeted interview. Regardless, we are ready to introduce the next topic.

Normally we will have more time, and in the following we will describe the structure and the different types of questions in further detail. Flexibility on our part will almost always be required. The interview may require us to move up and down the hierarchy, but Figure 15 illustrates the primary structure of the exploration and clarification phase.

The first thing we must do after the free recall phase is to evaluate our own plan in terms of the information that has emerged. It is possible that we will be obliged to adjust our planned exploration.

The free recall and our active listening enable us to assess whether the alternative hypotheses we developed in the planning phase have been strengthened, undermined, or even disproven. We may also have come up with new hypotheses. New topics may have arisen, while others are no longer of interest.

In this ongoing process, the interviewer must rely on his or her own preparations. To ensure that the interview corresponds with the relevant questions of the investigation, in keeping with the principles of abductive logic, the investigation of facts and use of the 6 Cs will be helpful.

We must have the list of hypotheses in the back of our mind while we are listening and collecting information. Without this awareness, we will not be able to ask the right questions to test the hypotheses. In this way, the 6 Cs serve as structural keys to ensure active listening.

We have listened to the free recall—and we will continue listening (collect). Is the information relevant, reliable, and sufficiently detailed? (check). Does it correspond with the other information we have? (connect). What impact does the information have on our hypotheses? Have any of them been refuted and have any new hypotheses emerged that must be tested? (construct). Which questions should I ask to ensure that we test the hypotheses further and that the information is reliable? (consider).

By viewing the information in light of the hypotheses we have already formed, it becomes easier to see the information needs we have yet to fill and the kinds of follow-up questions we must ask.

After the free recall phase, perhaps only one question remains about a given topic. For other topics, it could be that we must ask more questions. A central point about the structure is that if we always open a topic with a prompt providing a focus and parameters, we are more likely to be spared having to ask a lot of follow-up questions.

After the prompt, we move down the funnel and follow up on the free recall of the topic through exploratory questions, 5Ws+H questions, and clarifying questions where necessary ("Does this mean that …?"). If we have information that contradicts the interviewee's statement, we address this toward the end of the interview. For more on this, see the section "Strategic Presentation of Critical Information."

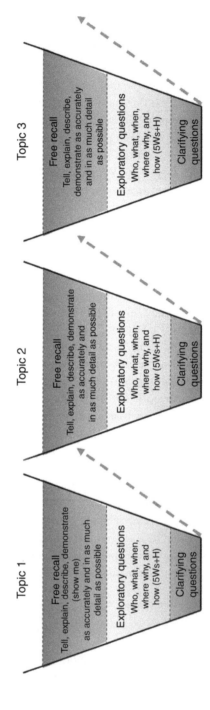

Figure 15 Structuring subject matter in the exploration and clarification phase. Inspired by Milne (2006).

The structure during the exploration phase functions in the manner of turning on lights in a darkened room. The neutral and open prompts at the very top of the hierarchy—*tell, explain, describe, demonstrate*—are like a ceiling light. We receive a lot of information, most of the things in the room become visible, but simultaneously, we will often not receive sufficiently detailed information. Everything on the table is perhaps not described in detail and the dark corners may be overlooked. It can also be a challenge if the person who is describing the room does not fully understand the parts of the room about which we are seeking information. Every part of the room is like a topic. As we move further down the funnel and begin asking the 5Ws+H questions, we replace the ceiling light with a powerful flashlight. The beam focuses on the details found in the part of the room—the topic—that is of particular interest. At the very end, when we have used the powerful flashlight, the 5Ws+ H questions, and achieved the clarity we need, we may find ourselves left with two or more alternatives. The smallest details are those that become visible first, when we twist the flashlight and the beam narrows: a specific, clarifying question. "Was it your wallet lying on the table?" Now we point the flashlight beam at the wallet, and only the wallet.

Transparent and Impartial

The prompts that we use to open up topics, how we can vary the use of them, and how we can connect them to 5Ws+H are illustrated in Figure 16.

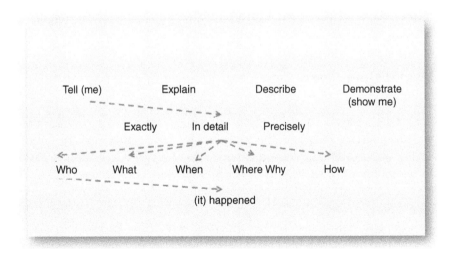

Figure 16 Alternative topic introductions. *Source:* Author.

As illustrated, the connections introduce different combinations that we can use as entryways to each topic. They all lead to an open prompt involving a minimum of influence on our part. Professional interviewers who have learned the method and have extensive experience in its application alternate the different combinations naturally. "Tell me exactly what happened after that. Describe exactly where you were standing. Explain in as much detail as possible how you experienced ..."

Everything that has been explained about asking questions during the free recall phase also applies during exploration. It is important to remember that the use of *tell, describe, explain,* or *show* must be communicated neutrally. As Elisabeth Loftus demonstrated in her studies of car crash witnesses, the reliability of the information we are collecting can be easily influenced by our questions. One word is enough. It doesn't matter if the question is open; it must also be neutral. "Describe the speed of the car when it crashed into the other vehicle" starts as an open question but is colored by an intention all the same. The open and neutral version could have been: "Describe the speed of the car at the moment of the accident." Alternatively, "when it bumped into" produces images of (and implies) a slow-moving car. "Smashed into" produces perceptions of high speed. "Describe the speed at the moment of the accident" offers no hints about the speed and is neutral.

The objective of asking neutral questions applies to all kinds of questions. Adhering to the theory to the letter throughout an entire interview is quite an achievement. You have come far if you successfully introduce topics using open and neutral prompts. Training and practice sessions followed by evaluations are required to make the method stick. What comes naturally is to converse the way we otherwise do in daily life. The professional interview requires a different approach.

5Ws+H Questions

The free recall of a particular topic will often not yield enough information. There may be questions that remain unanswered, or contradictions and misunderstandings, or the interviewee's explanation may be insufficiently detailed. During the exploration, you must therefore use the 5Ws+H questions: who, what, when, where, why, and how. When used properly—openly and neutrally—these questions open the door for more detailed information.

It can also be helpful to replace the word "why" with, for example: "What was the reason?" This is because the word "why" can in many cases sound like an accusation. The question "Why did you do that?" is sometimes understood as implying that maybe you shouldn't have done it. The question "why" can impede communication. It is less invasive to ask what the reasons might be, such as: "What was the reason you did that?" This implies that you may have had your reasons, and if so, I am interested in hearing about them. In other contexts, "why" can be replaced by "What was the idea behind that?" Another alternative can be: "What was the reason for …?" This invites the interviewee to explain and elaborate on the different reasons why a particular event came to pass. "Why," on the other hand, focuses more on motivation and can be experienced as being negative. "Why didn't you call for help?" implies that you should have called for help. The risk of a breakdown in communication is diminished if we rephrase the question: "What was it that stopped you from calling for help?" "I was terrified. He was holding the knife against my throat." The communication is not disrupted, and we have received an answer to our question.

The 5Ws+H questions can elicit both long and short answers. "What happened during production?" can trigger a long and detailed explanation, especially if the interviewee through the free recall instructions has understood that it is not only fine but actually preferable if they explain and elaborate. In other settings, the 5Ws+H questions trigger short answers. Toward the end of the exploration phase, short answers may be exactly what we want.

But if the interview is characterized by too many and prematurely posed 5Ws+H questions that are suitable for eliciting only short answers, the interview may have lost its potential as a source of reliable information before it really gets started. The questions "What is your name?," "When were you born?," "What is your address?," perhaps followed by clarifying questions "Were you there?" or "Do you know Lars?," introduce a dynamic through which the interviewee unconsciously understands that the nature of the interview is question and answer, question and answer. The interview will be quickly reduced to a ping-pong dialogue eliciting short answers.

Let us illustrate using a classic example from a police investigation. The police are questioning an eyewitness of a robbery. There is some urgency about getting information, such as about the getaway vehicle. The witness was standing outside the bank and got a good look at the car. Untrained detectives—especially if they are under pressure (in this case, time pressure)—can easily end up doing an interview like this:

"What color was the car?"
"What make of car was it?"
"How big was it?"
"How long was the car?"
"How old was the car?"
And so on …

The detective is essentially asking open 5Ws+H questions, but it is not effective. First, this type of interview takes a long time. The interviewer is talking just as much as the witness. Second, the procedure does not in any way enhance the interviewee's memory. On the contrary, here the interview jumps around at the behest of the interviewer (color, make, size, length, year). There is also a chance of incorrect information sneaking in here, even though the questions are apparently neutral and open.

It is not certain that the witness has any particular knowledge about car makes. The question "What make of car was it?" can lead to the witness more or less consciously deducing that it was a Volvo. The witness wants to help the police and answer their questions. The danger of such unintentional errors, often due to communication asymmetry, does not occur just in relation to the police. They can occur in all interactions in which the interviewee is eager to please or satisfy the person asking the questions. For example, if the interviews are about children who have experienced physical abuse, who doesn't want to help out? But we can also envision less-serious scenarios, such as a source who wants to go along with what the journalist is implying to help out and where the outcome is unreliable information. For the next question about the size of the car, the police risk causing the witness, who doesn't really have enough information about the car she saw, to start thinking about the size of a Volvo. After this interaction, the witness will have stored the memory of the incident with a Volvo in the starring role. There is a real danger of planting a false memory in the witness's memory.

Interviewers who are trained in the methods we describe here will perhaps spend 25 seconds on introducing the topic and then listen:

> "I would now like you to tell me everything you can remember about the car. Include all the details. Don't leave anything out. I would like you to describe the car in so much detail that on the basis of your description I will be able to identify the car in a parking lot where there are one hundred other cars. Do you understand how much detail I am looking for? When you are ready, describe the car in as much detail as possible."

Research shows that the 25 invested seconds—or 60 seconds at a relaxed pace—will in any case produce better results in the form of details and reliability. It takes no longer than that. When the witness starts talking and is allowed to explore his or her own memory freely, it is the witness, and not the interviewer, who is talking. As stated, there will then be a greater chance of our receiving information we didn't know that we didn't know. For example, the witness tells us that the car had a roof box, a sticker, or something else of this nature that we perhaps would not have asked about. It may well be that the witness will forget to say how old the car looked. That is completely fine, because we can ask about that after the witness has finished free recall. Then and only then do we follow up with "How old was the car?" With a good introduction, it may very well be that the rest of the ping-pong questions can be crossed off the list.

Clarifying Questions

At the bottom of the hierarchy of reliability, we find the clarifying questions. These are questions that are closed. If used incorrectly, they can be both leading and limiting, but when used properly, they have a function. Clarifying questions offer alternative answers. An example of this would be a yes-or-no question or a multiple-choice question. We use clarifying questions every day and all the time in our social interactions with friends, colleagues, and family. In this sense, it is not strange that they also emerge in professional interviews. "Did you enjoy going to school?" "How are you?" "Is it hot or cold outside?" Usually, such questions are fine. But when the required precision for the decisions we are going to make is as close to 100 percent on the mark as possible, this creates challenges and, in some situations, big problems.

If we use clarifying questions correctly, they have a function in professional interviews. They can be useful during the introduction but first and foremost toward the end of the exploration phase.

When eyewitness psychologists researched police interrogation methods for the first time, they immediately discovered that the police had no formal training and that they naturally brought their own social skills with them into interrogations. The police asked far too many closed and leading questions. In the research findings, the police detectives' manner of asking questions became the scapegoat for "everything that went wrong." The research had a down side. Training and manuals became too categorical. "Don't ask closed questions!"

When the British homicide detective Andy Griffiths did his PhD in forensic psychology, he decided to investigate this one-sided perception. He believed, based on his own long-term experience as a detective, that closed questions also have their place. In his doctoral work he introduced the category "appropriate closed questions" (Griffiths 2008). Today everyone who studies professional interviews agrees that on certain occasions and in response to certain phrases, closed questions are expedient.

Here we have chosen to call them clarifying questions. Most of them are suitable toward the end of every exploration of a topic, at the very bottom of the hierarchy. This is not because they necessarily produce unreliable information but because the questions don't elicit much information.

Clarifying questions can be especially expedient as a means of ensuring that we have met the information needs we have for a given topic. The interviewee may have given us a lot of information and we may have obtained many details, but nonetheless we need that final detail to reach the finish line. It can be a matter of a detail that we can't elicit by using 5Ws+H.

Think about the case against John. It is wholly fundamental to clarify whether or not John has been at the scene of the crime. For the topic "John's knowledge of the area," we therefore structure our exploration with an eye to determining whether John has for any reason been in the house or in the neighborhood. We have established that he has never worked at the house or in the garden. Neither does he know anybody in the area and hasn't spent time there for other reasons. And neither has he said explicitly that he has never been at the crime scene before the break-in on 24 Main Street. After having carried out thorough explorations, one clarifying question remains: "Have you ever been to 24 Main Street?" If he says yes, you explore further; if he says no, he is now locked into his account.

This procedure is particularly useful when the topic is critical in nature.

When consciously used to clarify something specific, we see that clarifying questions can serve many purposes. After summarizing, for example, it can be natural to make it clear that you have understood the explanation:

> "You told me you've had chest pain off and on for about two weeks. You also explained that you can't recall doing anything to set it off and that it's much the same each time. Have I understood your description of the chest pain correctly?"

Here the clarifying question also functions as a good, expedient entryway to the next topic: "Now I need to understand even more about the actual pain. Please describe it in as much detail as possible."

On some occasions it is necessary to determine whether or not a topic is relevant before we start free recall. The question can determine whether an interview is even required. In such a case the clarifying question will come first. Interviewing a board member about a decision made at the last board meeting can be a complete waste of time if the clarifying question "Did you attend the board meeting?" is not asked.

Clarifying questions can also have their place during the exploration phase. For example, "Was the decision you are talking about made before or after the board meeting?" As we will see later, a clarifying question like this can come across as very leading. If there is a danger that your wish for a quick clarification is in control here, we recommend that you choose a question from a higher level in the reliability hierarchy. In this case, the path can be by way of two exploratory questions: (1) "When was the decision made?" and (2) "When was the board meeting?" The answers will give us the information we are looking for, specifically whether the decision was made before or after the board meeting. Or we can receive an answer we hadn't expected when we asked the question: that the decision was made during the board meeting.

From the theoretical perspective of eyewitness psychology, it is reasonable to conclude that we should always choose the approach of the two open questions. It doesn't take long, does it?

Answer 1: "The decision was made in May."
Answer 2: "The board meeting was held in June."

The purpose of the clarifying, closed question is rendered immaterial. Asking two open questions is almost as quick. In reality, however, it is not always that simple. It is not given that the person will remember the date when the decision was made, but they will perhaps remember whether it was before or after the board meeting. In such situations, clarifying questions can potentially help us. Few people remember the date of the winter's first snowfall. Many more people will be able to give an answer to a clarifying question about whether the first snowfall occurred before or after Christmas. The connection increases the probability of remembering.

But if we are investigating a suspicion of insider trading, corruption, or something along these lines, the connection between the moment of the decision and the board meeting can seem leading and, in some situations, even be a giveaway.

Even when we use clarifying questions consciously and correctly, we must be aware how they in different ways will influence the person with whom we are speaking. Vulnerable individuals and children are especially susceptible to influence. A teacher, social worker, child welfare officer, psychologist, counsel for the victim, judges, or police detective would all be committing a cardinal error if they, for example, in a misguided attempt to clarify, were to ask a child: "Did daddy touch your penis or not?" When we aren't aware of the issues surrounding the use of clarifying questions, they can easily slide into the problematic categories that we discuss in depth in the following section.

Problematic Questions

There are several categories of questions that for different reasons are problematic and that we should therefore avoid. A common feature of these is that they elicit less information than their open alternatives and diminish the reliability of the answers. In addition to leading questions, which "put words into the mouth" of the person we are interviewing, problematic questions can offer multiple choices for answers, can have a negative implication, or have the effect of making the interviewee passive. Questions can be problematic if they are projections, a series of two or three questions, or long.

Leading Questions

Leading questions contain information that communicates something about the answer we are expecting to receive. In a conversation among friends, it is usual to help out or grease the wheels of the conversation, by suggesting answers we feel are plausible. Even if we start openly, we hasten to help out. "How are you doing?" "Yes, well …" "Are things perhaps a bit difficult now with him gone all the time?" "Yes, perhaps."

We must avoid this type of "help" in a professional interview. When we give a hint or suggest answers, we risk obscuring the correct information. Someone who has something to hide can simply choose a suitable answer, while someone who can't be bothered to do the tiresome job of thinking or remembering might choose the answer closest to the truth without elaborating on it by adding details. People who want to achieve a specific result can through leading questions understand what is the "right" answer and reply accordingly. This holds particularly true in asymmetric interactions such as a job interview or an interview about welfare benefits. It makes the information we receive less reliable. Even if the information we receive is correct, the question will make the information less credible because the person who answered responded to a hint or a proposed answer.

Unreliable answers to leading questions can occur both unconsciously and consciously. "Didn't you think it was a good plan?" Here the person asking the question is projecting his own thoughts about the plan into the question. The result can be that the person who responds consciously or unconsciously answers differently than they originally intended in order to avoid giving offence. The greater the asymmetry is in an interview, the stronger the influential force of such questions will be. This does not mean that leading questions function any better when we are carrying out interviews with a more balanced power structure. In interviews with greater symmetry, we also run the risk of leading, influencing, and irritating the interviewee with our questions.

When a class teacher at a middle school has a developmental interview with a troubled pupil and the pupil's parents, she has not necessarily consciously chosen to formulate her question as follows:

"I know you have been struggling to find your place here. But we are here for you, you know. All you have to do is speak up if you need some help from us. *But I think you are doing better now, aren't you?*"

There is nothing wrong with the empathy of this question. But there is something fundamentally wrong with the way the question is asked. It is leading, and the pupil will probably interpret it as meaning that the teacher wants a confirmation of her perception of reality. The answer will then often be:

"Yes, I'm doing a little better."

Even though it is absolutely not certain that he is doing better.

"That's good to hear! That's what we thought. Do you think we need to talk about it anymore?"

"No, we don't have to."

"Great! And I've noticed that you're doing better in math, too …"

If the teacher formulates the question more openly, clearly communicating her desire for the pupil to talk about his experience, she may receive a completely different answer.

"If you were to try and tell me a little bit about how you feel in class, what would you say then?"

"I don't really know …"

"No pressure. Just think a little bit about how it is when you're in the classroom."

"It's kind of scary."

"Okay, scary how so?"

"I'm afraid to say anything."

"What do you think is the reason for that?"

"Josefine and Elsa will laugh at me, for sure. Maybe not in class, but during recess."

"What is it that makes you think that?"

"They did it in elementary school and they keep doing it. It's just that now nobody notices it."

One or more leading questions in such an interview can have hugely negative consequences and lead to consequential errors.

Multiple-Choice Questions

These are also leading questions. Through multiple-choice questions, we lead the interviewee because we rule out all other alternatives beyond those we propose. In this way, the questions also become closed. "Were you driving at 40 or 50 miles per hour?" "Tall or short?" "Was it John, Paul, or Ringo?" There is always a 5Ws+H option that both can and should be used to create an opening to the information that interests us: "How fast were you driving?" "How tall was she?" "Who was it?" Multiple-choice questions are reminiscent of clarifying questions, but unlike expedient clarifications, the problematic version is more like what appears to be an innocent expression of curiosity that both could and should be formulated openly. From the perspectives of both eyewitness and decision-making psychology, the alternatives given can create problems due to what the related reference literature calls the "anchor effect"—an unconscious tendency to base oneself on the alternative offered by adjusting the answer according to "the anchor" that has been established: "What do you think? Are we talking about embezzlement in the amount of more or less than one million?" Maybe the interviewee was thinking that it was a matter of tens of millions but becomes uncertain and answers: "More than a million, maybe a few million."

In other words, there are several reasons why multiple-choice questions should be avoided, and as stated, there is always a more open alternative question we can ask about what we want to know: "How much money are we talking about?"

Closed questions. This is a blanket term for questions that allow only a few alternative answers. The most common are yes-or-no questions. Multiple-choice questions are also closed. A simpler description is that closed questions are all questions that are not open. They don't start with an interrogatory word (5Ws+H), but instead begin with a verb. "Are you tired?" Although closed questions are not necessarily leading, they produce more problems, problems corresponding with those of leading questions. They enhance neither the communication nor the interviewee's memory. The danger of slipping into a ping-pong dynamic, where you end up asking a long list of questions, increases. Our takeaway in this case is many short answers. Neither do we receive a response to what we don't ask about. The overhanging danger is that some of the closed questions will become leading.

Negatively charged questions. Another way in which we "help" is to ask negatively charged questions. "You perhaps don't remember who said what?" The subtext of the question is that it would have been nice if you remembered, but if you can't be bothered to think back, you don't have to. And that's fine. But in a professional interview, it's not fine. Because the purpose of the interview is to obtain information, we must ask questions that require answers: "I'd like you to describe for me exactly who said what in the meeting." The open question encourages the person with whom we are speaking to reflect: "Yes, who actually said what … I know that it wasn't Jens because …" Unlike negatively charged questions, open questions stimulate activation of the brain's network structure and as such are memory enhancing.

Passivity-inducing questions. This is a type of question we use a lot when socializing with others, but which can lead to the same problem as negatively charged questions: "Can you remember who said what?" By asking the question in this way, we don't require the other person to give it any thought. Instead, they are given the option of saying they don't remember. The interviewee can choose to be passive.

Questions containing projections. These are questions that contain our interpretations as interviewers. Through such questions we attribute our own feelings, motives, or characteristics to the other person. If, for example, we ask a fireman, "How does it feel to be such a big hero?" the question might serve its function, but only if our interpretation of his experience is correct. That he sees himself as a hero. And that is something we can't know until the fireman has told us so, voluntarily, without being prompted. If he doesn't view himself as a hero, he may even protest about such an assumption, "I'm no hero, I'm just doing my job." Then we won't receive an answer to our question. The objective was to learn something about how he feels when saving people. When we project our own views into our questions, we forget that it is the other person who is supposed to inform us of their feelings, motives, or experience. When we project, we present an interpretation that they can object to or accept without having to think, something they may choose to do rather than take on the task of delving into a difficult subject matter or what they actually and initially thought. If someone cries, instead of saying, "I understand that this is difficult for you," we can say instead, "I see that you're crying. What is the reason for that?" Or "What are you thinking about?"

In addition to the risk of our receiving information that has been influenced, questions informed by our projections undermine the ongoing conversation. By asking questions based on our interpretations, we can give the interviewee the impression that we aren't listening to them, that instead we are interpreting their words through the parameters of a preconceived notion. This can undermine the experience of empathy and respect, which in turn undermines trust and the motivation to share information.

Questions in a series. When we ask several questions in a row, there is a great risk of our not receiving useful information in response to any of them. "Why did you change your mind on this question, and when did you understand that you couldn't stand by what you said earlier? And have there been any reactions to your about-face?" The person who thinks the questions are uncomfortable or difficult to answer will choose to answer the easiest question. Even those who are willing to answer a series of two or three questions in a row can have difficulties remembering. If they answer the first question the best they can, they may have forgotten the second or third questions by the time they have finished. The information related to the different questions can be stored in different places in the network structure and therefore be more difficult to retrieve because the interviewee is obliged to "jump" back and forth between subjects without having the time or opportunity to concentrate or activate the right pathways in the structure. Then we must ask the question again anyway. The advice is simple: ask one question at a time.

Long questions. When a question is long, it can be difficult for the interviewee to understand what they are being asked. The longer the question, the greater the risk of it also containing information that influences the interviewee. This kind of information could be terms, information, conditions, hints, suggestions, words, and turns of phrase. We have already discussed spin. Long questions also provide openings that will enable the interviewee to spin. They can make it easier for the respondent to latch onto information found in the question and adapt their answer accordingly. It is also easy to suspect those who ask long questions of being more concerned about their own questions than the answer. The person asking the question uses the occasion to demonstrate his knowledge and analytical abilities. The question then often becomes just a monologue in disguise.

Sawatsky's Method

John Sawatsky uses a metaphor to illustrate the importance of good questions and neutrality. He likens the interview to a crystal clear window that becomes dirtier and dirtier, as leading questions, expansive questions, contentious questions, statements, and hypotheses are presented. The view is increasingly obscured. "Keep a clean window." The parallel to eyewitness psychology's analogy of pristine snow cover and footprints we describe in Part 1 is clear. Not only do problematic questions influence the interviewee's recollections and memory, they also have an impact on the reliability of the answers. Sawatsky holds that most questions asked by journalists today suppress rather than generate information. Sawatsky's method is outlined in the book *Talk Straight: Listen Carefully* (2001) by M. L. Stein and Susan F. Paterno. Here is a summary of his expert advice.

1. Ask neutral, open-ended questions. Start with questions about causes: "What happened?" Processes: "How did it happen?" Motivation: "For what reason did you do that?" Fill in the blanks: who, where, when. There are also a few traps we can walk into, even if our intentions are good and the question is open-ended. "How do you feel?" can produce good answers but can also be a trap. If you ask a mother who has just lost her child this question, an employee who just lost her job, or an athlete who has just achieved the victory of his lifetime ("How do you feel now?"), the question will almost always fall flat. This is because in the these situations, the interviewees don't know what they are feeling. They haven't had time to consider or reflect on it. The question can also be perceived as rude since the answer is often obvious and provokes a kind of counter question: "What do you think?" Sawatsky states you must wait until the source has had time to digest and reflect upon what has happened. Only then is it fitting to ask this type of question, and only then will the question perform its intended function.

2. The more a question huffs and puffs, the more it blows down. The more information journalists pack into a question, the more the information a source will leave out. "Less is more." Short questions elicit better answers; succinct, dramatic, focused responses. Sawatsky is adamant in his assertion that long, rambling questions will usually elicit lengthy, rambling, replies or curt, confused responses. Intricate questions containing opinions and hidden assumptions provide room for many interpretations, different kinds of answers, and an entire menu to choose from if the person doesn't feel like answering and would rather reel off a prepackaged message.

3. Help people to open up by using a clearly defined strategy. A strategic approach is especially important when the subject matter is difficult for the interviewee. An example about schoolchildren and food will illustrate this. A reporter was interested in testing a hypothesis that only one-third of the elementary school pupils in Edmonton, Canada, ate breakfast before coming to school. The reporter interviewed the children about the missing breakfast by asking direct questions: "Did you eat breakfast this morning? The answers were unreliable ("Yes, I did"), presumably because the children were socialized to deny both that they were hungry and that they had parents who didn't prepare meals for them. By asking a series of open-ended questions, with the objective of obtaining reliable information, a completely different outcome was achieved. "What was the first thing you did when you got up this morning? Then what? And then?" Follow up with similar questions until the story reaches the time when child arrived at school. If the pupil didn't mention a word about breakfast in his or her answer, it was reasonable to conclude that they hadn't eaten breakfast.

If the reporter had proceeded on the basis of this book's method by using free recall prompts, she would have instead started with "explain, describe, tell," rather than 5Ws+H questions. And if the exploration, including the 5Ws+H questions, hadn't obtained all the information, she could in closing ask the clarifying question: "Did you eat breakfast today?" Regardless, the reporter's open technique worked well and illustrates the strategic approach we are describing.

4. Establish agreement. Interviewers and sources must agree on some fundamental facts. Otherwise, the reporter will spend the better part of the interview convincing the source to accept their version of the story, through the use of mild coercion and leading questions. "You have to admit ..." "Is it really true that ..." For example, when the media had evidence that President Bill Clinton had had sex with an intern in the White House, the journalists should have first reached an agreement with Clinton on a definition of the term "sexual relations." Clinton was able to deny his flirtation quite easily by denying that what had transpired (or hadn't transpired) amounted to sexual relations.

5. Build the interview on the answers, not questions. People find it easier to say something voluntarily than to be forced to admit something. Instead of introducing another prepared question, it will therefore often be less intimidating if we follow up on what the source has said. When the source makes a claim, follow up by asking what she meant by it or if there is anything that supports her claim. "I think in fact those actions were way over the line." "Okay, how so?"

6. Put the burden of proof on the source. Follow-up questions are central in terms of acquiring more details and in-depth answers. As described earlier, base your follow-up on what has been said and ask the interviewee to elaborate, preferably using the exact words in the follow-up questions as those used in the answer when you are exploring. These can be words and phrases we have picked up on during the first free recall and exploration phases. By using exactly the same words, we avoid introducing new conditions into the interview and it becomes easier to get the interviewee to explain what they meant. We also show that we are paying attention and are interested in the answer.

In this way they will carry "the burden of proof" for their statements— they must explain what they have said. "When you say uncomfortable, what is it that you mean by that?" They thereby also become accountable and are simultaneously given ownership of their own statement. What they are telling us is not influenced by the introduction of new material. It isn't always necessary to use key words either; it can be sufficient to refer to them indirectly. "How so?" "What happened then?" "What was the reason for that?" This shows that we are listening, that we are curious and empathetic. But we must start with open questions, basing our questions on an answer other than yes/no.

When we ask closed questions, on the other hand, as interviewers we carry the burden of proof. This makes it easier, for example, for the interviewee to respond in keeping with his own planned message, to spin.

In an interview with the builder in charge of a project that went way over budget and was delayed many times, the journalists' questions were initially closed:

> "Does this final delay illustrate that you never should have taken on this huge job?" Here the interviewer carries the burden of proof. Besides, the question makes it very easy to respond "No."

This short answer fulfills the contract between interviewer and interviewee. A yes/no question has been asked, with an answer that is given. The interviewee is then free to supplement with a planned message. "This is a large and extremely complex project that would have been quite a challenge for anyone."

The interview continued in the same style, and the journalist received no new information about or explanation for the postponement of the building project. In a subsequent interview, the builder received an open, neutral, and precise question:

> "How would you personally characterize the overall work progress of the building project?"

> "Clearly we must acknowledge that there are a number of things that could have been done differently and better."

Here the burden of proof is activated. The interviewee has said that they could have done "things differently" and then it is merely a matter of follow up.

> "Such as what?"

> "We could have worked more efficiently during the planning and preparation phase."

Here another burden of proof is activated.

> "What do you mean by that?"

> "What we know is that this has been a formidable challenge and we should have employed more people at an earlier stage than we did."

The man first received so-called critical and tough questions, but this did not produce any results. But neutral, apparently simple questions elicited his own reflections and thereby new information. In short, to paraphrase Sawatsky, don't ask tough-sounding questions. An easy question to answer will often be the one that sounds tough (Are you racist?), while easy-sounding questions are often the tough ones (How would you explain that?)

The Top 10 Off-the-Shelf Questions

John Sawatsky has given examples of questions that in his studies functioned extremely well in many different situations. He calls them "off-the-shelf-questions," because they are questions that are handy to have in your personal interview inventory for use whenever you might need them. Here is a list of Sawatsky's "top 10 off-the-shelf-questions":

- What happened?
- Why is that? (Resist temptation to add "Is it because of X?")
- What do you mean? or What do you mean by that?
- What were (are) the options?
- How is that? or How is it that so-and-so can say X and do Y?
- What does this mean?
- How did you deal with that?
- What was the turning point?
- What did he (she, they) say?
- What is (was) it like?

How Do You Ask the Question?

In the establishment of rapport, we form the basis for trust and a shared under-standing of what we must do in the interview—ask questions—and of our role. But this rapport and trust is not established once and for all. Situations can arise, such as misunderstandings and communication breakdowns, because of which the rapport and trust must be reestablished during the interview. And to prevent communication breakdowns, it is important to think about *how* you ask your questions. What kind of intensity, tone of voice, and body language do you have? Do you have a twinkle in your eye and a smile, or are you behaving in an accusatory and aggressive manner? The style, of course, depends upon the subject matter and context. Body language is much more important when expressing feelings than when explaining a mathematical for-mula. Questions that start with *why* illustrate this well. "Why did you do that?" can as stated previously be perceived as an accusation. That is also why the police have rephrased it, in ways such as "What were the reasons for your choice of that strategy?" But it may be sufficient to adjust your tone of voice and body language and add a brief "do you think" at the end? "Why did you do that, do you think?" This is because there are many questions that can potentially seem harsh if expressed adamantly. "What do you mean by that?" "Give me examples of that!" and many other open questions or prompts are in and of themselves difficult to answer, because they require thought, reflection, and recollection. All questions should therefore be softened through tone of voice and the expression of genuine curiosity and kindness. The latter can be initiated simply by using the word "please."

"Please, tell me in detail what you saw that morning."

This approach must be calibrated through something as mercurial as personality or suitability. We are not making a bold statement when we say that the requisite flexibility comes more naturally to some interviewers than to others. Some people have a greater aptitude for empathetic communication. There are some people who have an easier time finding a rapport with others, who have an inherently gentle nature, and who on the force of their personality and approach are perceived as more trustworthy than others—before the work of trust-building has even commenced. Call it social intelligence if you like. The point of this model is that it is also supposed to compensate for any deficiencies we might have in the manner of naturalness and experience, also on this point. By following the procedure outlined here, it is easier to establish and maintain a good rapport with the interviewee, even if you are essentially a more introverted kind of person. It is also true that everyone can improve with practice and evaluation. For that reason, evaluation is also included as a phase of a professional interview.

In the chapter about planning and preparation, we saw that researchers from the University of Liverpool have identified what is required to persuade people who initially are unwilling to provide information. They found that the behavior and attitude of the person leading the interview had the greatest negative influence. *How* you ask questions, *how* you behave, and *how* you manage—or don't manage—to show empathy and genuine curiosity was decisive. "Bullshit doesn't work," as Alison et al. (2013) concluded in summarizing their analyses of thousands of hours of police interviews of terror suspects. Alison and his colleagues saw that the best interviewers seemed genuinely curious and didn't just appear to be curious. Here one finds the distinction between those who really endeavor to adhere to the method and those who just follow a formula.

Check: The Devil's in the Details

As explained, the purpose of a professional interview is to collect relevant, reliable, and sufficiently detailed information. The idea of a shortcut to the "truth" is tempting. That's why there is no shortage of stakeholders armed with new business ideas who will try to sell us the latest, most refined method or mechanism. Typically, the sales trick lies in the promise of access to "the truth" with 99.9 or 99.8 percent accuracy. In Part 1 we disclosed the findings of independent studies that tested the products being sold. Scientific studies reveal that there is no shortcut to the truth.

Because all the information we gather through professional interviews is of necessity shaped by human beings' subjective assessments and interpretations, we must do what we can to corroborate the information we collect. In the exploration and clarification phase, we have the opportunity to obtain details that can be verified.

"The devil is in the details" is a concept well known from crime fiction, television series, and movies. There is a reason for that. Detailed information that can be corroborated and substantiated by external facts has greater value than explanations that cannot. It is in the perspective of cross-checking that the degree of detail becomes relevant. The details of an explanation contribute to making it possible to verify the information and provide a more informed and secure basis for drawing conclusions (Rachlew & Fahsing 2015).

The most important thing we can do to test reliability is therefore to seek information that can be tested against external facts. Because there can be other explanations for the information that the interviewee gives than what they personally believe to be the case, or communicate, it is our task to ask follow up questions that are suitable for disclosing and testing other plausible interpretations of what they have experienced, observed, or claim to know.

An investor will need to acquire a lot of information about a company when considering a purchase of ownership shares. It is not sufficient to take the company at its word, accepting its assessment. The investor must collect detailed information about the figures forming the basis for the company's claims. Without such details, there is a greater risk of a bad investment. The objective must be to obtain details that can reveal background information. In this situation, an interview between the investor and the management of a company is an important source of information. It may well be that the company's own assessment is solid—the way a report to Child Protective Services can also prove correct—but we won't be able to determine this with sufficient certainty until we have enough details, details that can be corroborated through the information we have or will subsequently obtain.

To evaluate the reliability of the information we collect, we must obtain details that disclose the primary source, in other words, information providing as detailed a picture as possible of where, when, how, and under what circumstances the information arose or was initially made known. Using a fire scene investigation as an analogy is illustrative here: the investigators must establish where a fire started before they can say anything about its cause. If an interviewee tells us what was said in a meeting, the reliability of the information will clearly depend upon whether the person attended the meeting or has merely read the minutes.

When police collect information from eye witnesses, they gather information about factors they know will have an impact on the reliability of information elicited from the episodic memory of an interviewee. To ensure that the police don't forget this, a checklist has been created based on the acronym ADVOKATE.

Other professions can develop their own helpful checklists: What do we need to know? Which details must we clarify before drawing conclusions about key information? What questions must we ask to test the reliability of the information we collect? When dealing with eyewitness accounts, the police must make sure that their exploration procures answers to the following

A	Amount or length of time the witness had the suspect under observation
D	Distance between the witness and the suspect during the observation
V	Visibility conditions during the observation
O	Obstructions to the observations – whether they temporarily or partially inhibited the observation
K	Whether the suspect is known to the witness in any way
A	Any particular reason the witness has for remembering the suspect or event
T	Time the witness had the suspect under observation and the amount of time elapsed since the event
E	Errors in the description provided by the witness compared with the actual appearance

Source: R v Turnbull [1977] Q.B. 224, UK.

An essential aspect of such checklists is that an interviewee's inability to provide information is also to be documented: "The witness did not see any vehicles parked outside."

A real-life case from Oslo illustrates the importance of the checklist: A woman had reported a man she claimed had taken nude photos of her in her bedroom. The police went to the woman's apartment and there they received an explanation. The woman told them that she had been lying in bed naked, when she suddenly discovered that a man in the building directly across from her own apartment was standing in the window taking photographs of her with his mobile phone. She was sure of this. The police went across the street to the building and received an explanation from the man who supposedly had taken the photographs. The man's initial responses indicated that he didn't understand what the police were talking about. The police went over to the window and looked down towards the woman's bedroom window. There was a tree between the man's and the woman's windows. Due to the distance between the buildings and the position of the big tree, it was difficult even to see the bedroom window from the man's apartment and therefore also impossible to see what was going on inside. The tree had created a kind of keyhole effect: the woman could see the man clear as day from her window, while it was impossible for him to see her. It turned out that the man had been standing at the window at the time in question, with his telephone, but he hadn't taken any pictures. He had been texting with a friend. What the woman had believed to be the case was quite simply impossible.

Strategic Presentation of Critical Information

In the chapter about preparations, we introduced the term *critical information*— information that can be demanding for the interviewee to address during a professional interview. This can be information that indicates that the interviewee may have made a mistake, withheld information, or tried to cover something up. If the interviewee has not shared information that explains the critical information during free recall or our exploration, we have reached the phase of the interview when it can be appropriate to present information that we have held back for strategic reasons.

Before presenting the critical information, we must be certain that we have covered all other plausible explanations in our explorations. Let's go back to the case of the burglary suspect John whose fingerprints were found on the broken windowpane. In the exploratory phase we have investigated whether John had a legal right to enter the house, if he had been to a party there, if he had done work on the house, and so on. If John has ruled out all of these alternatives, we find ourselves in a situation where the only possible explanation for the fingerprint is that he is the burglar. Then and only then is it tactically correct to present the critical information.

The police are not the only ones who will experience receiving a statement that doesn't correspond with critical information in their possession. This will be the case for many different types of professional interviews. It is still interesting to note that police detectives who had been raised in the former interrogation tradition often experienced the situation as uncomfortable. They were trained to "confront" the person they were speaking with or blindside them by presenting the critical information. But the strategy we are describing here does not involve a confrontation and for that reason need not be uncomfortable for those asking the questions. At this point the interviewer has actively searched for alternative explanations, but hasn't found any, in contrast to former practice in which the confession—an admission—was often the goal of the interview. In keeping with the fundamentally abductive logic of our method, another, more open, mindset is stimulated: Maybe we have overlooked something? Maybe there is a straightforward explanation that we have failed to identify?

That is why we *present* the critical information and invite the interviewee to explain. The presentation of the critical information is done in the same way that we have asked our questions throughout the entire interview: with an attitude of genuine curiosity and inclusiveness. In the Child Protective Services case about the boy with the bruises, we would proceed as follows:

Thank you. Now I think it's suitable to summarize a bit before moving on: My understanding is that your son, Jonas, is an active boy, but that he can't be described as hyperactive. He is struggling a bit with some subjects and can be quiet at school, but he is content. He has, as far as you know, not been involved in any fights, he doesn't practice martial arts or extreme sports, skateboarding, BMX cycling or anything like that. Jonas doesn't have osteoporosis, hemophilia or any other such medical condition. He broke his arm when he fell off his bike last year, but beyond that he has not been involved in any other serious accidents.

As I said by way of introduction, here at Child Protective Services we have received a child protection alert from the school, and we have therefore started an inquiry. One thing the school mentioned in the alert is that they have observed on a regular basis that your boy comes to school with fresh bruises on his body and that he hasn't wanted to talk about the injuries. Health personnel have taken photographs of the bruises, there are several of them, all very visible, found on different parts of his body. What concerns us is that the bruises have occurred on different occasions. Now I would like you to tell me everything you know about these injuries.

In keeping with the strategy, the interviewer has throughout the entire interview sought information that could provide a natural explanation for the bruises, in other words, tried to determine whether the injuries could have been inflicted in some way other than through physical abuse. The parents have received the opportunity to speak freely about their son's upbringing. The interviewer has checked out relevant hypotheses through exploration of the subjects "extreme sports," "medical explanations," "accidents/incidents," but so far none of these inquiries have uncovered information that can explain the bruises. This of course strengthens the hypothesis of physical abuse, but there could still be another explanation for the bruises—causes that we haven't identified as alternative explanations.

The parents may have withheld information about issues that they find difficult to talk about. The boy might have an aggressive brother, or he may have begun practicing self-harm. Perhaps the information from the school is incorrect or the interviewer has misunderstood certain facts. Now the parents receive an opportunity to explain. Regardless, in the interests of obtaining more information about the subject in question, it is important to preserve an empathetic approach when presenting critical information, rather than becoming confrontational. An accusatory confrontation can break down communication at the end of the interaction, at the very moment when it is more crucial than ever to keep the conversation and the interview moving forward.

As stated earlier, there are a number of reasons why we postpone the presentation of critical information. First of all, a person with nothing to hide is given a chance to demonstrate his or her innocence, without being influenced by other information from the case. This will among other things counteract suspicions of fabricated or revised explanations. The strategy hereby strengthens both the reliability and the credibility of anyone who has no intention of withholding information. Second, the procedure makes it more difficult for the interviewee to withhold information. Invented, plausible explanations have already been ruled out. And finally, the most important point of all: the strategy stimulates an open mindset. We are looking for alternative explanations and hereby counteracting the insidious features of cognitive traps.

It goes without saying that when the parents are presented with the critical information, they may experience this as difficult. If there is a plausible explanation for the bruises, and the parents have unconsciously withheld this information, they will now have a chance to explain the cause of the injuries. As an interviewer you should in such a case include the explanation as a separate item in the evaluation of your own process. Should we have listed this explanation as one of the hypotheses during our preparations? Did we miss something, or did we simply not have the basis for doing so?

If the parents have no plausible explanation for the bruises and/or experience the situation as so uncomfortable that a breakdown in communication occurs, it is helpful to refer to the meta-contract formed during rapport establishment. In that contract we informed the interviewee(s) that we would eventually share the details of the child protection alert.

Summary

An interview without a strategy for the presentation of critical information deprives the interviewee of the opportunity to volunteer their own explanation. Simultaneously, a premature presentation of the critical information will make it easier for the interviewee to provide a false but plausible alternative explanation in the event they have something to hide.

Critical information can also surface during the interview, for example, if the interviewee provides information that does not correspond with information we have from other sources. There can be numerous causes for such discrepancies, but if the discrepancy is of significance for the case, process, or inquiry, it must be considered and treated as critical information. It must in other words be presented *after* new alternative explanations have been tested in the interview.

It can be extremely difficult to come up with all the plausible, alternative explanations for discrepancies that arise along the way, precisely because in this situation there is little or no time to generate the alternative explanations. It requires analytic, or "slow thinking" as Kahaneman describes the cognitive processes involved. It can then be a good idea to take a break—give yourself a moment to think: What can be the reason for the discrepancy? Which plausible and alternative explanations must I investigate *before* I point out the discrepancy? If such discrepancies arise during interviews that are a part of large-scale, complex processes, it can be expedient to take a break to think through the presentation or even to end the interview and start preparations for a new interview.

After the presentation of critical information, whereupon we encourage the interviewee to explain discrepancies, the interviewee may give us information intended to clarify the mismatch between the critical information and their own statement. Although the new information may offer an explanation, we may still be unclear about the connections. Regardless, we must immediately ask a follow-up question:

> Okay, so you feel certain that the poor reference your previous employer gave you is due to a conflict that arose when you demanded better safety gear for yourself and your colleagues. This is important information. Tell me everything about that conflict to help me understand.

Now "the conflict" has become an important subject that must be explored, down to the tiniest detail, so we can check and corroborate the interviewee's account. We can do so by interviewing other sources, through written correspondence that confirms or disproves the job applicant's explanation, and so on. After prompting the interviewee to "tell all," we must follow up with 5Ws+ H and clarifying questions as described earlier. "When did you send your request to management? How did they respond? Where can we find relevant documentation? Who can confirm this?" If the critical information pertains to a specific event, we must remember to ask all relevant control questions, such as by following a checklist similar to that presented earlier.

Perhaps the job applicant is completely in the right, perhaps not. This is what we must ascertain, and in front of you sits a key source of information. The more details we collect, the better our basis for making an informed decision.

When we present critical information, we must be prepared to explain where we got the information from. There are some legal exceptions—such as witness protection measures—but essentially, we are morally bound to reveal our sources and thereby ensure that the accused receives an authentic opportunity to refute any criticism or information that puts them in a difficult situation, a bad light, and so on. Anonymous tips pertaining to critical information must be investigated before they are introduced in the professional interview. If we can't reveal the source, the main rule is that neither can we present the tip. Procedures violating the ethical principle of transparency will quickly undermine trust in you and the organization you represent.

> Since the main rule of the method requires us to be completely open about the source(s) of the information we present, it is relevant to mention the issue of protection of sources in journalism. If you share information with a journalist and simultaneously make it clear that you cannot be revealed as the source, you can be granted protection as a source. If you are guaranteed such protection, this ensures that your identity will

not be disclosed. This principle can be considered a part of traditional media's "constitution" and ethical guidelines. If such protection did not exist, the media—and society—would miss out on important information, because sources would be reluctant to come forward out of fear of reprisals should their identity be disclosed. This principle is in many ways comparable to the professional secrecy required in many professions. An individual providing information must in certain situations be guaranteed confidentiality.

10

CLOSING THE INTERVIEW

Throughout the entire book we have drawn from the research of eyewitness and decision-making psychology. A substantial portion of the method is designed to help minimize the pitfalls and negative consequences of human beings' unconscious, cognitive simplification strategies. We must list and test alternative hypotheses to counteract tunnel vision and cognitive traps, and we must ask neutral and open questions to avoid influencing how the interviewee responds.

Now, in closing the interview, we can utilize and apply people's unconscious simplification strategies to our advantage. But in order to do so, we must understand and recognize the significance of closing the interview professionally. As you will see later, this is not difficult, but by ignoring or forgetting that the closing is also a key part of the professional interview, we risk destroying all the good work we have done.

For years Daniel Kahneman has studied how people remember their experiences. This research has culminated in the theory about "peak-end effect." Subsequent studies have confirmed the theory. A small improvement toward the end of an event can radically alter a person's experience of the event as a whole. What we remember from an event are the highlights and the ending.

The peak-end effect is an unconscious, cognitive simplification strategy that liberates and makes cognitive capacity more efficient by focusing on memories of the most intense moments and the end of an event (Kahneman 2011). The most obvious example would perhaps be childbirth. Despite excruciating pain over an extended period of time, the positive feeling that normally arises toward the end (when the baby is safely delivered) is so intense that it can offset the adverse after-effects of the pain endured throughout the process.

The duration of a professional interview has little impact on what we retain from it. A good, empathetic first impression is extremely important for successful implementation of the interview, but as illustrated in Figure 17, the first impression is less significant in terms of what is stored as a memory from

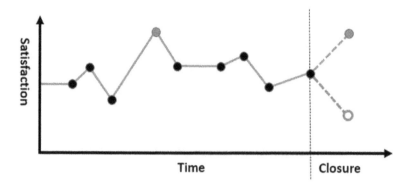

Figure 17 Peak-end effect. Inspired by Kahneman (2011).

the interview. The strongest memories attach themselves to experiences that stand out (peak) and to the end.

Research shows that an interview that is concluded in a positive way will be remembered as positive. Further, studies have revealed that a positive conclusion to a pleasant interaction creates a willingness to repeat the experience (Doll 2020). For you as a professional, for your organization, yes, your profession as a whole, a focus on the concluding phase of your conversations, interviews, or consultations will be of decisive significance to establishing and upholding the trust of customers, clients, users, or sources.

In light of this knowledge, it isn't difficult to understand that the closing phase was included in the model that researchers and the police developed in collaboration when reforming police interview methods. The argument we have made since the first page of this book is that it is irrelevant whether we call the interaction an interrogation, interview, consultation, or conversation. The psychology is the same in all cases and as highlighted by Kahneman: the experience of satisfaction or pain will be replaced by the memory of the experience.

When the End Is Good

The body of a fish can be used to illustrate a good story. The head is the prelude and the start. The tail is the closing and the point of the story. This also holds true for the professional interview. The head is the planning and preparation phase and the establishment of rapport; the body of the fish is the interview itself; and the tail is the closing and evaluation. If any of the parts are missing, we have neither a fish nor a professional interview. We have already explained the importance of the first two phases of the model. Earlier we have shown how important the first section of the tail actually is, namely, closing the interview.

An informative and solid closing of the interview can strengthen trust in and the reputation of professional interviewers and the organization or industry they represent. But in addition to this, closing the interview effectively will yield a series of specific benefits. We can obtain more information, we can corroborate our understanding of the information we have received, we can help the interviewee understand what has happened and what is going to happen, and we can establish parameters that will ensure even better interviews in the future.

More Information

Toward the very end of the exploration and clarification phase, as a transition to the closing of the interview, the questions can revisit former topics: "Is there anything we haven't addressed? Is there anything you would like to add?" In this way we can intercept information and details we had no awareness of or hadn't considered, which the interviewee has not yet shared. Such information may not have come up previously because we had no basis for perceiving its relevance and therefore did not ask about it.

We have explained how important trust is in a professional interview. Researchers who study interpersonal communication have identified a number of variables that determine what, where, when, and how we choose to share information with other people (Hargie 2018). Knowledge about interpersonal communication theories can also be misused. People can manipulate others into sharing more information than they otherwise would have done, such as by creating a false impression of "friendship," instrumental compassion, and so on. In Part 1 when we discussed ethical perspectives, we illustrated why the Norwegian police have denounced techniques of this nature and the underlying mentality. Fortunately, research shows that interviewers who *don't* have a hidden agenda and who are open and empathetic in their communication establish a form of trust that is more effective than a misguided and unethical approach (Meissner et al. 2012; Alison et al. 2013).

If for the interviewee the interview process itself is a key means of gaining trust in the interviewing party, then it is not inconceivable that the most difficult or the most important information will not be shared until the end. The closing phase of an investigative interview can thus be a crucial part of the information gathering achieved through professional interviews.

The police interviewed one of two Norwegians who had been charged for a large-scale art theft. In the interview, the suspect laid all his cards on the table. In other words, he gave honest answers to all the detectives' questions about the theft he had been apprehended for having committed. At the very end of the long interview, the detective asked: "Is there anything more you would like to say?" The man fell silent, and after a few moments, he asked if he could go to the lavatory. When he came back, he continued to sit in silence. It was clear that he was thinking, and the detective could see that he was struggling. For that reason, the detective didn't want to pressure him, so he just waited. After a minute and a half of silence, the suspect said: "We were inside there one more time. And we stole more paintings." This was information the police didn't have, so there was no apparent reason for the suspect to admit this. Afterward, the detective explained that it was because the suspect was in the mode. He actually wanted to explain himself. It was a budding seed that had been cultivated.

In addition to the chance of our obtaining new and important information, we demonstrate that the interviewee is the focus of the interview by asking the question "Is there anything more you would like to say?" We make it clear that it is important to hear everything the interviewee wants to share. In doing this, we also show empathy and respect.

As mentioned in the chapter "Exploration and Clarification," it can be useful to conclude each topic with a summing-up, before moving on. It can also be useful to summarize the entire interview at the end. We thereby ensure that all parties have a common understanding of what has been said in the course of the interview. It is also useful to repeat any agreements about what should be done and when it will be done, as a means of ensuring that everyone has understood. The summary, along with any notes or audio/video recording, will form the basis for the outcome of the interview, whether this be in the form of minutes, a journal entry, an article, an investigative interview report, a memo, or a ruling.

What Happens Next?

The close of the interview will contain important information about what happens next. In the same way that metacommunication at the beginning of the interview creates predictability, the information included in the closing phase creates an understanding about next steps, along with a feeling of predictability and security. Metacommunication about what happens next ensures that the interviewee is informed of and understands the subsequent, post-interview, process and that their needs have been addressed. The witness or suspect wants to know what will happen after the investigative interview and in the investigation. The source will want to know if an article will come out of the interview, if he or she will receive an email containing any quotes to be used for verification purposes, and when the article will be published. Patients will want to know when the doctor will be able to inform them of test results, if they will be required to take more tests, and when they can start treatment. The job applicant wants to know when he or she can expect a decision to be made and if so when and how it will be communicated. The majority of those who take part in a professional interview will have a need for this type of information. Without an interview methodology and training, the interviewer can easily forget about that need.

The pioneering researchers who evaluated the interrogation practices of the British police force stated that many of the detectives did not conclude their interviews in a professional manner (Baldwin 1992), which produced uncertainty and frustration. The interviewee was left with many unanswered questions. It can be difficult for the interviewee to remember or formulate questions at the tail end of an interview. If the interviewee thinks of a question only after the interview has ended, they may feel that it is too late to ask it. And if they wonder about something after they have left the interview, taking contact can seem odd or difficult. An important part of a professional interview is therefore to anticipate this and provide information about what comes next before finishing, including how the individual can contact the interviewing party, should the need arise. When we carry out a professional interview, we start a thought process. The interviewee will feel validated if offered the opportunity to contact the interviewer after the interview is over.

After having provided general information about the road ahead, preferably using a checklist based on the enterprise's experience with the type of information interviewees will typically need, we must always ask if the interviewee has any questions about the upcoming process. It's not certain that you have managed to cover all the bases or meet all manner of expectations. This simple measure is perhaps the most important in the final, closing phase. It is easy to forget, and this can cast a negative shadow over the entire interview.

In some situations, it can be important not to create false expectations with the final, open question: "Do you have any questions about what happens next?" It isn't necessarily the case that we can in fact answer the questions that may emerge. There are at least two ways of avoiding the creation of false expectations. First, you can manage expectations before asking the question. "I understand that you may have questions about what will happen next. I will certainly be able to answer some of them, though it may be difficult to provide a response to other questions today. I will answer to the best of my ability."

Another means of preventing the creation of false expectations is through mental preparations in which you try to imagine all the potential questions you might receive and prepare good answers for these in advance. In both cases it is important to acknowledge the question: "That's a good question. I understand why you would ask about that."

When you give the interviewee the opportunity to ask about something at the very end, their experience of you as an empathetic and understanding human being is reinforced.

Implementation

In the chapter "Engage and Explain—Establishing Rapport," we asked the question, "How would you want to be met?" The rule is equally valid when concluding the professional interview. Most people appreciate being accompanied to the door with a smile, a few kind words, and a warm handshake. Most of us can offer this regardless of the parameters of the professional interview.

We must maintain our concentration and the positive tone all the way to the end, both while we are obtaining the final pieces of information and when we explain what will happen next. We must avoid thoughts such as "Finished at last. Glad that's over with." We haven't finished until the interviewee has left the building or we have taken our departure. Thoughts of this nature can actually lower the level of professionalism or cause you to let down your guard. Then you could easily say things that are inappropriate at the end, which have not been suitably vetted or planned, but are instead an expression of your own feelings.

It's like driving a car. When we are driving through a complicated traffic situation, we concentrate on our driving. The focus is on arriving safely and doing what we can to avoid a collision or a fine. When we reach the garage and are going to park the car, the complicated situation is behind us. We have made it home without incident and can let down our guard. Our focus slips, and we put a dent in the car while backing it into the garage.

Set aside time for a good closing. If you don't have the time, explain this in a pleasant manner, so the other person will still feel valued. It can be helpful at this stage to refer to the management of expectations and time clarification done during the rapport establishment phase. During the wrap-up, take a moment to mention any positive topics or events that have been discussed during the interview. You can also say something about your experience of the interaction, as long as there's an emphasis on the positive. In many professional interviews, it is also appropriate to thank the interviewee for taking the time and trouble to participate.

If the situation and balance of power allows for it, we can ask how the interviewee experienced the interview: "How do you feel about today's interview?" This shows empathy, and you can learn something about their perception of you and your way of doing things. If we request feedback, we must of course be mentally prepared to receive negative input. An experience cannot be contested. This does, however, give you the opportunity to explain any extenuating circumstances. You also have the chance to apologize in the event you understand that you could and should have handled the critical episode in a better way. You can incorporate this feedback into the next phase of the interview: *evaluation*.

11

EVALUATION

When the interview has been terminated, the time has come for evaluation. There are predominantly two things that are to be evaluated: the information you have obtained and the implementation of the interview itself. Or to put this differently: the case and your communication process.

Feedback

Despite the efforts of many organizations to introduce sound performance assessment systems, there are still problems in ensuring employees receive timely, fair, and reliable evaluation and feedback. Inadequate feedback systems and cultures can also be found in professions for which the professional interview is an important tool. Unless compulsory procedures are introduced, self-evaluation will remain the most important form of assessment. However, when done properly, feedback from others can be enormously helpful. Regardless of how proficient and aware you may be, others can discern aspects of your process of which you are incognizant and where there is room for improvement.

When everyone at a workplace works according to the same method, this fosters a common language for and understanding of what good work entails and what can or should be changed. A consensus about method will simplify the evaluation process and make it more meaningful. An attitude of humility and a genuine wish to improve will facilitate good feedback. This requires a culture in which evaluation is defined as a joint undertaking, a culture that encourages constructive feedback and input that reinforces professional and sound conduct, because there is a consensus that this will improve the contribution of every employee. A misguided practice of giving feedback exclusively when somebody finds it fitting to point out mistakes will crush any and all attempts to increase professionalism in the workplace. Usually those who offer this kind of feedback are more interested in promoting themselves than in helping others to improve.

Many carry out professional interviews alone. In such a case, to acquire feedback, you could consider the following: asking a colleague to monitor the interview from another room (if appropriate equipment is available); recording the interview and asking a colleague to review it later; or asking the interviewee if it would be alright if a colleague sat in on the interview as an observer (explaining the reasons why and that the colleague would play no part in the interview itself). When this is not an option, you can discuss the interview before and after with a colleague. If you conduct an interview with a colleague present in the room, you can form an agreement in advance to evaluate and give each other feedback.

Feedback can be difficult, both for the person offering it and for the person on the receiving end. We all have different reactions to the positive and negative thoughts of others about our own work. For some people, hearing that they could do their job better can be an emotional challenge. Others find it difficult to accept praise. To prevent emotions from interfering with learning, it can be a good idea to have common ground rules for the communication of feedback. When both parties know what is going to happen and how, it is easier to be mentally prepared for the process.

There are many different guidelines for how we can best give and receive feedback. If your workplace has guidelines, use them. From an organizational perspective, it is essential that everyone have a shared understanding of what evaluation will entail. It is not enough that management merely facilitates this form of professionalization. They must actively encourage it and implement specific measures.

In order to illustrate this, we present here the guidelines developed for giving feedback on the investigative interviews done by the police.

Giving feedback

1. The party receiving the feedback should be interested in receiving it.
   Clarify whether feedback is wanted.
   Clarify the parameters (place, time, purpose, attendees, etc.)
2. Allow the party receiving the feedback to speak first.
   Listen, don't contradict or interrupt.
3. Be clear about the change of roles.
   "Is there anything else on your mind?"
   "Would you like to hear my thoughts?"
4. Describe observable facts from the situation and be specific.
   Start with something positive.
   Be clear about where there is room for improvement.
5. Describe your own thoughts and feelings, not those of the recipient.

"I felt that …"

"To me, it seemed as if …"

6. Have others check the contents of your feedback.
   Experts, lessons, written sources, etc.
7. Give feedback immediately.
   Avoid unnecessary delay.
   Here and now, then another meeting, if necessary.
8. Get feedback on your feedback.
   What can you do to improve your feedback?
   If the intention of giving feedback is not to help, it is best to abstain.

Receiving feedback

1. You must have a desire to improve: ask for feedback.
2. Listen to what is said. Make an effort to understand what it means to you.
3. Don't voice objections to the contents of the feedback.
4. You should thank the person who took the time to give you feedback.
5. Try to transform the feedback into milestones for personal change.
6. Bring the most important milestones with you in the next situation.
7. Be willing to ask for help in making changes.
8. Ask for new feedback.

Try to make the feedback session a conversation through which your colleague receives an opportunity to reflect as much as possible on the issues you raise. In this way, they can come up with solutions on their own. By asking the person receiving feedback to evaluate themselves first, you may find that they are more critical of themselves than you had intended to be. You may not have anything negative to say whatsoever and can instead focus on the positive. You can then work together in preparing a process that will promote development.

Sometimes a professional interview can be taxing, and afterward, those responsible for carrying out the interview may be tired. It such cases it can make sense to postpone the feedback session until the person in question is better prepared to receive an evaluation.

It is not always expedient to do everything all at once. The person offering feedback should not overload the recipient with absolutely everything in need of improvement. It is important that the person receiving the feedback experience mastery and that the suggestions for change be within reach. Select one or two themes to be worked on in the next interview. Developmental work should not be so overwhelming that it interferes with the task of gathering information in the next interview.

We may disagree with the feedback we receive, but we cannot dispute the experience of others. This can be challenging. What you can do, on the other hand, is explain why you made the choices you did. This increases your own awareness and can lead to good professional discussions.

Evaluation of the Process

Whether you are evaluating yourself or being evaluated by others, the check-list is the same. During the evaluation process, the phase model will be a helpful tool.

When we use the model, we can break the assessment down into manage-able parts, which makes it easier to be specific. This allows us to take every-thing we have learned about each individual phase and think through whether that knowledge was applied correctly. In short, what was done well? What could have been done better?

Did we do enough planning? Did I manage to establish a good rapport based on trust? Did I relinquish control to the interviewee and practice active listening? Was I flexible? Had I defined the correct topics, and did I explore these in the correct order? Were the questions asked in such a way as to influence the interviewee as little as possible? And were they asked so as to elicit as much information as possible? Did I disclose crit-ical information in a good way and at the right moment? Did I succeed in concluding the interview in an informative and confidence-inspiring manner?

Evaluation of the Case

It can be difficult to evaluate a case and its process separately. We notice this when the time comes to evaluate the information obtained through the interview. The primary question will be: "Did we meet the information needs identified in the preparatory phase?" "Did we achieve the purpose of the interview?" If the answer is no, the follow-up question will quite simply be: "What went wrong?" The answer to this question will often be related to the interview process.

During the case-related evaluation, there are at least two questions we must answer: "What information did we obtain?" and "What significance does it have for us?" To help us with the evaluation, we can use the 6C model from the chapter "Planning and Preparation," as explained in the following.

We have used the interview to obtain available information. When we ask the first question. "What information did we obtain?" we collect that information (Collect). Then we move on to the next step and consider the information's relevance, accuracy, and reliability (Check). Once we have assessed the value of the information, we comb ine it with the information we already have to gain an overview (Connect). This enables us to determine whether hypotheses have been strengthened, undermined, or disproven. We can then see whether there is a need for new hypotheses (Construct). The new information and its impact on the hypotheses will help us see the answer to the second question, "What significance does this have for us?" (Consider). We will then see whether we will need to carry out further interviews or to test the information we have in other ways, preferably in consultation with others (Consult). We can also see if we have enough information to reach a conclusion.

Skilled interviewers dare, take the trouble, and are able to self-evaluate—to be critical and simultaneously generous in the assessment of the work they have done. The best interviewers even manage to self-evaluate as they work, in terms of both the case and the process. They can thereby adjust their trajectory, improving the work process as they go along. "How is the rapport now?" "Am I asking questions well?" "Is the rapport in place or should I re-establish rapport?" "Am I achieving my purpose?" "Are the answers sufficiently detailed?" "Does the information corroborate what I already have?" As we can see, the investigative model employing the 6Cs creates a framework for working with the information of an entire case, a professional interview, and the evaluation of information after an interview.

This final phase is called *evaluation*. It could just as easily have been called *learning* because learning is the entire point of evaluation. A lot of learning occurs "by doing," in other words, as we are working. We see, there and then, what functions and what does not. Situations can arise that are teaching moments, such as when the rapport is broken. Perhaps we didn't immediately understand that it was something we said or did. Or we can experience that a particularly well-formulated prompt to talk about something in particular is immediately successful. In either case, if we aren't sufficiently aware of the specifics of what we are doing and have no method or agreed-upon terminology for the interview process, learning becomes more difficult. If we don't fully understand why an interview went well, our satisfaction can be short-lived, because we won't know how to go about repeating it. If an interview went badly, the next time around it will often turn out much better. But how? A thorough evaluation offers learning, insight, and improvement. The next interview will be even more professional. The information becomes more reliable, more relevant, and more detailed.

EPILOGUE

The suggestion to write this book came from a rather unexpected source. On July 22, 2011, the Norwegian financier Nicolai Tangen watched the events unfolding in his homeland Norway in a state of shock from London. At the time he was the head of a private hedge fund, AKO Capital. Several months after the horrific day in July and while the police investigation of the attack was underway, Tangen began considering the similarities between investigative interviewing and the meetings held by the financial analysts of AKO Capital. His curiosity was piqued. When he and his colleagues were assessing global investment opportunities, professional interviews were one of the most important tools they used to collect reliable information. How could he improve these processes? How could they obtain better information?

In the spring of 2012, Tangen contacted one of the authors of this book, Geir-Egil Løken, to learn more and explore whether it would be possible to arrange a collaboration. Tangen quickly understood the relevance of a research-based interview methodology for himself and his colleagues in the context of their work. The outcome of the collaboration was that the innovative Norwegian investigative interviewing technique was adapted to the parameters of the international world of finance.

AKO Capital began providing training in investigative interviewing, and since then all employees have attended courses to learn the method: fund managers and financial analysists as well as linguists and directors of market research. After having seen the value of the methodology in practice, Tangen also invited the investment company's clients to take part in a course. One of the participants claimed he should have taken this course 30 years ago and that the contents should be compiled into a book. Tangen agreed and encouraged Løken to write the book. In this way the first seed was sown, a seed that became the book you now hold in your hands.

While CREATIVE was adapted and shared with financial analysts in London, the second of the authors with police training, Asbjørn Rachlew, was contacted by the UN special rapporteur on Torture, Juan Méndez. Méndez wanted to submit a recommendation to the UN General Assembly in

New York for a collaboration on the development of a global set of standards for police questioning. Méndez has extensive experience with torture, first as a victim, later as a UN special adviser, but far less experience with good, alternative investigative interviewing methods. He therefore invited 40 experts from all over the world to attend a meeting. Each of the experts was allotted five minutes to present their recommendations. After this meeting, Méndez requested a report outlining the essence of CREATIVE. A few months later, he submitted his own recommendation to the United Nations, where he called for "the development of a global protocol for investigative interviewing." Méndez (2016) maintained that the global protocol should advocate the new, research-based interview methods—investigative interviewing—as best practice. These are the same interview methods that were embraced and further developed in Norway and which we have presented in this book. Méndez cited Fahsing and Rachlew's chapter on investigative interviewing in the Nordic region (2009), where CREATIVE is described. Two years after Méndez submitted his recommendation to the United Nations, the European Committee for the Prevention of Torture (CPT) resolved to implement a study on CREATIVE and Norwegian investigative interviewing practice. This culminated in a report being sent to the Norwegian government in which the development in Norway was highlighted as an example to be emulated in Europe (CPT 2019a). While this book was being written, the drafting of the global principles on effective interviewing was finalized (Méndez 2021) and advocated by the UN Human Rights Council in its resolution on torture (United Nations 2021). The principles are already referred to as "The Méndez Principles." One of the authors of the global protocol is also one of the authors of this book. The method and underlying knowledge are the same.

The book's third author, Svein Tore Bergestuen, works in the intersection of journalism method, storytelling, media consulting, and media criticism. After the book project was made known in Norway, an increasing number of media organizations have contacted us and shown a clear interest in the method, and how it can be adapted to the requirements of journalism. This occurred at a time when the press in Norway and the rest of the world was fighting battles on at least three fronts. The battle against fake news, the battle to uphold the credibility of traditional media outlets, and the battle for sustainable funding for good journalism. Increasingly more editors and journalists recognize that the method presented in this book ensures the collection of relevant, detailed, and reliable information in meeting with sources. Of equal importance is the fact that several editors and journalists hold that the method's ethical standards contribute to increasing the legitimacy, respectability, and credibility of each and every reporter, publication, and the media as a whole.

It is our hope and belief that you will find the method we have described and the underlying knowledge relevant for your needs and those of your profession. And remember, sometimes a reliable answer can mean the difference between life and death. As such, in acquiring that information, the best possible tools should be used. The purpose of this book has therefore been to make the professional interview even more professional.

Good luck!

ACKNOWLEDGMENTS

The three of us all owe a great debt of gratitude to our respective employers and collaborating partners, who have been extremely accommodating and flexible while we have been working on this project. We would also like to thank all our consultants and representatives from various professions who have been willing to discuss the professional interview with us and given us helpful input on the manuscript. A special thank you goes to those who have taken the time to read through parts of or the entire manuscript and provided valuable feedback.

But we are above all indebted to our life partners at home, who have shown incredible patience, night and day, for years. Thank you!

BIBLIOGRAPHY

Ahmed, N., Bestall, J., Payne, S., Noble, B., & Ahmedzai, S. 2009. "The use of cognitive interviewing methodology in the design and testing of a screening tool for supportive and palliative care needs." *Supportive Care in Cancer*, 17(6), 665.

Alison L. 1998. "Criminal rhetoric and investigative manipulation." Unpublished doctoral thesis, University of Liverpool.

Alison, L., Alison, E., Noone, G., Stamatis Elntib, S., & Christiansen, P. 2013. "Why tough tactics fail and rapport gets results: Observing Rapport-Based Interpersonal Techniques (ORBIT) to generate useful information from terrorists." *Psychology, Public Policy, and Law*, 19, 411–31.

Anonymous. 2017. "Nå skjønner jeg, etter mange år som doctor" [Now I understand, after many years as a physician]. *Tidsskrift for Den norske legeforening*, 12/13(June 27). DOI:10.4045/tidsskr.17.0095.

Ask, K. 2006. "Criminal investigation: Motivation, emotion, and cognition in the processing of evidence." Doctoral dissertation, Department of Psychology, Göteborg University. http://hdl.handle.net/2077/676. Accessed June 22, 2020.

Ask, K., & Fahsing, I. 2018. "Investigative decision-making." In *The Psychology of Criminal Investigation: From Theory to Practice*. Edited by A. Griffiths & R. Milne, pp. 52–73. New York: Routledge.

Ask, K., & Granhag, P. A. 2008. "Psykologiska påverkansfaktorer vid utredningsarbetet" [Psychological factors that influence investigative work]. In *Handbok i rättspsykologi* [Forensic psychology handbook]. Edited by P. A. Granhag & S. Å. Christianson, pp. 161–74). Stockholm: Liber.

Atkinson, R. C., & Shiffrin, R. M. (1968). "Human memory: A proposed system and its control processes." In *The Psychology of Learning and Motivation: II. Edited by* K. W. Spence & J. T. Spence. New York: Academic Press.

Baker-Eck, B., Bull, R., & Walsh, D. 2020. "Investigative empathy: A strength scale of empathy based on European police perspectives." *Psychiatry, Psychology and Law*, 27(3), 412–27. DOI:10.1080/13218719.2020.1751333.

Baldwin, J. 1992. "Video taping police interviews with suspects: An evaluation." Police Research Series Paper 1. H.O. Police Research Group, London.

Baldwin, M. W. 1992. "Relational schemas and the processing of social information." *Psychological Bulletin*, 112(3), 461–84.

Baron, J. 2008. *Thinking and Deciding*. Fourth Edition. Cambridge, UK: Cambridge University Press.

Bjerknes, O. T., & Fahsing, I. 2017. *Etterforskning: Prinsipper, metoder og praksis* [Criminal investigations: Principles, methods, and practice]. Bergen: Fagbokforlaget.

Bohart, A. C., Elliott, R., Greenberg, L. S., & Watson, J. C. 2002. "Empathy." In *Psychotherapy Relationships That Work: Therapist Contributions and Responsiveness to Patients*. Edited by J. C. Norcross, pp. 89–108. Oxford: Oxford University Press.

Bower, G. 1967. "A multicomponent theory of the memory trace." In *The Psychology of Learning and Motivation*. Edited by K. W. Spence & J. T. Spence, vol. 1, pp. 229–325. New York: Academic Press.

Brannon, S. M., & Gawronski, B. 2016. "A second chance for first impressions? Exploring the context-(in)dependent updating of implicit evaluations." *Social Psychological and Personality Science*, 8(3), 275–83.

Bull, R. 2001. Video interview for investigative interviewing instructors. KREATIV [CREATIVE]. Norwegian Police University College.

Bull, R., & Rachlew, A. 2020. "Investigative interviewing: From England to Norway and beyond." In *Interrogation and Torture: Research on Efficacy, and Its Integration with Morality and Legality*. Edited by S. Barela, M. Fallon, G. Gaggioli, & J. Ohlin, pp. 171–96S. Oxford: Oxford University Press.

Campbell, A. 2007. *The Blair Years: The Alastair Campbell Diaries*. New York: Knopf.

Canter, D. V., & Alison, L. (eds.). 1999. "Interviewing and deception." In *Profiling in Policy and Practice. Vol. I*, pp. 3–21. Aldershot, UK: Dartmouth.

Chaplin, J. P. 1985. *Dictionary of Psychology*. Perfection Learning Corporation. New York: Dell.

Cook, T. 2019. *Senior Investigating Officers' Handbook*. Fifth edition. Oxford: Oxford University Press.

CPT. 2019a. CPT/Inf. 2019. 1. Report to the Norwegian Government on the visit to Norway carried out by the European Committee for the Prevention of Torture and Inhuman or Degrading Treatment or Punishment (CPT) from 28 May to 5 June 2018. Strasbourg, January 17, 2019, pp. 16–19.

———. 2019b. CPT standards. CPT/Inf 2019 9—part. Preventing police torture and other forms of ill-treatment—reflections on good practices and emerging approaches. Extract from the 28th General Report of the CPT.

CPT. 2002. CPT standards. 12th General Report on the CPT's activities, CPT/Inf/E (2002) 1—Rev. 2013.

Cuff, B., Brown, S., Taylor, L., & Howat, D. 2016. "Empathy: A review of the concept." *Emotion Review*, 8, 144–53.

Dawson, E., Hartwig, M., Brimbal, L., & Denisenkov, P. 2017. "A room with a view: Setting influences information disclosure in investigative interviews." *Law and Human Behavior*, 41. DOI:10.1037/lhb0000244.

Denzin, N. K., & Lincoln, Y. S. 2011. *The SAGE Handbook of Qualitative Research*. Los Angeles, CA: SAGE.

Doll, K. 2020. "What is Peak-End Theory? A psychologist explains how our memory fools us." PositivePsychology.com. https://positivepsychology.com/what-is-peak-end-theory/. Accessed June 22, 2020.

Drew, P., & Heritage, J. (eds.). 1992. "Analyzing talk at work: An introduction." In *Talk at Work: Interaction in Institutional Settings*, pp. 3–65. Cambridge: Cambridge University Press.

Dyregrov, A., & Raundalen, M. 2002. "Det første møtet: intervjuing av barn med krigstraumer" [The first encounter: Interviewing war-traumatized children]. In *Det kliniske intervjuet: En handbook* [The Clinical Interview: A Handbook]. Edited by M. H. Rønnestad & A. von der Lippe. Oslo: Ad Notam Gyldendal Forlag.

Eagly, A. H., & Chaiken, S. 1998. "Attitude structure and function." In *The Handbook of Social Psychology*. Edited by D. T. Gilbert, S. T. Fiske, & G. Lindzey, pp. 269–322. New York: McGraw-Hill.

Ebbinghaus, H. 1885. "Memory: A contribution to experimental psychology." http://psychclassics.yorku.ca/Ebbinghaus/index.htm. Accessed June 22, 2020.

Eriksson, A., & Lacerda, F. 2007. "Charlatanry in forensic speech science: A problem to be taken seriously." *International Journal of Speech, Language and the Law*, 14(2), 169–93.

Fahsing, I. A. 2016. "The making of an expert detective: Thinking and deciding in criminal investigations." Doctoral thesis. Department of Psychology, University of Gothenburg.

Fahsing, I. A., & Rachlew, A. 2009. "Investigative interviewing in the Nordic region." In *International Developments in Investigative Interviewing*. Edited by T. Williamson, B. Milne, & S. P. Savag, pp. 39–65. Devon, UK: Willan.

Fallon, M. 2017. *Unjustifiable Means: The Inside Story of How the CIA, Pentagon, and US Government Conspired to Torture*. New York: Regan Arts.

Fisher, R., Geiselman, E., & Raymond, D. S. 1987. "Critical analysis of police interview techniques." *Journal of Police Science and Administration*, 15, 177–85.

Forst, B. 2004. *Error of Justice: Nature, Sources and Remedies*. Cambridge, UK: Cambridge University Press.

Gallo, C. 2014. *Talk like TED. The 9 Public-Speaking Secrets of the World's Top Minds*. New York: St. Martin's Press.

Gawande, A. 2009. *The Checklist Manifesto: How to Get Things Right*. New York: Metropolitan Books.

George, R. 1991. "A field and experimental evaluation of three methods of interviewing witnesses and victims of crime." Unpublished master's thesis, Polytechnic of East London, London, UK.

Granhag, P. A., Ask, K., Rebelius, A., Öhman L., & Mac Giolla, E. 2013. " 'I saw the man who killed Anna Lindh!' An archival study of witnesses' offender descriptions." *Psychology, Crime & Law*, 19(10), 921–31.

Granhag, P. A., Fallon, M., Vernham, Z., & Giolla, E. M. 2018. "Detecting deceit via verbal cues: Towards a context sensitive research agenda." In *The Psychology of Criminal Investigation: From Theory to Practice*. Edited by A. Griffiths & R. Milne, pp. 179–202. London: Routledge.

Griffiths, A. 2008. "An examination into the efficacy of police advanced investigative interview training." Unpublished doctoral thesis, University of Portsmouth.

Griffiths, A., & Rachlew, A. 2018. "From interrogation to investigative interviewing: The application of psychology." In *The Psychology of Criminal Investigation: Theory into Practice*. Edited by A. Griffiths & R. Milne, pp. 154–78. London: Routledge.

Griffiths, L., & Milne, B. 2006. "Will it all end in tiers? Police interviews with suspects in Britain." In *Investigative Interviewing: Rights, Research, Regulation*. Edited by T. Williamson, pp. 167–89. Devon: Willan.

Grimstad, E. 2015. *Gransking. Ved mistanke om korrupsjon og andre former for økonomisk kriminalitet i arbeidsforhold* [Investigating. Upon suspicion of corruption and other forms of financial crime in the workplace]. Oslo: Gyldendal Norsk forlag AS.

Gubrium, J. F., Holstein, J. A., Marvasti, A. B., & McKinney, K. D. (eds.). 2012. *Handbook of Interview Research*, 2nd ed. Thousand Oaks, CA: SAGE.

Gulbrandsen, P., & Finset, A. 2019. *Skreddersydde samtaler* [Tailormade Interviews]. Oslo: Gyldendal

Handgaard, B. 2008. *Intervjuteknikk for journalister* [Interviewing Techniques for Journalists]. Oslo: Gyldendal.

Hargie, E.W. 2018. *The Handbook of Communication skills*, 4th ed. London: Routledge.

Holgerson, A. 1998. *Huvudvittnets identifisering av Christer Pettersson i Palme-målet—en vittnespsykologisk analys* [The principal witness's identification of Christer Pettersson in the Palme case—a witness psychology analysis]. Research report from Eyewitness psychology research laboratory, Institute of Pedagogy, Stockholm University. ISSN 1104-8948. Report no. 3. https://www.rettsnorge.com/artikler/301001Palme.htm. Accessed June 22, 2020.

Holmberg, U. 2004. "Police interviews with and suspects of violent and sexual crimes: Interviewees' experience and interview outcome." Doctoral thesis. Stocholm: Stockholm University.

Holmberg, U., & Christianson, S-Å. 2002. "Murderers' and sexual offenders' experiences of police interviews and their inclination to admit or deny crimes." *Behavioral Sciences and the Law*, 20, 31–45.

Horvath, A. O., & Bedi, R. P. 2002. "The alliance." In *Psychotherapy Relationships That Work: Therapist Contributions and Responsiveness to Patients*. Edited by J. C. Norcross, pp. 37–69. Oxford: Oxford University Press.

Høyesterett. 2003. *Rt. 2003 s. 549* [Norwegian Supreme Court Report].

Huff, C. R., Rattner, A., & Sagagrin, E. 1996. *Convicted but Innocent: Wrongful Conviction and Public Policy*. Thousand Oaks: SAGE.

Jakobsen, K. K. 2010. Afhøring af sigtede. En undersøgelse af dansk politis afhøringspraksis [Interrogating suspects. An investigation of the Danish police force's interrogation practice]. Politiets Videncenter. Rigspolitiet, Copenhagen.

———. 2019: "Empathy in investigative interviews of victims: How to understand it, how to measure it, and how to do it?" *Police Practice and Research*, 22(3), 1–16.

———. 2021. "Objektivitet og empati i avhør av fornærmede. En kvalitativ undersøkelse av norske politiavhør" [Objectivity and empathy in police interviews. A qualitative study of Norwegian police interviews]. Doktoravhandling forsvart ved Det juridiske fakultet, Universitetet i Oslo. Nr. 170, PhD thesis, Faculty of Law, University of Oslo.

Jakobsen, K. K., Langballe, Å., & Schultz, J. H. 2017. "Trauma-exposed young victims: Possibilities and constraints for providing trauma support within the investigative interview." *Psychology, Crime and Law*, 23(5), 427–44.

Jensen, B. F. 2011. "Hospital doctors' communication skills: A randomized controlled trial investigating the effect of a short course and the usefulness of a patient questionnaire." Doctoral thesis, Institute of Clinical Medicine, University of Oslo.

Kahneman, D. 2011. *Thinking, Fast and Slow*. New York: Penguin.

Kant, I. 1895. *Fundamental Principles of the Metaphysics of Ethics*. Translated by Thomas Kingsmill Abbott. Excercere.

Kassin, S., Drizin, S., Grisso, T., Gudjonsson, G., Leo R., & Redlich, A. 2009. "Police-induced confessions: Risk factors and recommendations." *Law and Human Behaviour*, 34(1), 3–38.

Kongsvik, L. T. 2014. "Lær kommunikasjon—bli en bedre lege? Intervju med Bård Fossli Jensen" [Learn communication—become a better doctor]. *Tidsskrift for Den norske legeforening*. 22(November 11), 134.

Koudenburg, N., Postmes, T., & Gordijn, E. 2011. "Disrupting the flow: How brief silences in group conversations affect social needs." *Journal of Experimental Social Psychology*, 47(2), 512–15.

Kvale, S., & Brinkmann, S. 2015a. *Det kvalitative forskningsintervju* [The Qualitative Research Interview]. Oslo: Gyldendal Akademisk.

———. 2015b. *InterViews: Learning the Craft of Qualitative Research Interviewing*, 3rd ed. Thousand Oaks, CA: SAGE.

Lai, L. (1999). *Dømmekraft* [Judgement]. Oslo: Tano Aschehoug.

Lamark, H. 1997. *Som journalister spør: en undersøkelse av intervju som arbeidsmetode i nyhetsjournalistikk* [As Asked by Journalists: About the Interview as a Work Method in News Journalism]. HBO-report, 4, Bodø University College.

———. 2001 *Som journalister spør. Om intervju som arbeidsmetode i nyhetsjournalistikken* [As Asked by Journalists: About the Interview as a Work Method in News Journalism]. Kristiansand: IJ-forlaget

Langballe, Å., Trøften Gamst, K., & Jacobsen M. 2010. *Den vanskelige samtalen. Barneperspektiv på barnevernarbeid. Kunnskapsbasert praksis og handlingskompetanse* [Difficult Conversations. The Child's Perspective on Child Welfare]. Norwegian Center for Violence and Traumatic Stress Studies (NKVTS). Report 2.

Lattimore, K. L. 2013. "The effect of seating orientation and a spatial barrier on students' experience of person-centered counselling." Master's thesis presented to the Faculty of the Graduate School of Cornell University.

Leavy, P. 2014. *The Oxford Handbook of Qualitative Research*. New York: Oxford University Press.

Leslie, I. 2017. "The scientists persuading terrorists to spill their secrets." Interview with Laurence Alison, *Guardian*, October 13. https://www.theguardian.com/news/2017/oct/13/the-scientists-persuading-terrorists-to-spill-their-secrets. Accessed June 22, 202.

Lieberman, M., Rock, D., Grant Halvorson, H., & Cox, C. 2015. "Breaking bias updated: The SEEDS model." *Neuro Leadership Journal*, 6 (November), 4–18.

Loftus, E. 2018. "Eyewitness science and the legal system." *Annual Review of Law and Social Science*, 14, 1–10.

Loftus, E., & Palmer. J.C. 1974. "Reconstruction of automobile destruction: An example of the interaction between language and memory." *Journal of Verbal Learning and Verbal Behavior*, 13, 585–89.

MacFarlane, B. 2006. "Convicting the innocent: A triple failure of the justice system." *Manitoba Law Journal*, 31, 403–83.

Magnussen, S. 2017. *Vitnepsykologi 2.0* [Witness Psychology 2.0]. Oslo: Abstrakt forlag.

Magnussen, S., & Stridbeck, U. 2001. "Vurdering av troverdighet. Hva sier forskningen?" [Assessing credibility. What does the research say?]. *Tidsskrift for strafferett*, 1, 81–97.

McLean, P. 1973. *A Triune Concept of the Brain and Behaviour, by Paul D. Maclean. Including Psychology of Memory and Sleep and Dreaming.* Paper Presented at Queen's University, Kingston, Ontario, February 1969, by V. A. Dral et al.

Meissner, C. A., Redlich, A. D., Bhatt, S., & Brandon, S. 2012. "Interview and interrogation methods and their effects on true and false confessions." *Campbell Systematic Reviews*, 13(1), 1–53.

Melinder, A. 2004. "Perspectives on children as witnesses." Doctoral dissertation. Institute of Psychology, University of Oslo.

Méndez, J. E. 2016. *Interim Report to the General Assembly* (A/71/298). Submitted by the Special Rapporteur on torture and other cruel, inhuman, or degrading treatment or punishment, Juan E. Méndez, in accordance with Assembly resolution 70/146. Geneva: United Nations. https://digitallibrary.un.org/record/839995/files/A_71_298-EN.pdf. Accessed January 1, 2021.

———. 2021. "Principles on effective interviewing for investigations and information gathering." https://www.apt.ch/en/resources/publications/new-principles-effective-interviewing-investigations-and-information. Accessed May 25, 2020.

Milne, B. 2006. Tier 3/5 "Enhanced Cognitive Interview." Presentation for Institute of Criminal Justice Studies.

Ministry of Justice, 2003. "Lydopptaksprosjektet 1998–2003". Justisdepartementet, Norge. [Recording of police interviews—a pilot study 1998–2003).

Mueller, P. A., & Oppenheimer, D. M. 2014. "The pen is mightier than the keyboard: Advantages of longhand over laptop note taking." *Science*, 25(6), 1159–68.

Nettavisen. 2003. "Anna Lindh knivstukket" [The stabbing of Anna Lindh]. September 10. https://www.nettavisen.no/nyheter/utenriks/anna-lindh-knivstukket/134524.html. Accessed June 22, 2020.

Nickerson, R. S. 1998. "Confirmation bias: A ubiquitous phenomenon in many guises." *Review of General Psychology*, 2, 175–220.

Norwegian Ministry of Justice. 2003. Lydopptaksprosjektet 1998–2003. Styringsgruppens anbefalinger. Justis-og politidepartementet. Norge [The audio recording project 1998–2003. Recommendations of the Steering Group. Former Norwegian Ministry of Justice and the Police].

Olcaysoy Okten, I. 2018. "Studying First Impressions: What to Consider?" Student notebook. Association for Psychological Science. January 31.

Öhrn, H. 2005. "Berätta din sanning: en förhörsledares projekt i förhör med misstänkt person" [Speak your truth: an interrogation leader's project on the interrogations of suspects]. Doctoral thesis. Institute of Pedagogy, Stockholm University.

Osato, E., & Ogawa, N. 2003. "Effects of seating positions on heart rates, state anxiety, and estimated interview duration in interview situations." *Psychological Reports*, 93(3), 755–70.

Packer, H. L. 1969. *The Limits of the Criminal Sanction*. London, UK: Oxford University Press.

Rachlew, A. 2002. "Interview strategy." Presentation at the 7th International Conference on Investigative Psychology, University of Liverpool, June 13.

———. 2003. "Norske politiavhør i et internasjonalt perspektiv" [Norwegian police interviews in an international perspective]. *Tidsskrift for Strafferett*, 4(2003), 400–39.

———. 2009. "Justisfeil ved politiets etterforskning—noen eksempler og forskningsbaserte mottiltak" [Errors of justice in police investigations—some examples and research-based counter measures]. Doctoral thesis, Faculty of Law, University of Oslo.

———. 2017. "From interrogating to interviewing suspects of terror: Towards a new mindset." Expert blog, Penal Reform International. https://goo.gl/7Hk9gn. Accessed June 22, 2020.

Rachlew, A., & Fahsing, I. 2015. "Politiavhøret" [The Police Interview]. In *Bevis i straffesaker* [Evidence in Criminal Cases]. Edited by R. Aarli, M. Hedlund, & S. E. Jebens. Oslo: Gyldendal Akademisk.

Rachlew, C., & Rachlew, A. 2009. "'Ja, han ligner—tror jeg'—Om utpeking av gjerningsmenn" ["Yes, he resembles him—I think." On identifying perpetrators]. *Tidsskrift for Strafferett*, 9(2), 153–89.

Ramsey, R. J. 2003. "False positives in the criminal justice process—an analysis of factors associated with wrongful conviction of the innocent." Doctoral dissertation, Division of Research and Advanced Studies of the University of Cincinnati, Division of Criminal Justice. https://etd.ohiolink.edu/apexprod/rws_etd/send_file/send?accession=uci n1044985710&disposition=inline. Accessed June 22, 2020.

Riksadvokatens publikasjoner [Office of the Public Prosecutor]. 2015. *Norsk politi og påtalemyndighets behandling av straffesakene mot Sture Bergwall. Hva kan vi lære?* [The Norwegian police and the prosecuting authority's handling of the criminal case against Sture

Bergwall. What can we learn?]. Report from task force, publication no. 3. Submitted September 21.

Riksadvokatens rundskriv [Director of Public Prosecution]. 1999. Circular letter, Part II no. 3.

Ritzer, G. 2008. *The McDonaldization of Society 5*. Los Angeles, CA: Pine Forge Press.

Rollins, J. 2009. "The influence of two hospitals' designs and policies on social interaction and privacy as coping factors for children with cancer and their families." *Journal of Pediatric Oncology Nursing* 26(6), 340–53.

Royal Commission on Criminal Procedure. 1981. Cmnd 8092. London: HMSO. https://onlinelibrary.wiley.com/doi/abs/10.1111/j.1467-923X.1981.tb02800.x. Accessed June 22, 2020.

Rusconi, E., & Mitchener-Niessen, T. 2013. "Prospects of functional magnetic resonance imaging as a lie detector." *Frontiers in Human Neuroscience*, review article, 7, 1–12.

Sawatsky, J. 1999. "Avansert intervjuteknikk" [Advanced interviewing techniques]. Lecture presented at Norwegian Institute of Journalism. Fredrikstad, Norway.

Schacter, D. L. 2001. *The Seven Sins of Memory: How the Mind Forgets and Remembers*. New York: Houghton Mifflin.

Schneider, M. 2019. "The fly on a pane of glass: Paradoxes of transparency." In *Contested Transparencies, Social Movements and the Public Sphere: Multi-disciplinary Perspectives*. Edited by S. Berger & D. Owetschkin. London: Palgrave Macmillan.

Shepherd, E. 1991. "Ethical interviewing." *Legal and Criminological Psychology*, 18, 46–56.

Simon, D. 2012. *In Doubt*. London: Harvard University Press.

Stanford Encyclopedia of Philosophy. 2016."Kant's moral philosophy." https://plato.stanford.edu/entries/kant-moral/#HumFor. Accessed January 10, 2021.

Stein, M. L., & Paterno, S. F. 2001. *Talk Straight—Listen Carefully: The Art of Interviewing*. New Jersey: Wiley-Blackwell.

Strand, K. 1998. *Spørg bedre. Interview og interviewteknik i radio og tv* [Ask Better Questions. Interviewing and Interview Techniques for Radio and TV]. København, Copenhagen: DR Multimedie.

Stridbeck, U. 2020. "Coerced-reactive confessions: The case of Thomas Quick." *Journal of Forensic Psychology Research and Practice*. https://doi.org/10.1080/24732850.2020.1732758.

Sullivan, T. P., Vail, A. W., & Anderson, H. W. 2008. "The case for recording police interrogation." *Litigation*, 34, 1–8.

Szalita, A. 1976. "Some thoughts on empathy." *Psychiatry*, 39(2), 142–52.

Thagaard, T. 2018. *Systematikk og innlevelse* [Systematic Thinking and Empathy]. Bergen-Sandviken: Fagbokforlaget.

Tjora, A. H. 2017. *Kvalitative forskningsmetoder i praksis (3. utg.)* [Qualitative Research Methods in Practice. 3rd ed.]. Oslo: Gyldendal Akademisk.

Toreno, E., Thompson, J., & Cotton, R. 2009. *Picking Cotton: Our Memoir of Injustice and Redemption*. New York: St. Martin's Press.

Tranøy, K. E. 2017. Hypotese. Definisjon Store norske leksikon. Vitenskapsteori. (The Large Norwegian Encyclopedia). https://snl.no/hypotese?source=post_page Accessed Juni 22, 2020.

Tulving, E., & Thomson, D. M. 1973. "Encoding specificity and retrieval processes in episodic memory." *Psychological Review*, 80, 352–73.

United Nations. 2021. General Assembly. Human Rights council. 46th session. (A/HRC/46/L.27).

Universal Declaration of Human Rights. 1948. United Nations.

Verlinde, E., de Laender N., de Maesschalck, S., Deveugele, M., & Willems, S. 2012. "The social gradient in doctor-patient communication." *International Journal for Equity in Health*, 11(12), 1–14. [PubMed]

Von der Lippe, A., & Rønnestad, M. H. 2011. *Det kliniske intervjuet Bind 2—Praksis med ulike klientgrupper* [The Clinical Interview. Vol. 2. Practical Experience with Diverse Client Groups]. Oslo: Gyldendal.

Vrij, A. 2008. *Detecting Lies and Deceit. Pitfalls and Opportunities*. 2nd ed.. Chichester, England: John Wiley.

Waddington, P. A. J., & Bull, R. 2007. "Cognitive interviewing as a research technique." *Social Research Update*, 50, 1–4.

Wale, T. 1996. *Innføring i journalistikk* [Introduction to Journalism]. 5th revised ed. Fredrikstad: Norwegian Institute of Journalism.

Welch, B. 2014. "The idea is to gather the richest possible ingredients to serve readers." In *Interviewing: The Oregon Method*. Edited by P. Laufer, pp. 1–16. Portland: University of Oregon.

Wessel, E. 2013. "Ekspert: Nesten umulig å avsløre om vitner lyver" [Expert: Almost impossible to disclose that a witness is lying]. Interview in *Bergens Tidende*. May 16.

Wessel, E. O., & Bollingmo, G. C. 2007. "The emotional witness—a study of judgments of credibility." Doctoral thesis, Institute of Psychology, Faculty of Social Sciences, University of Oslo.

West, I., Bull, R., & Köhnken, G. 1994. Advanced interview development course trainers' manual. Merseyside Police Interview Development Unit.

Williamson, T., Milne, B., & Savage (eds.). (2009). *International Developments in Investigative Interviewing*. Cullompton: Willan.

Willis, J., & Todorov, A. 2006. "First impressions: Making up your mind after a 100-ms exposure to a face!" *Psychological Science*, 17(7), 592–98.

INDEX

Note: "n" denotes note number.

Lightning Source UK Ltd.
Milton Keynes UK
UKHW012341171222
414057UK00003B/115